VISIONS OF EMPIRE

VISIONS OF EMPIRE

Political Imagery in
Contemporary American Film

STEPHEN PRINCE

Praeger Series in Political Communication

New York
Westport, Connecticut
London

Copyright Acknowledgment

The author and publisher gratefully acknowledge permission to use the following material:

"LAI 'Platoon' Message." Used by permission of the Chrysler Corporation, Highland Park, MI.

Library of Congress Cataloging-in-Publication Data

Prince, Stephen, 1955–
    Visions of empire : political imagery in contemporary American
film / Stephen Prince.
        p.   cm. — (Praeger series in political communication)
    Includes bibliographical references and index.
    ISBN 0–275–93661–9 (alk. paper). — ISBN 0–275–93662–7 (pbk.)
    1. Politics in motion pictures.   2. Motion pictures—United
States.   I. Title.   II. Series.
    PN1995.9.P6P73   1992
    791.43'658—dc20   91–44449

British Library Cataloguing in Publication Data is available.

Library of Congress Catalog Card Number: 91–44449
ISBN: 0–275–93661–9 (hb.)
        0–275–93662–7 (pbk.)

First published in 1992

Praeger Publishers, One Madison Avenue, New York, NY 10010
An imprint of Greenwood Publishing Group, Inc.

Printed in the United States of America

∞™

The paper used in this book complies with the
Permanent Paper Standard issued by the National
Information Standards Organization (Z39.48–1984).

10 9 8 7 6 5 4 3 2 1

For My Parents

Contents

About the Series

Those of us from the discipline of communication studies have long believed that communication is prior to all other fields of inquiry. In several other forums I have argued that the essence of politics is "talk" or human interaction.[1] Such interaction may be formal or informal, verbal or nonverbal, public or private, but it is always persuasive, forcing us consciously or subconsciously to interpret, to evaluate, and to act. Communication is the vehicle for human action.

From this perspective, it is not surprising that Aristotle recognized the natural kinship of politics and communication in his writings *Politics* and *Rhetoric*. In the former, he establishes that humans are "political beings [who] alone of the animals [are] furnished with the faculty of language."[2] And, in the latter, he begins his systematic analysis of discourse by proclaiming that "rhetorical study, in its strict sense, is concerned with the modes of persuasion."[3] Thus, it was recognized over twenty-three hundred years ago that politics and communication go hand in hand because they are essential parts of human nature.

Back in 1981, Dan Nimmo and Keith Sanders proclaimed that political communication was an emerging field.[4] Although its origin, as noted, dates back centuries, a "self-consciously cross-disciplinary" focus began in the late 1950s. Thousands of books and articles later, colleges and universities offer a variety of graduate and undergraduate coursework in the area in such diverse departments as communication, mass communication, journalism, political science, and sociology.[5] In Nimmo and Sanders' early assessment, the "key areas of inquiry" included rhetorical analysis, propaganda analysis, attitude change studies, voting studies, government and the news media, functional and systems analyses, technological changes, media technologies, campaign techniques, and research techniques.[6] In a survey of the state of field in 1983, the same authors and Lynda Kaid, found additional, more specific areas of concerns such as the presidency, political polls, public opinion, debates, and advertising to name a few.[7] Since the first study, they also noted a shift away from the rather strict behavioral approach.

Today, Dan Nimmo and David Swanson assert that "political communication has developed some identity as a more or less distinct domain of scholarly work."[8] The scope and concerns of the area have further expanded to include critical theories and cultural studies. While there is no precise definition, method, or disciplinary home of the area of inquiry, its primary domain is the role, processes, and effects of communication within the context of politics broadly defined.

In 1985, the editors of *Political Communication Yearbook: 1984* noted that "more things are happening in the study, teaching, and practice of political communication than can be captured within the space limitations of the relatively few publications available."[9] In addition, they argued that the backgrounds of "those involved in the field [are] so varied and pluralist in outlook and approach, . . . it [is] a mistake to adhere slavishly to any set format in shaping the content."[10] And more recently, Swanson and Nimmo called for "ways of overcoming the unhappy consequences of fragmentation within a framework that respects, encourages, and benefits from diverse scholarly commitments, agendas, and approaches."[11]

In agreement with these assessments of the area and with gentle encouragement, Praeger established in 1988 the series entitled "Praeger Studies in Political Communication." The series is open to all qualitative and quantitative methodologies as well as contemporary and historical studies. The key to characterizing the studies in the series is the focus on communication variables or activities within a political context or dimension. Scholars from the disciplines of communication, history, political science, and sociology have participated in the series.

I am, without shame or modesty, a fan of the series. The joy of serving as its editor is in participating in the dialogue of the field of political communication and in reading the contributors' works. I invite you to join me.

Robert E. Denton, Jr.

NOTES

1. See Robert E. Denton, Jr., *The Symbolic Dimensions of the American Presidency* (Prospect Heights, IL: Waveland Press, 1982); Robert E. Denton, Jr. and Gary Woodward, *Political Communication in America* (New York: Praeger, 1985, Second Edition, 1990); Robert E. Denton, Jr., and Dan Hahn, *Presidential Communication* (New York: Praeger, 1986); and Robert E. Denton, Jr., *The Primetime Presidency of Ronald Reagan* (New York: Praeger, 1988).

2. Aristotle, *The Politics of Aristotle*, trans. Ernest Barker (New York: Oxford University Press, 1970), p. 5.

3. Aristotle, *Rhetoric*, trans. Rhys Roberts (New York: The Modern Library, 1954), p. 22.

4. Dan Nimmo and Keith Sanders, "Introduction: The Emergence of Political Communication as a Field," in *Handbook of Political Communication*, Dan Nimmo and Keith Sanders, eds. (Beverly Hills, CA: Sage, 1981), pp. 11–36.

5. Ibid., p. 15.

6. Ibid., pp. 17–27.

7. Keith Sanders, Lynda Kaid, and Dan Nimmo, eds. *Political Communication Yearbook: 1984* (Carbondale, IL: Southern Illinois University: 1985), pp. 283–308.

8. Dan Nimmo and David Swanson, "The Field of Political Communication: Beyond the Voter Persuasion Paradigm" in *New Directions in Political Communication*, David Swanson and Dan Nimmo, eds. (Beverly Hills, CA: Sage, 1990), p. 8.

9. Sanders, Kaid, and Nimmo, p. xiv.

10. Ibid.

11. Nimmo and Swanson, p. 11.

Series Foreword

Political scholars have historically recognized the social power of the mass media. The influence and role of the mass media in the electoral and governing processes have greatly increased over the last forty years. Today, the mass media have become the "central nervous system" for our society and the major source of public information about politics. The social power of the media is probably at an all time high. Today's media can quickly and efficiently attract, focus, and direct attention to social problems. They serve as our primary channels for public persuasion and mobilization.

Much of the power and influence of the mass media go beyond their messages to include the unique form and requirements of the specific medium. Television, for example, requires a special adaptation of the message, which should be simple, dramatic, visual, involving, and tied to an individual (Denton, 1988). By the early 1980s, Dan Nimmo and James Combs (1983) noted that few people learn about politics from direct experience. They argue that political realities are mediated through mass and group communication. The impact upon social behavior, according to Joshua Meyrowitz (1985), is the reorganization of social settings in which people interact simultaneous with the weakening of the relationship between "physical place and social place" (ix). Thus, physical presence is no longer a prerequisite for first-hand experience of the world. For Nimmo and Combs, the result is the "creation, transmission, and adoption of political fantasies as realistic views of what takes place" (xv).

Even political reporting, according to Murray Edelman (1988), has become mere "spectacle" that "continuously constructs and reconstructs social problems, crises, enemies, and leaders" (1). As a result, "accounts of political issues, problems, crises, threats, and leaders now become devices for creating disparate assumptions and beliefs about the social and political world rather than factual statements'' (10).

Neil Postman (1986) extends the argument claiming that politics, education, religion, and journalism must conform to the ''show business'' demands of today's media. Public discourse has become ''dangerous nonsense'' (16) where all subject matter is presented as entertaining, there for our amusement and pleasure (87). We just may, in Postman's words, be ''amusing ourselves to death.''

Within the academic community, there has always been a great debate about the specific effects of media upon our political process. I think the absence of medium effects in most research does not mean the absence of media effects. Perhaps the term ''media effects'' connotes too strong a deterministic notion and ''media influence'' is more palatable.

There are three principal ways the mass media influence American politics (Denton and Woodward, 1990, 148–162). The mass media collectively exert a considerable influence on determining the agenda of topics for public discussion, debate, and action. Not only is there a limit to the number of issues or topics that should or can receive public attention, but the selection of specific concerns increasingly lies with the mass communication industries rather than with citizens or public officials. It is difficult for politicians to initiate, establish, or maintain social agendas without the help and participation of the mass media industries. Politicians increasingly find themselves responding to rather initiating public issues. This rather strong position, however, does not negate the use of the media by politicians and government officials to convey ideas or share information with the public. Rather, the point to note is the symbiotic and interdependent relationship politicians and the public have with the media.

The media also give form and substance to world events: They construct the political realities to which we respond. Through the media we learn what is good or bad, right or wrong, strong or weak, just or unjust. In addition to telling us what to think about, the media thus influences us how to think. Even the reporting of facts requires subsequent judgment from the viewer. Reporters act as narrators and interpreters, often assessing the motives and consequences of political actions or events. Although we see our leaders more often, we also hear them less. Seldom do politicians and leaders speak for themselves—except in the form of short sound bites.

Finally, the media reduce abstract or ideological principles to human, personal components. Political issues and actions are linked to individuals. Rather than choose among policies or ideologies, we select among actors. This ''personalizing'' nature of the mass media has contributed. according to some, to the decline and lack of interest in party organizations and citizen participation in general.

Of course, it is important to remember that the term "mass media" is a plural concept and includes all the various news and entertainment media such as newspapers, films, magazines, radio and television programs, and music, to name a few. Today, as perhaps never before in our nation's history, there is a strong relationship between politics and popular forms of communication (Savage and Nimmo, 1990).

Despite the collective influence of the mass media, scholars initially avoided systematic study of the more popular forms of communication and politics. The focus has been limited to campaigns and clearly defined political messages. As the field of political communication grew and became more diverse, the focus of studies expanded to include a variety of contexts, messages, and media. Indeed, in the most recent assessment of the field of political communication, Dan Nimmo and David Swanson (1990) encourage that "the study of political communication would do well to move away from context-based conceptions of itself, particularly the unicentric campaign touchstone, toward an organizing framework grounded in basic questions about how communication and politics intersect" (11). This broader perspective recognizes the role of the popular media in reflecting the concerns, issues, myths, and values of the larger society.

Stephen Prince provides one of the most comprehensive analyses of contemporary political filmmaking. Cinema provides a wonderful landscape to assess the social concerns of a nation. According to Robert Savage (1990), movies are "parasocial vehicles revealing the very parameters of human society" and thus provide the "iconographic shorthand for political communication" (119–120).

The study of politics and film incorporates several dimensions. First is the relationship between the film medium and society. As Prince emphasizes, topicality has been essential to the popularity of Hollywood movies. To keep current with the audience, Hollywood productions routinely draw from contemporary political agendas and issues, portraying them at times explicitly, at other times implicitly. Prince situates prominent cycles of Hollywood productions—films dealing with the Cold War, with revolution in Latin America, with the Vietnam war, and with the declining health of the American economy—in relation to prominent political agendas and controversies during the 1980s.

As popular film responds to topical political issues, it must symbolically encode these into cinematic form. This is another dimension of the study of politics and film Prince emphasizes. He explores how filmmaking in the Hollywood industry is subject to firm limits upon the ways characters, stories, and images can be used to comment upon, and to represent, political issues and perspectives. His book explores Hollywood's interest in topical filmmaking and Reagan's social initiatives. According to Reagan, it was "morning again in America." The new day brought a renewed sense of moral purpose for America and its actions both at home and abroad. American films were quick to respond. In some cases, they recreated history while others articulated a partisan view, and some even challenged current social values and political assumptions. Collectively, the films of the Reagan era reflect some of the most important political, social, and economic issues of the time.

In his thoughtful and penetrating analysis, Prince helps us understand the political imagery of the era and the kinds of political forms available to contemporary American filmmakers. Reagan made us feel at ease while the national debt soared and the number of homeless and poor increased at an alarming rate. We now seem to be discovering the "placebo effect" of the Reagan era. American cinema was a major player in the process. The significance of this volume lies in the way it clarifies Hollywood's customary approaches to political representation and shows how the limits of those representations are a function, finally, of politics rather than cinema.

Robert E. Denton, Jr.

REFERENCES

Denton, Robert E., Jr. *The Primetime Presidency of Ronald Reagan*. New York: Praeger, 1988.

Denton, Robert E., Jr. and Gary Woodward. *Political Communication in America: Second Edition*. New York: Praeger, 1990.

Edelman, Murray. *Constructing the Political Spectacle*. Chicago: University of Chicago Press, 1988.

Meyrowitz, Joshua. *No Sense of Place*. New York: Oxford University Press, 1985.

Nimmo, Dan and James E. Combs. *Mediated Political Realities*. New York: Longman Press, 1983.

Nimmo, Dan and David L. Swanson. "The Field of Political Communication: Beyond the Voter Persuasion Paradigm." In *New Directions in Political Communication: A Resource Book*, ed. David Swanson and Dan Nimmo. Newbury Park, CA: Sage Publications, 1990.

Postman, Neil. *Amusing Ourselves to Death*. New York: Penguin Books, 1985.

Savage, Robert. "The Stuff of Politics Through Cinematic Imagery: An Eiconic Perspective." In *Politics In Familiar Contexts*, ed. Robert Savage and Dan Nimmo. Norwood, NJ: Ablex Publishing Corp., 1990.

Savage, Robert and Dan Nimmo. *Politics in Familiar Contexts*. Norwood, NJ: Ablex Publishing Corp., 1900.

Acknowledgments

Nothing changes so fast as the flux of daily political events, even if the cultural traditions and frameworks within which those events are embedded are more durable and resistant to change. Accordingly, one of the challenges in writing a book on political representation in contemporary Hollywood film is the sometimes breathless task of trying to keep pace with major events that can develop, and even be concluded, so quickly. As I began the research for this book, for example, Iraq and Kuwait were at peace with one another. When I wrote the final chapter, Kuwait's oil fields were on fire and hundreds of thousands of Iraqis lay dead from U.S. and allied firepower. A more dramatic example of this problem is apparent in the fate of the Soviet Union. As this book was going to press, a question emerged about whether or not the Soviet Union would continue to exist as a union, or as a new arrangement of confederated republics. Although the term Soviet Union is used in this book, it is done so in full acknowledgment of swiftly changing events.

Not only do topical events unfold at a rapid pace but they can be quickly eclipsed in the popular mind. The intense anti-Sovietism of the early Reagan years, for example, has been replaced by a new, more cordial, and supportive U.S.-Soviet relationship. One of the important functions to be served by a book like this, therefore, is in recalling political features of the not-too-distant past as a means of contextualizing Hollywood film productions as well as of securing this past against the steady erosion of new developments.

This is a book on film, but in contextualizing the films of the 1980s I have attempted to sketch selected features of the political background against which Hollywood production occurred. In reconstructing these features from the vantage of a different era, I necessarily placed myself in relation to both the films and their time. In other words, the accounts and analyses that follow are not without their own political position and point of view. It would be spurious to pretend otherwise, especially in a book on a subject as notoriously personal as the movies.

The filmmakers, actors, and political personalities of the 1980s who figure in the pages that follow must be acknowledged as among the major influences on this book because their work and lives helped to create in a very real way the world and the culture we inhabit.

I would like to thank Robert Denton, the series editor, for his interest in a volume on political imagery in contemporary Hollywood film and for his enthusiastic encouragement. I would also like to thank my colleagues in the Department of Communication Studies at Virginia Polytechnic Institute and State University for the supportive environment they create on a daily basis. Teresa Darvalics assisted with her word-processing skills.

VISIONS OF EMPIRE

Introduction: A Decade of Political Representation

Despite the Hollywood film industry's ambivalent relationship with political subjects and content, the 1980s was a very good decade for political filmmaking, if that is measured in terms of the volume of productions engaging political issues and the explicitness with which they did so. To take just a few examples, Hollywood films spoke to us about the conflicts in Central America (*Under Fire, Salvador*), the need for a strong American military (*Top Gun, Iron Eagle*), the Soviet menace (*Red Dawn, Rambo III*), the use of anticommunism as a vehicle for domestic political repression (*Daniel*), the uncertain legacy of the political Left in American society (*The Return of the Secaucus Seven, The Big Chill, Running on Empty*), the crisis of farm foreclosures (*Country, The River*), the avarice of the world of high finance (*Wall Street*), and the social fragmentation and anomie afflicting diverse groups and breeding alienation, bitterness, and homicidal rage (*The River's Edge, Talk Radio, Colors*). These and other subjects vied with blockbuster fantasies (*Ghostbusters, Batman*) for the attention of the nation's moviegoers, and although the blockbusters generally eschewed contemporary social realities in favor of beguiling imaginary worlds, many other productions chose instead to confront and engage the issues of their day. It is with those films that this book is concerned.

To look for, and expect to find, political material in Hollywood films may seem to be a chimerical undertaking. After all, didn't Hollywood proclaim that messages were more suited to Western Union than to films? Yet, throughout the 1980s, as in earlier decades, popular movies were tied so closely to the desires and anxieties of their audiences that they could not do otherwise than embody and refract the currents of social and political culture that helped define the era to which they belonged. As a vehicle of popular culture conceived and marketed to appeal to large numbers of people, movies are inevitably part of a collective cultural landscape. Trying to specify the nature of this relationship between film and culture, however, has always involved problems of linkage and causation. The question of where the influence lies and in which direction— whether it moves from movies to society or the reverse—has been a persistent problem, but it is probably irresolvable and finally may not be very informative. As the editors of an anthology studying the interplay between Hollywood film and American political history pointed out, ''In most cases it is impossible to discover whether films served more to shape popular attitudes or to reflect them.''[1] As noted, however, it has been a classic issue with which studies of movies and politics have tried to grapple. The problems that can arise from strict or prescriptive attempts to resolve it are decisively embodied by Siegfried Kracauer in his classic study of 1920s German cinema, *From Caligari to Hitler*. Kracauer contended that film reflects the collective cultural consciousness (or unconscious) and that its images prefigure and embody the logic and direction of social development. Thus, German films of the interwar period, he maintained, predict the rise of Hitler. Analytic hindsight, of course, is perfect perception, and Kracauer could decode the films knowing full well where Germany would be in the 1930s. Moreover, anticipating this, he could be selective about the films he chose and the images he selected to support his more general hypothesis.

For a number of reasons, posting such a strong, if not perfect, correlation between trends in film and society is insupportable. The intentions or effects of aesthetic doctrines are almost always far richer than the political platforms to which they may be attached or which may, on occasion, motivate them. Given films or doctrines may embody both progressive and reactionary tendencies. Was the expressionism Kracauer studied, for example, progressive or reactionary? On film, perhaps, a case can be made that *The Cabinet of Dr. Caligari* (1919)—a key film in the expressionist cycle—is an authoritarian parable, but on the other hand Fritz Lang—a major expressionist director whose *Metropolis* (1926) was one of Hitler's favorite films—fled from the Nazis to America, despite being offered an important position in the Nazi film industry. Outside the cinema, the expressionist images of the artist Georg Grosz clearly embody a radical antifascist critique. Aesthetics may on occasion be expressive of, or homologous with, political frameworks but are not always reducible to them.

To put this issue in another way, visual images and narratives are polyvalent. Films are frequently ambiguous, especially Hollywood films because of their need to appeal to wide and diverse segments of the public. We will examine this phenomenon at greater length in Chapter 1, but here it will be sufficient to note that the economic imperatives of

Hollywood productions, their need for broad appeal, often lead them to violate or contradict or mute the logic of a straightforward presentation of sets of social values or political frameworks or positions. This is one reason why a perfect correlation does not exist between trends in Hollywood films and society or politics. Yet another reason is Hollywood's own long-standing belief that entertainment values must take precedence over whatever social messages or values a given film might embody or convey. To recognize this distinction, however, is not to imply that the studios' entertainment tradition is itself free of social orientation or political assumptions. Indeed, throughout this book, we will see that the structures of the Hollywood image and narrative intersect in often influential ways with the content of a given film, providing, in a sense, its rhetorical inflection.

Despite its commitment to a tradition of entertainment, and despite the ambiguous linkages between film and society, aesthetics and politics, American film has consistently sought out topicality. Kevin Brownlow has emphasized the extraordinary attention devoted during the early silent era to social problem films dealing with crime, drugs, prohibition, censorship, poverty, women's suffrage, political corruption, and sexual morals.[2] During the sound era, the social problem film was a durable and persisting production category found at all the major studios, and it was didactic in tone and representative of overt social criticism in its tackling of crime, unemployment, gangsterism, racism, and political and business corruption. As Peter Roffman and James Purdy point out in their study of this category of productions, the social problem film was tied to the currents of progressive politics and social concern in America from the depression to the onset of McCarthyism in the 1950s, after which the social problem film began to decline as the studios timidly fell into line during the political chill of the Cold War.[3] But this was a temporary retreat. The late 1960s and early 1970s saw a renewed wave of topical filmmaking, in the wake of the Vietnam war and the counterculture. Moreover, throughout the 1980s, despite the economic dominance of the blockbusters, American films were often extremely topical in their focus.

In part, this was a legacy of the Reagan period. Indeed, it would be more surprising had film not responded and embodied the anxieties and controversies of that era because it was, politically, a highly self-conscious time. Ronald Reagan's election to the presidency was presented by his campaign managers, by the media, and by other analysts as a political revolution, a decisive and profound political shift in the culture that would result in a major realignment and revision of the role and administration of government. Consonant with this, Reagan's administration was, for better or worse, an activist one, cutting social services, deregulating business, and promulgating the view that less government was better government. Responses to these policies were predictably intense, further heightening the political self-consciousness of the period. With the Reagan political agenda at the center of public discussion and debate, and with the administration's own need to promote and consolidate that agenda, ideological production and dispute were especially acute during the period. This self-awareness, and these issues and controversies, found their way into the era's popular films in myriad ways, some of the most pertinent of which are examined in the chapters to come.

Political visions and discourse could be found in the expected places in Hollywood films of the 1980s, as in the cycle of productions that reexamined America's involvement in Vietnam. But topical references and concerns might also appear in unlikely places. A routine police thriller like *The Last of the Finest* (1990), for example, unfolds as a formulaic action film about the efforts of a crack antinarcotics squad to stem drug traffic in the United States. (Dates following film titles are release dates. Films released in 1990 would, in general, have been in production in 1989 and can, accordingly, be considered works of the 1980s.) But the climax of the film reveals the villains to be U.S. politicians running drugs to finance the Contra war against Nicaragua. An elaborate drugs-for-weapons scheme is unearthed, and its organization points to the highest levels of U.S. government. The film ends with one of the drug traffickers, a White House aide, appearing on television to deny administration complicity in the operation. He speaks in front of the nation's flag, as George C. Scott's General Patton did in an earlier film. The White House official's denial, however, is contextualized by the narrative as a blatant lie, and the flag imagery places this corruption at the center of the nation's political institutions and discourse. "Giving unconditional support [to the Contras]," the aide says, "is, in my opinion, the most fundamentally American thing we can do to keep alive the spirit of freedom and truth." This speech, in the film's surprising and abrupt political conclusion, clearly suggests that public appeals to anticommunism and the support of "freedom" in Central America are covers for corrupt political realities and relationships. This turn in the film's narrative is clearly associated with the persistent, if during the 1980s quite muted, allegations that the administration was indeed using drug money to finance its war against Nicaragua and with subsequent suggestions of political complicity in Panamanian General Manuel Noriega's drug operations. That these openly critical perspectives could find their way into a routine genre film offers some indication of the importance of political experience in the culture of the period.

A more blatant illustration of the intensity and contentiousness with which the era's political agendas were fraught can be found in the reception of Tri-Star's *Air America* (1990), a comic action film about the operations of the CIA-funded airline during the secret war in Laos, an adjunct of the Vietnam conflict. The film is a poorly plotted, episodic collection of explosions and aerial stunts starring Mel Gibson and Robert Downey. Its irreverent tone was partly the work of screenwriter John Eskow, who had contributed material to "Saturday Night Live." Eskow described the film as "a fun, zany thing for the whole family, with laughs aplenty and big things blowing up."[4]

But it wasn't the film's juvenile comedy that aroused the ire of some leading newspapers. It was the film's suggestion that the secret war in Laos was funded via a drug smuggling partnership involving the CIA, U.S. military officials, and corrupt Laotian generals, in which Air America pilots smuggled guns for heroin, with some personally profiting from the deal. So concerned about this view of the war was *The Wall Street Journal* that it ran an op-ed piece against it. The article all but accused the film and its makers of manufacturing Communist propaganda. It called the film's plot "so moronic and mendacious that it might more logically have been distributed by Red Star Studios in Hanoi rather than Tri-Star Pictures in Hollywood."[5] Calling the film a "political obscenity" that could have been taken from "Jane Fonda's Hanoi diaries," the article was motivated by an acknowledged fear that the film might help supply the pop historical memory of the war for future generations. The film's crime, for the authors, was that it plants "the black hats squarely on the wrong heads." This fear is a curious one, given the large number of films about Vietnam that appeared after 1986 which idealized the U.S. effort in that war. The critical view of the war expressed by *Air America*, however juvenile its terms, is very much an anomaly among the period's films, most of which present a very loving evocation of the patriotism and devotion to duty of U.S. soldiers. The intense anger of the article, in fact, and its targeting of a single film, ironically indicate how constrained were the political perspectives of the period's Vietnam productions. When a single film like *Air America* did stray far outside those frameworks, it could be roundly condemned. It didn't seem to matter how amateurish or badly made the film was. Ideological fidelity counted for something.

The political intensity of the 1980s, then, established a frame within which film production might occur, as well as the reception that might be accorded given films. The remainder of the book tries to relate selected cycles of films to the period's often turbulent political concerns. Before describing the specifics of this project in more detail, a brief discussion of how I am construing political film is in order. Some film scholars have suggested that the linearity of Hollywood narratives, the "invisible" editing style of Hollywood films, or the projection environment itself (called "the apparatus") may express or embody political relationships or ideologies based on the way these styles or environments may call forth a certain kind of viewing and viewer.[6] Some scholars have maintained that Hollywood films, whether superficially informed by right-wing or left-wing perspectives, actually collapse these political distinctions by elaborating a core set of traditional American myths (revolving around such attributes as the frontier, marriage, home, family) whose function it is to resolve and reconcile political alternatives and differences.[7] While we will have occasion to note, and indeed to emphasize, the constraints and limitations operating upon the representation of political material in American film, we will also emphasize that the Hollywood cinema is not ideologically univocal. In the chapters to come, we will see that a certain space and range existed in the cinema of the 1980s for differing ideological inflections and portrayals of the period's political issues. We will also have ample occasion to note the ways that film conventions and formulas intersect with, limit, and often deform the political material to which they have been attached or which they structure and inform.

Our general position, however, will be that political representation and ideology in film are a matter of content and the ways it is inflected by image, narrative design, and other attributes of style. Rather than suggesting that continuity editing, for example, necessarily embodies, a priori, an ideological framework or position, we will see how the stylistic structures of Hollywood movies may be deployed to express and portray a range of political material. Implicit in this recognition is the principle of rule-governed expression. Rules constrain as well as empower, and this dialectic tension between expressive potential and limitations will be a central theme in our discussions. The conventions of continuity editing work to establish basic principles of coherence in film narratives, and their much-discussed "transparence" may have less to do with the ideological values they are said to embody and express and more with their capability to serve as structural analogues of real-world visual experience.[8] As such, they may then be used to construct narratives (although continuity editing is not the only editing system capable of constructing narratives) that express ideologies or address political issues. In the chapters to come, we will be very concerned with the stylistic structures available to American filmmakers, and we will be developing a portrait of a highly constrained film tradition with respect to political representation. The sources of these constraints have economic roots in the film industry's organization and the intellectual frameworks operative in American politics and society, as well as in the industry's preference for certain kinds of stories and visual styles. But these boundaries also define a space where topical representation may occur, and we will be interested to sample the range of voices, images, propositions, and discourses contending there. Robert Sklar noted this tension between conserving and critiquing in the American cinema when he wrote that despite the extent to which American movies have reflected established ideologies, they have also "altered or challenged many of the values and doctrines of powerful social and cultural forces in American society, providing alternative ways of understanding the world."[9]

We will be emphasizing, then, expression within a limiting field. In addition, our understanding of political film will place it in a broader category than that which usually applies when discussing "propaganda" films. Propaganda films, like Leni Riefenstahl's *Triumph of the Will* (1935) or Frank Capra's *Why We Fight* series (1942–1945), typically offer a fairly naked display of ideological values or political positions, and they have been widely studied. A great deal of literature exists on the Nazi cinema, for example, as well as on the didactic Soviet cinema of the 1920s. Many of these films assert a clear political line quite directly, and if they do so by deliberate factual omission or distortion, they are generally labeled propaganda. Moreover, as Harold Lasswell pointed out in his classic essay on the subject, propaganda includes as one of its aims the attempt to influence behavior or attitude. For Lasswell, "Propaganda in the broadest sense is the technique of influencing human action by the manipulation of representations."[10] While some of the films to be examined in this book—*Red Dawn* or *Rambo: First Blood Part II*, for example—offer clear and explicitly partisan political statements, it is doubtful that they, or any commercially produced and marketed Hollywood films, have as their raison d'être the influence of the audience's attitudes and behavior. The reasons for this have to do with the industry's economic need to appeal to the diverse segments of a heterogeneous public. (The industry's strategies for doing this will be examined in a subsequent chapter.) Furthermore, Hollywood has traditionally been suspicious of the inclusion of overtly partisan political positions in its films, preferring instead to emphasize entertainment values and, when necessary, to permit political issues to speak through the dominant entertainment formulas.

If not in the sense of overt propaganda, then, how are we to understand the political nature of Hollywood film? The answer is in an indirect, mediated, and symbolic process whereby Hollywood films reference salient clusters of social and political values and, through the operations of narrative, create a dialogue through and with these values and, on occasion, transform or revise them (within the world of the narrative). Hollywood entertainment films may embody, question, or critique constellations of established social values that underlie out attitudes and assumptions about real historical, social, or political events or conditions (e.g., the Vietnam war, corporate and consumer society). By recognizing that contemporary narrative films, manufactured as entertainments with mass appeal, must necessarily draw upon and rework salient cultural values, the political implications of such films become clearer. "Political" is understood here not just in terms of parties and electoral institutions, or the design of overt propaganda, but as the realm of collective values and fantasies that underlie and inform socioeconomic systems and behavior in the real world. To the extent that Hollywood entertainment films dramatize these systems and this behavior and allude to real historical events, and do it by way of appeals to collective desires and fantasies, such films are deservedly seen as political works. They are, in most cases, not propaganda films, but they do tell us a lot about contemporary American social anxieties and the range of cinematic devices that may be used to structure political messages.

The aims of the book, then, are twofold. First, the book will provide a close analysis of the political imagery in major categories and genres of American films of the 1980s. Since we are dealing with a visual medium, the analysis will proceed by closely examining the structure of the imagery in these works and the ways that imagery is integrated into narrative patterns. This will allow us to emphasize the *cinematic* nature of political film and to describe the range of permissible and impermissible formal structures available to contemporary American film in its political dimension. We will see, in fact, that American narrative films are sharply constrained in the kinds of visual and narrative structures they can use to describe the contours of social and political worlds. The constraints of the "entertainment" film tend to channel the efforts of filmmakers into sharply defined narrative and visual patterns, and the book will describe the multileveled tensions issuing from this: tensions between historical events and their cinematic representations, between the films and the dominant cultural values to which they respond and which they occasionally question, and between the images within a given film and the Hollywood formulas it uses and the overt messages it tries to send. Political visions in contemporary films are often quite messy. Because cultural attitudes may be fluid and tied to historical events that are in flux, the efforts of a given film to articulate a political vision, and by doing so to pin down these attitudes and events, frequently yields a movie that is full of interesting tensions and contradictions. (These tensions also distinguish such works from the propaganda films, which tend to be more ideologically homogeneous.)

In describing these tensions, the book will engage its second aim, which is to offer a more general mapping of the kinds of political forms available to contemporary American filmmakers. What is the range of models of political filmmaking that American films have drawn upon in the 1980s? We will see that this is a more limited range than is available to European or Third World filmmakers and that these constraints have much to do with the nature of the Hollywood entertainment film. For filmmakers working outside the United States, self-reflexive, overtly interrogative forms have been powerfully influential and persuasive. In these, the filmmaker does not seek to portray his film as a self-contained illusion, as "real life," but emphasizes its real status as a deliberately created series of images that make intentional reference to historical or social events. Such a strategy tries to encourage the viewer to be more critical of both the depicted events and their depiction. This tradition is almost totally lacking in American fictional films, and one goal of the book will be to examine the cinematic strategies used in its stead.

This book is not intended as a history of American political films in the 1980s. Its aims are less comprehensive and more specific. The analysis tries to show how, and to some extent why, Hollywood films have been constrained in talking intelligently about contemporary society and politics. Since the book does not aim to be a history of the period, a few methodological remarks about the design of its focus are in order. Because the understanding of political film employed here is an inclusive one, it could be extended and applied to a wide range of films and genres. For example, certain key films of the 1980s, such as *Back to the Future* (1985) and *Field of Dreams* (1989), seem to be intimately connected with the zeitgeist of the decade, particularly with the nostalgic myths incarnated by the Reagan-era political culture and the desire for retrieval of and reconciliation with a past conceived in idealized and romanticized terms. In both films, the protagonists are able to magically reenter this familial and cultural past and rearrange it to suit the needs of the present. Marty McFly (Michael J. Fox) in *Back to the Future* travels back in time, and Ray Kinsella (Kevin Costner) is able to mystically re-create the past in an Iowa cornfield of dreams. Both meet their parents again and, in doing so, are able to reclaim their boyhood. Both films are claimants to that blend of folklore and memory, history and nostalgic mythology, that imperative never to grow up, that Garry Wills saw as central to 1980s America.

Other key films of the period include, of course, the work of Steven Spielberg and George Lucas, who established successful careers through emotionally charged appeals to adolescence and childhood. The mystical faith placed in "the force" and the fear of the power of "the dark side" that organizes Lucas's *Star Wars* trilogy is a cinematic analogue of the politically dichotomous visions of the period, clearly evidenced by the degree to which names and terms derived from Lucas's series entered the political lexicon of the time (e.g., "Star Wars," "evil empire"). Spielberg's more recent box-office struggles (*Empire of the Sun, Always*) may indicate how important the culture of the period was in sustaining his work.

Because, then, our understanding of political film is an inclusive one and because many productions during the 1980s intersect in myriad ways with the political and cultural agendas of the period, I have chosen to restrict the present discussion mainly to films that deal with overtly political topics rather than those, like *Back to the Future* and *Field of Dreams*, which are implicitly symbolic of the period's political culture. Thus, we will consider cycles of films that examined the Cold War struggle between the United States and Soviet Union and its allies, the revolutions in Latin America, the U.S. role in Vietnam, and the social ills and pathologies of domestic urban society. Each of these areas was a major topic of discussion and debate, occupied a major place on the political agenda of the period, and was addressed by a significant body of films. We will want, then, to integrate the films with the corresponding political agendas.

A second principle of selection was also employed. In order to create the space for a detailed analysis of each of the production cycles, the sample of films examined was, for the most part, drawn from *Variety's* list of all-time box-office champions.[11] *Variety's* criteria for inclusion are those films which paid more than $4 million in domestic rentals to their distributor. Selecting from this list provided a means for narrowing the universe of films available for discussion in a way that would permit sustained focus and analysis and that would differentiate major productions from the sometimes numerous minor offshoots concerned with a given political topic. If one is interested in political films and, especially, the saliency of given cinematic forms for political messages, then it can be useful to examine films that are widely seen. Some caveats, however, are in order. No purely "reflectionist" assumptions are being made here. That is, by examining top box-office draws, I am not assuming that such films are necessarily popular because they reflect popular fears and desires. They very well may do that, but the structure of the film industry today is such that it acts as a very restrictive gatekeeper. With inflationary, upwardly spiraling production costs, and with competition from the ancillary markets of video and cable television, film production for the theatrical market has today come to emphasize a fairly narrow range of film categories and genres. This restriction is due as much to the nature of the industry as to audience tastes. While it is important, therefore, to study those films which are being widely seen, we should not confuse this popularity with a necessary reflection of audience desire. Furthermore, the theatrical market no longer furnishes all, or even most, of a given film's revenue. Some films are seen more widely on video than in the theaters, thereby qualifying the usefulness of theatrical revenue data for establishing the popularity of a given film.

Despite these considerations, however, theatrical revenue data do provide one source of information for evaluating the public visibility of a given film production vis-à-vis the topics it addresses, and in this limited context they can be useful in providing an initial basis for establishing representative films for discussion. But, because of the foregoing considerations, I have not restricted the films under discussion to the *Variety* list. It provided an initial basis for selection and was, in turn, supplemented with additional films that had an obvious bearing upon the political topic under discussion. Examining the film treatments of the revolutions in Latin America, for example, entailed going beyond and outside of the *Variety* list because the films in that cycle—*Under Fire, Salvador, Romero,* and others—did not gross enough to appear on the list, but they do constitute a distinct cycle of productions that addresses a major item on the period's political agenda: the roots of the conflicts in Latin America and the U.S. role therein. In addition to going beyond the *Variety* list, I have also, on occasion, treated the boundaries of the decade in a slightly fluid fashion in order to pursue a discussion of the antecedents of a given film cycle or its extensions. Thus, discussion of the Vietnam war productions of the 1980s begins with a consideration of the films produced on that subject in the 1970s, especially such late 1970s productions as *The Deer Hunter*, *Coming Home*, and *Apocalypse Now*, in order to see how the films of the 1980s diverge from or are compatible with the imagery and narratives of these earlier productions. By employing a flexible set of selection criteria, then, I have tried to direct a sustained focus on the major films in four topical areas of production.

Chapter 1 establishes the theoretical framework relevant for the subsequent analyses by considering some basic features of the political landscape of the Reagan period and the structure of the contemporary film industry as it bears upon attempts at topically engaged filmmaking. Traditional Hollywood attitudes and practices in past decades regarding politics and film are also discussed, and theories about political representation and the place of ideology in film and other communications media are examined.

Chapters 2 through 5 focus upon major cycles of political films, each chapter in essence a case study of a given cycle. Chapter 2 examines the new Cold War films, those 1980s productions which played upon fears of the Soviet menace or Soviet expansionism. *Rambo III*, *Invasion USA*, *Red Dawn*, *Top Gun*, and others offered portrayals of international power bloc relations that accommodated and supported, in often explicitly self-conscious terms, the objectives and assumptions of Reagan-era foreign policy. The aggressively ideological tone of these films placed them to some extent outside the dominant entertainment formulas of the Hollywood tradition and closer to the propaganda productions briefly undertaken by the industry in the wake of the House Committee on Un-American Activities hearings during the 1950s.

The civil wars and peasant revolutions in Latin American countries such as El Salvador, Nicaragua, and Guatemala were major items on the foreign policy agenda of the early 1980s, and public discussion of these events was charged with Cold War tensions. The specter of Vietnam reappeared on the domestic political landscape, as the prospect of direct American troop involvement in El Salvador or Nicaragua seemed a real possibility. Chapter 3 examines the small group of films—*Under Fire*, *Salvador*, *El Norte*, and others—that addressed the wars in Latin America and the ways they explained the origins of the conflict and the U.S. role therein.

In the late 1970s and continuing throughout the 1980s, American fiction films began trying to come to grips with the Vietnam war, constructing various histories and mythologies of that war and its effects upon the United States. These evolving accounts are examined in Chapter 4 as examples of the symbolic reconstruction of social memory. The films are grouped according to the differing modes of historical understanding and explanations they offer.

One of the most interesting developments in the 1980s was the politicization of the science fiction film. A cycle of films emerged that offered critical commentaries on the pathologies of contemporary urban society and capitalism. *Blade Runner, Aliens, Robocop, Total Recall,* and others used the garb of fantasy to project existing social conflicts into a heightened future form, envisioning dystopian futures where corporate and military states have extirpated democratic aspirations. The degree of political explicitness and critique available in these fantasy films is compared in Chapter 5 with what was possible in the Cold War, Vietnam, and Latin America films. This comparison will allow us to evaluate the role of fantasy as a structural mediator of political content because this dystopia cycle works upon its political referents in a less direct and immediate fashion than do the films in the other production cycles.

The Afterword assesses the efficacy, for modes of political address, of the visual and narrative conventions employed by these four film cycles and seeks to establish some general conclusions regarding the potential for political representation in contemporary Hollywood films.

By focusing on the ways recent American films have sought to represent contemporary social and political issues, the book aims to provide an analysis of the political imagery in 1980s American movies and an exploration of those cinematic structures available (and unavailable) to American filmmakers interested in visualizing contemporary politics. The politics of the 1980s offered a renewal of the claims of American empire, that is, of a commitment to a vision of the United States as the leading economic, military, and political power in the world, one capable of exerting an undiminished influence over international affairs and the maintenance of its interests overseas. But, as we will note in later chapters, the social infrastructure of the United States is in crisis, perhaps signaling the beginning of a decline. To what extent did our films join the prevailing call to empire or seek alternatives? To answer that, we now need to enter more deeply into the cinematic and political fictions of the period.

NOTES

1. John E. O'Connor and Martin A. Jackson, eds., *American History/American Film,* (New York: Frederick Ungar, 1988), p. xxiv.

2. Kevin Brownlow, *Behind the Mask of Innocence* (New York: Knopf, 1990).

3. See Peter Roffman and Jim Purdy, *The Hollywood Social Problem Film* (Bloomington: Indiana University Press, 1981).

4. Quoted in " 'Air America' Hits Turbulence," *Variety,* September 10, 1990, p. 78.

5. Peter B. Kann and Phillip Jennings, "Trashing History: Did Hanoi Make This Movie?" *The Wall Street Journal*, August 28, 1990, p. A8.

6. The key essays arguing this position are in Phillip Rosen, ed., *Narrative, Apparatus, Ideology* (New York: Columbia University Press, 1986). For a counter-argument and critique of this position, see Noel Carroll, *Mystifying Movies: Fads and Fallacies in Contemporary Film Theory* (New York: Columbia University Press, 1988).

7. See, for example, Robert B. Ray, *A Certain Tendency of the Hollywood Cinema, 1930–1980* (Princeton: Princeton University Press, 1985).

8. Questions about the relationship between editing codes (and pictorial codes in general) and real-world visual experience have received a great deal of investigation and discussion. See, for example, J. B. Deregowski, "Real Space and Represented Space: Cross-Cultural Perspectives," *Behavioral and Brain Sciences* 12 (1989), pp. 51–119; Julian Hochberg and Virginia Brooks, "Pictorial Perception as an Unlearned Ability: A Study of One Child's Performance," *American Journal of Psychology* 75 (1962), pp. 624–628; Paul Messaris, "To What Extent Does One Have to Learn to Interpret Movies?" in *Film/Culture*, ed. Sari Thomas (Metuchen, NJ: Scarecrow, 1982), pp. 168–183.

9. Robert Sklar, *Movie-Made America* (New York: Random House, 1975), p. 316.

10. Harold W. Lasswell, "Propaganda," *Encyclopaedia of the Social Sciences*, vol. 12 (New York: Macmillan, 1934), p. 521.

11. "All-Time Film Rental Champs," *Variety*, February 21, 1990, pp. 183–218.

Chapter One

Hollywood, Politics, and Media Study

In an era of instant electronic journalism where the sound bite frames the memorable image, our collective portraits of the world may be as much a product of images as of real political experience. At a time when the media consultant is a fixture of campaigns, is virtually an invisible running mate, and the 30-second television spot can make or break a candidate, the two seem to be merging so that political discourse often becomes a language of images. The embodiment of these trends throughout the 1980s, of course, was Ronald Reagan, popularly known as "the great communicator," a president who used television, radio, and the press quite successfully to consolidate both his presidency and his political agenda. With President Reagan, in fact, it was sometimes difficult to tell where real life began and movie images ended. Although never there himself, Ronald Reagan described a black sailor at Pearl Harbor, gallantly cradling a machine gun in his arms, who "stood on the end of a pier blazing away at Japanese airplanes that were coming down and strafing him," to explain why the military forces ended segregation during World War II.[1] And despite the fact that segregation in the military was not abolished until several years *after* the war, Reagan claims to "remember the scene. It was very powerful."[2] The anecdote is described as a scene, a movie image, yet is meant to retain all of its "alleged" historical significance.

This merging of cinema and reality is apparent in many of Reagan's memories. As Garry Wills points out, Reagan seems to recall his time in the Los Angeles movie colony during and after World War II as if he had fought overseas.[3] Despite spending the war years in the United States, Reagan seemed to imagine himself in the thick of things, with the fighting men. In his most amazing statement, he claimed that he had filmed the Nazi death camps as part of his war duties with the Signal Corps and had kept one of the films in case one day he had to prove to skeptics that the Holocaust was real.[4] He titled his autobiography *Where's the Rest of Me?* after his favorite line from his favorite film, *King's Row*, identifying himself with the legless playboy Drake McHugh.[5] In 1985, after enjoying *Rambo: First Blood Part II*, he enthusiastically announced that he knew what to do the next time American hostages were taken in the Middle East. As his popularity in the polls (prior to the Iran-Contra scandal) indicated, Americans didn't seem to mind this confusion. His mix-ups were emblematic of the political and cultural atmosphere of the decade, and it is in this context that they are of interest for us.

Michael Rogin suggested that "Reagan's easy slippage between movies and reality is synechdochic for a political culture increasingly impervious to distinctions between fiction and history."[6] As the "Reagan revolution" came to office with just 29 percent of the eligible electorate's vote, yet claimed to represent a landslide of popular opinion, the decade saw the loss or blurring of important distinctions between fiction and history, ideology and fact. While presiding over a massive transfer of wealth, during which the personal income of the poorest one-fifth of the population decreased by 9.8 percent while the income of the wealthiest one-fifth increased by 15.6 percent,[7] Reagan was able to publicly identify himself with Franklin Roosevelt and invoke populist rhetoric. He compared the Nicaraguan Contras to the nation's Founding Fathers, the Nazi SS soldiers at Bitburg cemetery to the Jewish victims of the Holocaust, arms control agreements to the appeasement of Hitler at Munich—passing over the important historical and political differences. Discussing this, political correspondent Sidney Blumenthal finds that "The abuse of history was one of the era's defining features."[8] Blumenthal points out that in Reagan's worldview, facts were simply unimportant. Reagan presided over an "America of the mind," informed by an ideology that had the timeless appeal of a dream as it invoked a mythical past. "Reagan has faith that we are always the same and that the place remains the same. . . . Among the virtues of the promised land is its vagueness."[9] Blumenthal argues that as a veteran of the entertainment industry, Reagan is a hero of consumption rather than of production, promoting a symbolic politics of national transformation and economic growth through faith and appearances, rather than through self-denial and sacrifice (qualities entailed by the older ideals of production). "Reagan represents consumption without guilt. . . . He allows us to have whatever we want so long as we give credence to an obsolescent ideology. He's a permissive father."[10]

The muting of ideological alternatives, of political discourse and history, during the Reagan period resulted in part from the lack of an institutionalized political opposition. Faced with a resurgent political Right, liberals and Democrats acquiesced in the resurrection of a new Cold War at the beginning of the decade, with its unfortunate tendency to view international conflicts as the result of Soviet expansionism. As Alan Wolfe points out, "By choosing to make its foreign policy on grounds established by its opposition, liberals simply delayed their own de-legitimation. Having sacrificed any alternative to a foreign policy of anti-communism, they were used up and discarded by the electorate, which in 1980 turned to those who had been establishing the foreign policy framework from near the start of the postwar period."[11]

Inevitably culture, too, reflected in myriad ways the contours of the decade's political and imaginary landscape. In the cinema, as we shall see, films embodied as well as responded to the changing political tides in Washington. Conjoining the two realms, symbolic mediator of politics and cinema, was Ronald Reagan, the trained Hollywood actor-cum-politician. To what extent did the political culture of the period influence American filmmaking, eliciting films that earnestly embodied the terms of its discourse or sought instead to critique, satirize, or condemn? Subsequent chapters attempt to address this question. Before that can be done adequately, however, some theoretical and historical background must be established. Accordingly, this introductory chapter examines three topical areas that bear upon political representation in the American cinema, past and present. First, we will examine the structure of the contemporary film industry and its consequences for political filmmaking, as well as the sets of industry attitudes and practices that have historically governed political representation in American film. Second, we will consider political culture in the 1980s, the major contours of the decade's political landscape that would inspire and influence the social content in myriad Hollywood films. Finally, we will need to examine the sociology of mass media scholarship and criticism as they have addressed political representation, the links between society and media content, and the place of ideology in film and other media of communication. In doing so, we will attempt to locate contemporary work in film studies within a larger tradition of mass media scholarship. These discussions will help establish a historical frame and some theoretical parameters for our subsequent examination of political imagery in contemporary American film.

In order to explore the importance of the symbolic politics of the 1980s as a frame for understanding the discourse of the era's most popular films, we need first to look more closely at the structure of the film industry during this period and its effects upon political and social representation. This is not just a question of the extent to which the film creations of George Lucas and Steven Spielberg embodied the political culture of the Reagan period.[12] The structure of the industry itself can incline production in certain directions rather than in others, helping to establish norms and conventions that govern social and political representation. The contemporary film industry is part of an integrated network of conglomerated corporate activity. The major studios are owned by parent companies that have diversified into related leisure-time markets. An initial wave of consolidation occurred in the 1960s when Universal was acquired by Music Corporation of America, Paramount by Gulf and Western, United Artists by Transamerica Corporation, Warner Brothers by Kinney Services (which then created Warner Communications, Inc.), and MGM by real estate financier Kirk Kerkorian. Sales, new acquisitions, and mergers of film studios have continued, especially since the emergence of blockbuster production in the 1970s demonstrated the enormous profit potential of film production. Coca-Cola, for example, relinquished Columbia Pictures Entertainment, and Sony snatched it up for $3.4 billion. Warner's parent company recently merged with Time, Inc., to create an unprecedented concentration of media outlets.

Developing in tandem with this concentration of ownership have been the newer markets for film, termed the "ancillary" markets, primarily videocassettes and cable television. In the mid-1980s, returns from video rentals and sales surpassed box-office revenues. In 1989, the video business brought in more than $11 billion, compared with about $5 billion for theatrical revenues.[13] Control of the ancillary markets—and the need to keep them supplied with product[14]—is a spur to diversification. Robert Gustafson has shown how Warner Communications, Inc. (WCI), operates through a series of mutually reinforcing multiple profit centers, each one of which can aid the others.[15] During the 1980s WCI could market consumer products in the areas of recorded music (Warner Brothers, Atlantic, and Elektra/Asylum/Nonesuch Records), films (Warner Brothers film and television production, Warner Home Video, Warner Bros. Distribution), publishing (Warner Books, Mad Magazine, D.C. Comics), cable (The Movie Channel), consumer electronics (Atari), and such other operations as The Franklin Mint. Control of these areas permits WCI to enforce policies of price discrimination, that is, to segment consumers into different markets and charge them different prices for similar goods (i.e., depending on whether the film is seen in a theater, on cable TV, or on a VCR).[16] Moreover, as Gustafson shows, a hit film can generate a TV show (Warner's Alice Doesn't Live Here Anymore was the basis for the Warner TV series), and Warner books like All the President's Men can lead to Warner movies. Most spectacularly, Warner comic characters like Superman and 1989's top hit, Batman, can become the subjects of movies. Sound tracks can be marketed on Warner record labels and the video versions can be released on Warner Home Video. Spin-off products can appear as Knickerbocker dolls or Atari games, or be licensed to other manufacturers through Warner's Licensing Corporation of America. And all of this predates the merger with Time, Inc., which carried its own obvious advantages, such as a feature article promoting Warner's Batman.

While WCI is one of the most spectacular examples of the interlocking "leisure-time" market, the general trend of consolidation that it represents is a basic principle in today's Hollywood, and it has had a marked effect on the kinds of movies that are made. Fundamental to the maintenance of this system is blockbuster production and the mushrooming phenomenon of "product placement" and related product tie-ins. In the 1980s, Hollywood production emphasized the manufacture of film blockbusters, movies that are frequently expensive to produce but that generate staggering sums of money at the box office. *The Godfather*, with its huge gross revenue in 1972, was an augury of things to come. But it was Steven Spielberg's *Jaws* in 1975, tied in to a mountain of related products (books, records, dolls, T-shirts, hosiery, jewelry, etc.) that seemed to officially announce the onset of the blockbuster era. Spielberg himself, and his pal George Lucas, would be the key players developing and defining the blockbuster film style: technically polished and aggressively manipulative images, heavily dependent on special effects, reducing narrative to a simple succession of "wow" episodes, and, most significantly for the era's political culture, presenting Manichaean struggles between good and evil.[17] Between them, Spielberg and Lucas are responsible for eight of the top ten all-time film rental champions: *E.T.*, *Star Wars*, *Return of the Jedi*, *The Empire Strikes Back*, *Jaws*, *Raiders of the Lost Ark*, *Indiana Jones and the Last Crusade*, and *Indiana Jones and the Temple of Doom*.[18] The other two top ten films—*Batman* and *Ghostbusters*—are clearly in the Spielberg-Lucas mold.

The rush to blockbuster production had become so pervasive a feature of the industry by the end of the decade that the chairman of Disney Studios, Jeffrey Katzenberg, issued a 28-page memo castigating the "atmosphere of near hysteria" stimulated by the blockbuster climate. "It seems that, like lemmings, we are all racing faster and faster into the sea, each of us trying to outrun and outspend and outearn the other in a mad sprint toward the mirage of making the next blockbuster."[19] *Batman* spectacularly demonstrated just how much money could be made, and how quickly, in the blockbuster sweepstakes. Released in the summer of 1989, by year's end it had returned to its distributor over $150 million (rental returns are only about 40–50 percent of the box-office gross). *Batman*, in fact, was the quickest-grossing movie in Hollywood history and certainly helped make 1989 the highest-grossing ($5 billion) year ever. In its first weekend, June 23–25, it grossed $40 million.[20] In five months, it had grossed $250 million, and in the first six weeks of video release earned $400 million.[21]

Like *Teenage Mutant Ninja Turtles* a few months later, *Batman* set off a marketing craze as shopping malls and retail outlets were blitzed with books, clothing, jewelry, records, and other tie-ins. While the product tie-in is now an essential form of integration between advertising and the movies, product placement inside movies is also a firmly established part of the industry. Movie theater patrons resist the inclusion of ads before the start of the feature but do not seem to object when the ads are placed inside the film itself. E.T. eats Reese's Pieces, Darryl Hannah thaws her Haagen-Dazs inside a microwave in *Wall Street*, and Sally Field drinks Coke and asks for "an Extra-Strength Tylenol" in *Murphy's Romance*. The Teenage Mutant Ninja Turtles not only eat Domino's pizza but also get a discount when it arrives late, a plug for which Domino's reportedly paid a sum in the mid-five figures.[22] In old Hollywood, by contrast, operating under the Production Code Administration and the Advertising Code Administration, studios avoided the use of advertising in their films (although stars regularly endorsed products in the pages of popular magazines). Writing in 1947, Ruth Inglis observed, "Although occasionally high-pressure publicists for national products try to inject their sponsors' wares into films and at times bribe studio employees to achieve their ends, every effort is made to avoid unnecessary close-ups of radios and other items showing the name of the product, outdoor scenes showing advertising signs or billboards, and dialogue mentioning trade names."[23]

A handful of agencies handle most of the placements in major films today, generally for a flat fee. However, interesting and mutually lucrative arrangements frequently can be worked out. For the Tom Cruise vehicle *Days of Thunder*, Paramount worked deals where, in exchange for product placement, manufacturers like Chevrolet and Hardee's would plug the film in their own ads. A spot for Hardee's, airing as the film broke nationally, opened as if it were a preview of the film by showing the movie's title and footage of the racetrack, and only then launched into a pitch for hamburgers and a deal whereby Hardee's patrons could get little toy race cars with their burgers.

Proponents of product placement extoll the practice for two reasons. One is that it's very inexpensive compared with other forms of advertising. One product placement executive noted,

The average film can realize $200,000 in product placements. . . . If [the film earns] $20-million, which is average, you've reached 5.5 million people, and more importantly, when it is seen around the world—on video, HBO, maybe primetime TV—it's incredibly cost-efficient. When you're talking $10,000 to $50,000 [for a placement], the cpms are pennies. It's $400,000 for a 30-second spot, and people feel good when they see impressions in movies. It pays to have Tom Hanks driving a Subaru.[24]

Proponents also point out that product placement helps to create a greater sense of *realism* in a film. Al Ruddy, who produced *The Godfather*, talks about why it was so important for the Teenage Mutant Ninja Turtles to eat Domino's pizza: "That scene is funny because kids know Domino's Pizza, and they know you get money off when it's late. Also, when you have fantasy characters and can ground them in reality like that, it's great for the movie. . . . You can't have Mel Gibson picking up a pack of Ajax cigarettes and drinking Aqua beer, because people won't believe it."[25]

Commodity consumption thus becomes an index of realism for some films, rather than the characters, stories, or the issues a film might present. For proponents of the practice, Mel Gibson isn't believable unless he is shown surrounded by familiar brands. Yet this practice can be aesthetically detrimental. The need for prominent product display (background displays or incidental use have "negligible value," according to one placement executive[26]) can overwhelm narrative by interrupting it so our gaze may linger on the brand name. Moreover, as advertisers and their wares invade films, issues of creative control arise. Mark Crispin Miller, who has examined these problems, notes that the much-vaunted realism accruing from product placement is actually an antirealism which works to the detriment of the film: "Usually, however, 'product placement' does not seem 'natural' at all but is, in fact, deliberately anti-realistic: its sole purpose is to enhance the product by meticulously placing it within the sort of idealized display that occurs nowhere in real life but everywhere in advertising . . . the label or logo always shines forth like the full moon."[27]Advertisers, moreover, routinely try to match their products with the characters and stories that will give them the best showcase.[28]

In some cases, product merchandising can heavily influence the box-office success of a film. The first Teenage Mutant Ninja Turtles movie bombed on its release in Japan because there were no product tie-ins on toy store shelves to support the film. Despite lots of publicity, theater attendance was sparse. American copyright holders would not sell the Japanese the rights to merchandise based on the film's characters at a reasonable sum, the film's Japanese distributor claimed, attributing the movie's failure to lack of merchandise support.[29] We can now see why so many of the biggest contemporary films are cartoon-like or involve cartoon or mechanical characters: *Dick Tracy, Batman, Superman, E.T.*, the *Star Wars* series, *Jaws*, the Ninja Turtles. These characters, with their distinctive, stylized appearances, lend themselves easily to duplication as myriad product lines, much more easily than do ordinary-looking human beings or even the "old" Hollywood stars. Try to imagine Gregory Peck or Katharine Hepburn pictures on hamburger wrappers or bookbags, but you can easily picture R2D2 or Batman on lunch boxes. The extraordinary success of comic book films like *Batman* and *Dick Tracy* has stimulated a rush of development deals to bring to the screen Barbie, the Flintstones, Captain America, Dr. Strange, Iron Man, the Fantastic Four, Green Lantern, and others.[30] Universal has even registered the title "Nintendo: The Movie," just in case it can find a way of turning this phenomenally popular video game into a film.[31]

The use of popular film characters as advertisements for related product lines functions globally as a part of multinational economics. Describing how its film, video, and recorded music products were used in countries ranging from the United States, England, and Germany to Taiwan, Kenya, New Guinea, and Thailand, Warner Communications' 1982 annual report proudly described WCI's part in helping to create a global web of inter-linked cultural and commodity consumption: "There is a natural demand for entertainment the world over, and WCI's products have become an integral part of many different cultures in a variety of ways. . . . One reason for the success of Warner Communications internationally is the fact that its products know no geographical boundaries."[32]

Relationships between culture and commerce, film characters, and commodities, are being reorganized in the era of the blockbuster as an economy of advertising comes to regulate film production and its representations of our cultural life in new ways. Some films become ads, and characters like E.T. become products. Since it has already been suggested that a merging of the real and the symbolic was a hallmark of the Reagan presidency, we should ask about the consequences of these separate but analogous trends for the representation on screen of contemporary social and political life. To what extent does the cartoon or fantasy format in film facilitate or exclude possibilities for political representation? What have traditionally been Hollywood's attitude and practice regarding political filmmaking? It is important to recall some of the golden periods of the American cinema—the late 1930s and 1940s, the late 1960s and early 1970s—to reflect that film has, in the past, frequently been able to work as an oppositional medium to the society (e.g., Warner Brothers' gangster cycle of the 1930s or the films of Arthur Penn, Sam Peckinpah, and Stanley Kubrick in the 1960s and 1970s, all of which were quite popular in their day). Writing about Hollywood prior to the era of conglomeration, Ian Jarvie noted that Hollywood films were not always conservative or centrist in their outlook: "America had a strong tradition of social criticism and this made it respectable to expose, denounce, and impugn. What movies supplied were a new medium, a very elaborate series of conventions and genres, and an unparalleled discipline of form which gives film content a disturbing force."[33] He noted that films of the 1930s and 1940s "were as thematically rich as the world has ever seen."[34]

By contrast, the Spielberg-Lucas productions of the 1980s, and the cycles of films they inspired, set out to reassure their audiences with comforting narratives of virtue rewarded and evil defeated, stories about the need to submit to benevolent authorities who will take care of us as parents take care of children. That *Batman*, the major blockbuster of 1989, seemed so initially different from the optimistic fantasies of Spielberg or Lucas and could have been discussed as a grim and dark film reflecting the era of crack epidemics, homelessness, and relentless corporate acquisition[35] reflects the general absence of an authentically critical filmmaking in our time. Moreover, it ignores the way the film's handsome and triumphant hero and beautiful heroine, and the imagery of the powerful hero protecting the city, constitute familiar and reassuring formulas that help to cancel the film's brooding set design. Even Jack Nicholson's villain is such a blatant star turn as to become a figure of mirth and fun, a joker. Dark and disturbing films simply do not become blockbusters.

The blockbuster trend has reinforced and helped to legitimate in new ways a long-standing political and social caution on the part of Hollywood. Although, as noted, greater room and flexibility may have seemed to exist in the industry for the oppositional film in prior decades, a history of Hollywood could still be written emphasizing its cautionary policies and willingness to curb film content when faced with pressure groups of various stripes. Hollywood film production has a long tradition of extraordinary sensitivity to threats of public outcry, and if we take a look at some of the decisive moments in this history, we can better understand how the current crisis in film content has some of its roots in prior policies.

The major development curbing and regulating film content came with the establishment of the Production Code Administration (PCA) by the Motion Picture Producers and Distributors of America (MPPDA) in 1934 to enforce the principles of the Production Code, which had been adopted in 1930. Members of the MPPDA agreed that no studio film would be distributed unless it had been approved by the PCA. In practice, this meant that scripts would be submitted to the PCA prior to filming and that the PCA would review the finished film and be able to suggest changes before the picture was released. Compliance was essentially voluntary, and this enabled some producers and studios in the late 1940s and 1950s to ignore the PCA and to take films that would have been objectionable—for example, Otto Preminger's *The Moon Is Blue* and *The Man with the Golden Arm*—straight to theaters without a PCA seal, thereby helping to bring about the downfall of the PCA. Moreover, by the 1950s, studios had lost control of their first-run theaters, government censor boards were under attack by the courts, and in 1952 the Supreme Court finally granted films the same First Amendment protections that media like newspapers and magazines had long enjoyed (following a Court decision in 1915, films had been excluded from this protection on the grounds that they were strictly a business).

During its heyday in the 1930s and 1940s, the Production Code drastically restricted acceptable motion picture content.[36] The Code argued that motion pictures, because of their vividness and popularity, had a moral and educational responsibility to the public, which, it was assumed, was held in thrall by movies and could be unduly influenced by their content: "No picture shall be produced which will lower the moral standards of those who see it." Thus, crime was not to be presented in a sympathetic light nor its methods dwelt upon, nor could its perpetrators escape punishment. Liquor was not to be shown unless essential to the plot, human and "natural" law were inviolate, religion was to be respected, and its ministers could not appear as comic characters or villians. Revealing costumes were off-limits, the treatment of bedrooms had to be "governed by good taste and delicacy," "use of the flag shall be consistently respectful," "excessive and lustful kissing" could not be shown, and the "sanctity of the institution of marriage and the home" was to be upheld. The restrictions were legion and often seemingly trivial, helping to produce a falsely idealized, distorted portrait of human life on movie screens. Anthropologist Hortense Powdermaker satirically noted the huge gulf between daily life and the movie world: "Most people take for granted that marriages are consummated, that toilets are in bathrooms, that cows have udders, that sexual perversions exist . . . and do not think that references to them are necessarily vulgar. . . . The Code simply does not belong to this world."[37]

A major source of pressure on Hollywood in the 1930s came from the Legion of Decency, which had instituted its own ratings system, declaring studio products to be either morally unobjectionable, and therefore fit for Catholics to see, or morally objectionable in part for all. In the worst cases, films were condemned outright and were considered off-limits for Catholics (who constituted an audience in the millions and, therefore, the threat to studios of substantial loss of revenue). Two of the men who had authored portions of the Production Code were affiliated with the Catholic Church, so it is not surprising to find a philosophy consistent with Catholicism in certain portions of the Code. The Code, for example, prohibited adultery in almost all cases and stipulated that adulterers must be punished for their transgression. In a letter to a producer, PCA head Joseph Breen explained his objections to a novel proposed as a basis for a film: "The male lead . . . commits adultery in a flagrant fashion. The Code says that adultery as a subject should be avoided. When adultery is absolutely necessary for the plot, there must be ample compensating moral values, in the nature of a strong voice for decency, of pointed suffering, of actual punishment of the guilty. We fail to find these values in the story we have read."[38]

Among the most common reasons for the Legion of Decency to find a film morally objectionable were a frivolous treatment of marriage or divorce and the presence of "suggestive" scenes or dialogue. Of 157 major studio pictures released between 1939 and 1945 and classified as objectionable in part for all, the Legion found that 131 contained suggestive scenes, 32 presented a light treatment of marriage, and 26 presented divorce as a theme or situation.[39] Between 1936 and 1943, the Legion placed 53 releases on its condemned list, all but one of which were independent productions or foreign films rather than major studio releases.[40] The exception was Howard Hughes's *The Outlaw*, initially released without a PCA seal of approval. These figures help to indicate the relationship between the PCA and the Legion. PCA approval was important for the studios because it helped to ensure that a film would not be condemned by the Legion of Decency.

Both the Production Code and the Legion of Decency were the results of a prolonged period in the 1910s and 1920s of social agitation over allegedly indecent film content, during which many attempts were made by citizens' groups and state and local agencies to censor the movies.[41] Outside censorship was what the industry most feared so, in effect, it agreed to curb itself to prevent the government from doing so. A consistent assumption throughout much of this activity was that the movies exerted a hypnotic power over their audience and, through processes of modeling, would encourage audience members to imitate what they had seen on screen, to the detriment of society. The Production Code noted that the grandeur of the movies "arouses more intensely the emotional side of the audience" and that, psychologically, "the larger the audience, the lower the moral mass resistance to suggestion." A pamphlet produced by the Legion of Decency echoed the idea: "Many films, by their insidious and attractive presentation of false standards, induce their patrons to change their lifelong convictions and to believe that, occasionally, at least, certain sins are virtues and certain virtues are sins."[42] Similar ideas are found in the Payne Fund Studies, conducted in the early 1930s. The most extensive social scientific investigation of the movies undertaken to that point, these studies comprised eight volumes of research on the effects of movies on children and youth, and found some evidence of behavioral and attitudinal effects in such areas as delinquency and sexuality. Summarizing the results of the studies, W. W. Charters noted that movies "owe their power over children chiefly to the factor of emotional possession."[43] Watching a film, a child "loses ordinary control of his feelings, his actions, and his thoughts. . . . He is possessed by the drama."[44] Although these studies exerted minimal influence over subsequent empirical investigations of mass media content,[45] it is worth noting that the concepts of modeling and emotional persuasion still inform contemporary investigations of the media.[46]

In succumbing to popular pressure and instituting the Production Code, then, Hollywood was acknowledging the power of pressure groups and the fear of film's vivid modeling powers that lay behind them. Behind this retreat lay the desire for political and economic stability essential to continued profits, and the next time the industry was threatened by similar circumstances—charges of corrupt social or political content in films, beyond which loomed the threat of censorship—its response was identical: retreat, partnership with the pressure groups, and intensified self-policing. This time the charges were strictly political and came from

the House Committee on Un-American Activities (HUAC). Activated by
the Cold War commenced under Truman, HUAC investigated Hollywood
in 1947 and again in 1952, ostensibly concerned that Hollywood was in
danger of being taken over by Communists (although the headlines that
were garnered by interviewing famous stars and the careers to be made
by attacking the New Deal liberalism of FDR in the changed postwar world
were in many ways more powerful motivations for the hearings than the
unproven charges that Hollywood was about to go Red). Ronald Reagan,
who as president of the Screen Actors Guild had instituted loyalty oaths
for members and was convinced, then as now, that the Communist threat
to Hollywood was real, provides the orthodox view:

The Communist plan for Hollywood was remarkably simple. It was merely to
take over the motion picture business. Not only for its profit . . . but also for a
grand world-wide propaganda base. In those days before television and massive
foreign film production, American films dominated 95 percent of the world's movie
screens. We had a weekly audience of about 500,000,000 souls. Takeover of this
enormous plant and its gradual transformation into a Communist gristmill was
a grandiose idea. It would have been a magnificent coup for our enemies.[47]

Charges of Red propaganda centered on a handful of pro-Russia films
produced as part of the war effort—*Mission to Moscow, Song of Russia*—
and on a select few films deemed to have objectionable political content,
such as a critical view of the rich or an advocacy of populist values. The
evidence of on-screen propaganda was typically trivial. To support her
contention that *None but the Lonely Heart* was communistic, for example,
Lela Rogers, Ginger's mother, offered to cite for the committee a telling
line: "The mother in the story runs a second-hand store. The son says
to her . . . 'You are not going to get me to work here and squeeze pennies out of little people who are poorer than we are.' "[48] Rogers objected,
"We [Americans] don't necessarily squeeze pennies from people poorer
than we are."[49] Even friendly witnesses often had a hard time finding
evidence to support their charges of Communist propaganda. Gary
Cooper, for example, while maintaining that Hollywood films were being
spoiled by Red propaganda and claiming that he had found many scripts
with a Communist bias, could not think of a specific title (in Cooper's
case, this was because, he said, he read most of his scripts late at
night!).[50] The industry as a whole was reluctant to smear particular films
(better to sacrifice a few directors or screenwriters), but the very notion
that Hollywood films were espousing an explicit philosophy was patently
contrary to official industry practice. As Richard Maltby has noted, "conventional Hollywood wisdom regarded films about politics as box-office
poison, since anything controversial was liable to move the cinema out
of its safe and profitable territory as entertainment into more dangerous

areas. If the movies began to express their opinions about politics, politicians might want to express, and enforce, their opinions about the movies."[51]

Appeal to the widest audience was the basis for profit maximization, and this often entailed—then, as it does now—avoiding political controversy: "That the industry sought to make its entertainment safe, and therefore depoliticized, is clear. That it had economic motives for doing so is equally evident."[52] Hollywood's notorious attitude toward "messages" is that they were better sent by Western Union than by films. During World War II, producer Walter Wanger (*Foreign Correspondent*), president of the Motion Picture Academy of Arts and Sciences, told the Office of War Information to stop pressuring Hollywood to make propaganda films. Pointing out that audiences are quick to spot explicit political messages in films and are mainly seeking diversion, Wanger argued that well-made entertainments were more important for the public's spirits and the war effort. He succinctly stated Hollywood's credo: Audiences "are willing to be moved by genuine storytelling—anything that legitimately warms the heart and stirs the spirit. . . . They are not willing to be bored by clumsy pictures. . . . Any 'truths' you wish to impart, with and in the drama, had better be skillfully integrated."[53]

This historical background enables us to better contextualize the political potential of contemporary filmmaking. The contemporary blockbuster formula, by emphasizing in an unprecedented way film's status as a merchandised product and its links to the surrounding culture, can be seen, in part, as a functional outgrowth of Hollywood's traditional desire for politically nonprovocative entertainment and for the kind of social and political stability, vis-à-vis public attitudes toward the industry, that is conducive to business success. By tying films to mass-marketed products in newly intimate ways, blockbusters are insulated, to some extent, from cultural criticism because the films themselves are the hubs of huge wheels of tied-in products and affiliated sponsors. In addition, projects slated for blockbuster status are far less likely to adopt a politically oppositional stance because of the need to appeal to a huge market. The blockbuster film might be harder to single out as a discrete and anomalous cultural product, the way HUAC singled out the pro-Russia wartime productions or earlier pressure groups could mobilize around productions like *The Outlaw*. These films could be separated from the established culture because there was not yet a structural confusion between them. By contrast, blockbuster films become the culture to the extent that they are giant engines of the consumer economy. Through legions of interconnected products, they are insinuated in myriad ways into the lived texture of daily life, as any parent knows who has seen their home engulfed by the paraphernalia of Ninja Turtle fever.

As we have seen, Hollywood films have traditionally been reluctant to explicitly engage political issues. The adoption of the Production Code

and subsequent cooperation with the HUAC investigations typified
Hollywood's interest in avoiding the kind of controversy that could lead
to censorship and its tendency to produce films embodying centrist social
values while avoiding ideological extremes. Blockbuster production was
well suited to the industry's economic need to appeal to a diverse audience
and to the industry's social cautiousness. Blockbuster films typically represent the world with a simplified dichotomy of good versus evil, and the
cartoon characters who populate them are appropriate embodiments of
this reductive perspective. In the manufacture of entertaining fantasies,
and the use of films to integrate chains of products, sponsors, and viewers,
culture and free-market economics become indistinguishable. The
blockbluster structure is amenable to assimilating and expressing the
political world in a reductive frame, and one of the issues we will consider in the coming chapters is whether blockbuster production is acting
to restrict the range of acceptable political representation in the American
cinema. What are the relationships and tensions that prevail between
topical representations and the emphasis of blockbuster production upon
formulaic spectacle? To what extent does visual spectacle, typical of
blockbuster films but now an influence as well on non-blockbuster productions, inflect or deflect political content? Not all of the films we will
be examining in the coming chapters are blockbusters. With each of them,
however, we will be concerned with the ways that their formal design
facilitates and structures given sets of political frameworks while deny-
ing others.

Exploring these issues and problems entails situating Hollywood films
within the decade's political landscape. Their cinematic designs and social
content are not only a function of the nature of the contemporary film
industry and its traditions regarding topical representation. They are also
a function of the era's political agendas, its analytic categories and contending ideological frameworks. The films examined in the subsequent
chapters alternately endorse and criticize these agendas, and their operations in this respect need to be placed in relation to salient features of
the era's political culture. As previously noted, the intensity and frequency
of topical representation in the American cinema of the 1980s was itself
a function of the era's defining political contentiousness and ideological
explicitness. As a deliberate attempt to return national economic policy
to an era before Roosevelt and the New Deal, the Reagan period was
distinguished by an extraordinary amount of ideological production. This
was partly due to Reagan's own tendency to view the world ideologically,
but it was in larger measure a product of the highly successful efforts
by the Right to mobilize a constituency that could command the national
agenda at both local and national levels—or, as John Dolan of the National Conservative Political Action Committee put it, "to take control
of the culture."[54] Learning a host of lessons from the Goldwater defeat

in 1964, the Right began a long process of organization and dissemination of conservative views through think tanks and publications like the Heritage Foundation, the American Enterprise Institute, *Conservative Digest, Policy Review, National Review, Foreign Affairs, Commentary*, and others. The Right was not a unified bloc, but was split into an Old Guard of traditional conservatives (e.g., William Buckley), a neoconservative wing of converted former liberals,[55] and a grass-roots and more extreme New Right movement of rapidly developing potency, each with a somewhat distinct set of policies and agendas. Direct mail guru Richard Viguerie was a key player in the growth of the New Right, the power of which was mobilized through a loose network of single-issue groups whose animus about disparate issues like busing, gay and women's rights, abortion, gun control, and prayer in the schools could be roused and focused by manipulative direct mailings. While many of these New Right groups were too crude and extreme to be permitted a close identification with the Reagan administration, much of the impression that the country had swung to the right during the 1980s was nevertheless due to their high visibility. Anita Bryant's crusade against gay rights, Phyllis Schafley's anti-ERA Eagle Forum, Jerry Falwell's Moral Majority, and diverse others became celebrity players in domestic political dramas.

Single-issue campaigning, a key to the rise of the Right, was a consequence of the growth of political action groups and their penchant for targeting narrowly defined segments of the electorate. The highly emotional, visible, and symbolic issues of abortion, school prayer, pornography, and gay rights furnished a very effective basis for political agitation, one that proved to be far more effective than more traditional appeals. Viguerie noted, "We never really won until we began stressing issues like busing, abortion, school prayer and gun control. We talked about the sanctity of free enterprise, about the Communist onslaught until we were blue in the face."[56] Appeals to anger, fear, and hostility, rooted in symbolic issues that were perceived as threats to traditional family life, were a prime method for generating funds. John Dolan admitted that the shriller the appeal, the more hostility a fund-raising letter could arouse, the easier it was to get money.[57]

The success of a politics of symbolism and narrow self-interest depends on a fragmented electorate that has lost a sense of common needs and interests and is concerned with sheer economic survival: "Where relative prosperity or impoverishment may hang on the timing of a house purchase or the fact of working in (say) the aerospace rather than the auto industry or having been born in 1940 rather than 1950, the sense of commonality of experience and needs disintegrates."[58] Furthermore, symbolic politics can hold a primary appeal for groups who feel marginalized by the dominant movement and direction of society. As James McEvoy points out, "symbolic politics are the politics of groups that enjoy relatively greater representation that newly challenging groups but which are somewhat marginal with respect to their relations with the dominant segments of the society."[59] Throughout New Right political activity—and neoconservative thought as well—is an anxiety about where the country is heading and an attempt to defend a cultural agenda on which abortion, women's rights, or gay rights have little or no place. These anxieties, as Peter Steinfels discusses in his analysis of neoconservatism,[60] are partly rooted in the perception of a growing adversarial culture whose constituents—radical students, women's libbers, gays, "bohemian" artists and intellectuals—are seen as threats to vested forms of social authority. The anxieties and hostilities that underlie symbolic politics, once roused, are not easily extinguished. Although the Reagan period is now over and the Cold War has diminished with the recent changes in the Soviet Union and Eastern Europe, so that anticommunism no longers looms as the rallying point it once did, New Right groups are finding themselves bereft of an important, long-standing symbolic basis for organizing and are searching for new bases. Accordingly, during the Bush presidency, symbolic politics has remained a major presence on the cultural landscape. Thus, we find a great deal of attention being directed toward issues of obscenity and censorship in the arts. The artists involved—feminist and gay performance artists, photographers, and black rap groups—are precisely the kinds of groups the New Right perceives as part of the adversarial culture.[61]

Attempts to chart a new direction for American society during the period also centered on the international arena and debates about foreign policies. Here, the adversarial culture was defined in terms of the policies of détente, human rights, and military disengagement associated, as signs of an alleged national weakness, with the post-Vietnam and Carter years. A key document of the period was Jeane Kirkpatrick's *Commentary* article "Dictatorships and Double Standards," written at the end of the Carter period as a criticism of what she saw as a demeaning U.S. posture of "continuous self-abasement and apology vis-a-vis the Third World."[62] For Kirkpatrick, excessive concentration on policies of human rights and an insufficient tolerance of the repressive policies of dictatorial regimes friendly to U.S. interests had cost the United States important strategic allies in the shah of Iran and Nicaragua's Anastasio Somoza. Her distinction between "authoritarian" (friendly to the United States) and "totalitarian" (unfriendly) regimes rested on the assertion that the authoritarian regime, however repressive, doesn't disturb the indigenous cultural patterns and ways of life. Thus, she suggested that in such countries "the miseries of traditional life are familiar, they are bearable to ordinary people who, growing up in the society, learn to cope, as children born to untouchables in India acquire the skills and attitudes necessary for survival in the miserable roles they are destined to fill." By contrast, Communist regimes "claim jurisdiction over the whole life of the society and make demands for change that so violate internalized values and habits that inhabitants flee by the tens of thousands."[63] This distinction rested upon a certain amount of selective perception; it was indifferent, for example, to the egregiously repressive policies of such virtual police states as Guatemala and El Salvador (both friendly to the United States) throughout the 1980s.

Kirkpatrick's distinction between the authoritarian and the totalitarian regime, and her defense of the former, furnished an important theoretical pillar for Reagan-era foreign policy. She had ended her article with a call for a renewed global projection of U.S. power that would not necessarily avoid the use of military force. This call for renewed policies of Third World intervention was heeded by the Reagan administration, which placed the CIA back on a more active footing following the cutbacks in personnel and data-gathering capabilities of the 1970s. Furthermore, foreign policy in the Reagan years was predicated on the need to stop perceived Soviet aggression throughout the world. Anticommunism became, as it had been in the 1950s, an important rallying point for the Right as Truman-era conceptions of monolithic communism were revived and the bipolar terms of Kirkpatrick's analysis found expression in administration practice. In the logic of the period, most points of conflict in the world were reducible to the U.S.-Soviet contest. Anxieties about monolithic communism, however, were somewhat out of fashion. The Vietnam war had intervened between the old and new Cold Wars, and attitudes toward U.S. intervention in the Third World had changed in the 1970s. It would be difficult to sell a new Cold War using the ideological terms of the old one. Thus, a new political construction entered the cultural discourse of the era: "terrorism," a term which functioned essentially as a synonym for communism but was sufficiently new and vivid that it could carry a great deal of political freight, unlike the somewhat discredited anticommunism of Truman-era politics.

The omnipresent threat of terrorism became a major theme in the new Cold War. The danger of terrorism was discerned in the most politically and geographically diverse regions, and the Soviet Union was allegedly its sponsor. In Latin America: "Gathered in Nicaragua already are thousands of Cuban military advisers, contingents of Soviet and East Germans and all the elements of international terror—from the PLO to Italy's Red Brigades."[64] In the Caribbean: "The Soviet-Cuban militarization of Grenada, in short, can only be seen as a power projection into the region."[65] In the efforts to end apartheid in South Africa: "the Soviet armed guerrillas of the African National Congress, operating both within South Africa and from some neighboring countries, have embarked on new acts of terrorism inside South Africa."[66] Mainstream media helped to disseminate perceptions of the terrorist threat. Reader's Digest Press copublished Claire Sterling's *The Terror Network*, a pop-cultural analysis

of "an inexorably advancing enemy"—a secret army of international
terrorists waging war against Western democracies. "Guerrilla
International," as she called it, was under the direct sponsorship of the
Soviet Union, whose expansionist policies required the weakening of
Western democracies.[67] *U.S. News & World Report* offered a cover story
titled "Terrorism: Russia's Secret Weapon?" in 1981 which proclaimed
that the "problem of global terrorism is growing worse" and that the
Soviet Union lay behind everything from the PLO, Cuba, guerrilla
movements in Guatemala, El Salvador, and Colombia to the Red Brigades,
SWAPO (the Southwest Africa People's Organization), the African
National Congress, and neo-Nazi fascist groups in Europe.[68]

Such indiscriminate perceptions are examples of what Michael Rogin
called "political demonology." "The demonologist splits the world in
two, attributing magical, pervasive power to a conspiratorial center of
evil. Fearing chaos and secret penetration, the countersubversive
interprets local initiatives as signs of alien power. Discrete individuals
and groups become, in the countersubversive imagination, members
of a single political body directed by its head."[69] Political rhetoric
through much of the decade tended to demonize the Soviet Union.
For President Reagan, the Soviet Union aimed for nothing less than
world conquest and, with its minions, was "the focus of evil in the
modern world."[70]

The dominant symbolic motifs of the Reagan period, then, portrayed
a society under threat. America and the family were besieged by
resurgent forces of chaos and disorder: communism, terrorism, gay and
women's rights, school busing, abortion, and so on. Twentieth-century
America had gone astray. Internationally, concern for human rights
and a perceived reluctance to use military force were aiding the Soviets'
plans for world conquest and leading the United States to abandon
its authoritarian Third World friends. Domestically, God had been
thrown out of the classroom, society had lost its spiritual bearings, and
homosexuality, abortion, and pornography threatened the body politic.
As Reagan observed, "modern-day secularism [was] discarding the tried
and time-tested values upon which our very civilization is based."[71]
All were threats to a nostalgic vision of an America of small government, small business, and local communities organized around family
and church. The Reagan "revolution" was an attempt to turn back
the clock to a mythical and more pristine America, to a time when
traditional authority was not challenged by oppositional racial, sexual,
political, or economic interests. This vision of the past, of course, was
a political construction rather than a historical reality. This is why
symbolic politics came to play such a large role in the Reagan period.
Their powerful emotional appeals might substitute for a real past. As
Garry Wills has written:

If one settles, instead, for a substitute past, an illusion of it, then that fragile construct must be protected from the challenge of complex or contradictory evidence, from any test of evidence at all. That explains Amerians' extraordinary tacit bargain with each other not to challenge Reagan's version of the past. The power of his appeal is the great joint confession that we cannot live with our real past, that we not only prefer but need a substitute.[72]

To what extent did Hollywood films of the period participate in these symbolic politics, in the construction of a synthetic past and a political consciousness congruent with the tides of official culture? The chapters that follow attempt to examine this question by focusing on three areas which were at the center of national debates and cultural energies: a new Cold War tied to visions of an aggressive Soviet menace; perceived threats of subversion in our "backyard," Latin America; and lingering questions about the meaning of the Vietnam war. In addition, a fourth chapter will explore the frequently critical, sometimes oppositional views of contemporary life that occasionally found their way, as projections of dark future worlds, into science fiction films of the period. These offer gloomy, dystopian visions of social and economic collapse and seem to indicate a crisis of belief that the future—and, therefore, the present—no longer remains under our control.

Exploring the ways Hollywood films portrayed these political topics and agendas necessarily raises larger issues about the relationship of ideology and visual representation, about political content and its structuring by the mass media. Since the cinema is one of the contemporary media of mass communication, an understanding of the theoretical place ideology has assumed, and the problems it has raised, in media studies can help us to establish some of the necessary linkages between film and society that we will need to consider when attempting to understand the space available for political filmmaking in the commercial cinema. A great deal of literature exists on this topic, replete with its share of controversies and disagreements.[73] Some of the basic questions involve the ways that film and other media or cultural products can be said to model or communicate the social and political values of their time. Where in the film or media product do these values characteristically lie? How do they get "in" there? Should ideology be understood in the old, original Marxian sense (from *The German Ideology*) as an upside-down, distorting image produced as if from a camera obscura? Or is the ideological image itself fissured and fractured, contested by other voices and perspectives in the film or cultural text, resulting from the multiplex, multivoiced nature of the society, where diverse classes, races, and genders contest with each other over the social construction of reality? Did the cinema respond to the cultural politics of the 1980s with a body of ideologically closed and homogeneous films or with more diverse political perspectives? To what extent can one speak of a "dominant" ideology, a concept borrowed by contemporary critics from the work of European Marxists like Antonio Gramsci, in a society where class structure is not nearly as visible and as historically palpable?[74] A brief review of the major traditions of American mass media scholarship with reference to their conceptions of how the media construct their messages and with what effect will help to clarify and situate the issues of cinematic representation as part of a broader tradition of inquiry into the relationships of media and society. Along the way, I will indicate where work on ideology in film studies fits into these traditions.

Initial formulations of the relation of the mass media and society early in the century, in the 1910s and 1920s, were influenced by the apparent demonstrations of the power of propaganda in World War I and were informed as well by nineteenth-century European sociology with its theories of social anomie, alienation, and mass society, as well as by powerful stimulus-responses theories of human psychology.[75] The result was a picture of all-powerful media injecting messages into an undifferentiated public, each member of which absorbed and reacted to these messages in an identical manner. This was the hypodermic theory of media effects. As study of the mass media developed, however, this initial formulation was soon rejected. In the 1940s, Paul Lazarsfeld, Robert Merton, and others began to elaborate an alternative media studies paradigm that was to hold dominant sway in American media sociology until the 1960s. The empirical work of Lazarsfeld and his colleagues substituted for the all-powerful media of the hypodermic theory a view that saw the media (film, newspapers, magazines, radio, and later television) as far more modest contributors to social and cultural life. The media were seen as embedded within and secondary to interpersonal networks of social influence and persuasion. From a study of the 1940 presidential elections, Lazarsfeld and his colleagues formulated the "two-step flow" theory of media influence which suggested that "ideas often flow from radio and print to the opinion leaders and from them to the less active sections of the population."[76] This idea was expanded in a study of consumer decision making among a group of housewives conducted in Decatur, Illinois, in 1944–1945. Examining how these housewives decided what fashions and hair styles, grocery products, movies and political issues to buy, attend, or follow, Lazarsfeld and Elihu Katz argued that media messages were filtered through the opinions and recommendations of influential friends whom the housewives trusted and whose recommendations were decisive. From this suggestion, they elaborated a horizontal model of social influence in which "concentrations of opinion leaders . . . can be located in varying densities in each of the different life-cycle types, in almost equal densities on every status level, and generally among the more gregarious people in those groups."[77]

Note that this model omits consideration of pyramidal, structural relations of power within society and the question of how the media may operate to legitimate such arrangements. In fact, opinion leading is defined as opinion following, since the opinion "leaders" are those who get their ideas from the media in the first place.[78] Furthermore, its theoretical conception of media effects is absorbed within an unexamined consumerist framework. Soap flakes, movies, and political issues are conflated into a single plane of decision making. In this, the administrative functions of the research are apparent. The study was commissioned by a popular magazine publisher who wished to learn how to reach a target audience more effectively; accordingly, the research has difficulty coming to terms with its own role in extending the science of marketing. As Lazarsfeld's occasional collaborator Robert Merton noted, "Mass communications research developed very largely in response to market requirements. The severe competition for advertising among the several mass media and among agencies within each medium has provoked an economic demand for objective measures of size, composition, and responses of audiences (of newspapers, magazines, radio and television)."[79] These demands, he noted, "have also helped shape the categories in terms of which the audience is described or measured."

The limited effects model of American media sociology was somewhat compromised by its administrative role as an agent of advertisers and marketers who wished to find new ways of segmenting the audience and learning how viewers made their decisions. These limitations can be seen in the paradigm's absence of a theory of political and social legitimation, of what Gramsci had termed hegemony, whereby the flow of ideas through the media might be shaped and regulated in accordance with domestic or international political needs. As C. Wright Mills noted in his classic critique of this paradigm, which he termed "abstracted empiricism": "The idea of legitimation is one of the central conceptions of political science, particularly as the problems of this discipline bear on questions of opinion and ideology. The research on 'political opinion' is all the more curious in view of the suspicion that American electoral politics is a sort of politics without opinion."[80] A cardinal tenet of this paradigm, presented in 1960 by Joseph Klapper in his review of the literature, *The Effects of Mass Communication*,[81] was that the mass media had little or no significant effect on the popular mind or political decision making. Effects were defined in terms of *changes* in attitude or behavior impelled by the media, and when the research had difficulty finding these, a notion of restricted media effects was elaborated. The major media effect, it was suggested, was to reinforce already held beliefs or attitudes, not to change them. As Lazarsfeld and Merton stated in a classic article, "Media of mass communication . . . have been effectively used to canalize [reinforce] basic attitudes, but there is little evidence of their having served to change these attitudes."[82]

Ironically, Lazarsfeld and Merton acknowledged that mass media work to "render mass publics conformative to the social and economic status quo," yet they failed to follow the political implications of this, instead suggesting that popular theories of the media tend to overemphasize their power. While their admission and the reinforcement-effect component of their theory place the empirical paradigm close in some respects to concepts of ideological hegemony familiar in critical theory (e.g., in the work of the Frankfurt school),[83] the classical empirical tradition lacked the critical recognition of structured social power, of class, and a concept of ideological function and effect. As C. Wright Mills and others have suggested, this paradigm limited theory by restricting its formulations to what could be statistically proven. The Frankfurt school émigré T. W. Adorno briefly tried to reconcile critical theory and American empiricism in a short collaboration with Lazarsfeld, but eventually decided they could not be married, sardonically concluding, "When I was confronted with the demand to 'measure culture,' I reflected that culture might be precisely that condition that excludes a mentality capable of measuring it."[84] Resulting from the marketing and administrative mission of classical American empiricism was a restricted portrait of the linkages between the mass media and society, particularly how content passing through the media is regulated and shaped, and how personal or communal patterns of media usage may impact upon the content of the media. More recent work within the empirical tradition has attempted to sharpen scrutiny of these linkages, and to move away from a limited-effects model. In the 1960s and 1970s mass communications scholarship began to move back toward a view of powerful media effects. Discussing the revival of interest in media effects in this later "third" period of research, Denis McQuail points out that this shift was explicitly identified by Noelle-Neumann's slogan, derived from the title of her 1973 article, "return to the concept of powerful mass media."[85] Accordingly, the two-step flow has been supplanted by newer theories and perspectives: theories of agenda-setting by the media, of the ways that media content may be inflected by audience usage patterns and the gratifications sought, of the conditions creating media dependency in an audience, of the influence of media ownership and internal operations upon the production of content, and an attempt—cultivation analysis—to conjoin empirical work with critical theory and ideology.[86]

Controversies over the classical sociological paradigm of media scholarship, then, helped to produce a major shift within the field beginning in the 1960s. European and Marxist theories of hegemony and ideology, and the critical, nonempirical tradition of which they were a part, also began to find a growing niche within mass media and communications scholarship.[87] As these newer approaches began to be applied to traditional areas of mass media research, the pluralistic model of society that had been implicit in the earlier schools of media research, a model which had been heavily influenced by sociological functionalism and which viewed society as a harmonious and consensus-based system, now began to compete with views of society that stressed differentiation of strata—classes, races, genders—and the fractures and fissures in the ideological realm which struggles among these groups for the social construction of reality necessarily produced.

Ideology thus became a crucial theoretical tool in this portrait of society because social differences and struggle might assume symbolic forms and be fought at the level of ideas within the cultural arena and through its products. Unlike its initial formulations by Marx and by theorists like Georg Lukacs, for whom ideology was simply a set of false ideas existing in consciousness and distorting a true portrait of the social relations of production, newer understandings of ideology stressed its concrete, material dimension. Rather than simply a set of ideas projected by a ruling elite, as in the old Marxist formulations, ideology now came to be seen as a semiotic phenomenon inhering in the audiovisual signs of communication. Those signs themselves could bear the marks of ideological struggle, as different groups or classes contended over the semantic meaning of a given sign or term. As a tangible and concrete political sign, the American flag stimulated a great deal of debate in 1990 as battles were fought over the legitimacy of flag-burning as a form of protest and, by extension, over the meaning of the nation, of patriotism, and of whether social and political protest must have a preordained form. As the Russian linguist V. N. Volosinov pointed out in 1929, "differently oriented accents intersect in every ideological sign. Sign becomes an arena of class struggle."[88] As we have been noting, though, not just class struggle but struggle among virtually any set of contending, socially significant groups may be carried out at the level of the semiotic sign. Moreover, unlike the formulations of the hypodermic theory or the two-step flow, recent work has stressed how semiotic signs undergo a process of decoding just as they have been encoded at the production end.[89] Thus, they can be fought over by different social groups who decode the signs according to their own social agendas and experiences. The dispassionate views of homoerotic life in Robert Mapplethorpe's photographs, for example, were construed as threats to the family and to social morals by groups who would censor or ban these images.

By locating social and political values at a material level inside the structure of the sign and by emphasizing that signs are by no means necessarily univocal, we can derive a flexible and powerful model of the interconnections between social forces and mass media content. By looking closely at the structure of the sign—in our case, at the structure of visual and narrative codes—we can proceed to explore the relationship between the social and political culture of the Reagan era and important film images of the period. Film occupies a rather special place within the array of the mass media. As a popular and emotionally powerful medium, it has been intimately connected with the currents of our national and political history. The Prohibition era spawned the gangster film. The youth movement of the 1960s spawned the rebel heroes of *Easy Rider* and *Bonnie and Clyde*. During World War II, the movies enthusiastically joined the Allied cause and helped form a cinematic home front. Working with film was rather like writing history with lightning, as Woodrow Wilson noted. As discussed earlier, reformers have always been concerned that film enters rather too intimately into the lives of its viewers, influencing their feelings, beliefs, and behavior in often untoward ways. As a medium, film is uniquely gifted in its ability to mirror and refract the national mood and events, and not only because of the extraordinary emotional power with which it speaks. While cautioning against any simple theories of how movies and society intersect, Ian Jarvie points out that the special conditions of film production help to establish an important point of contact and linkage between film and society. As a group effort and product, the result of negotiated decisions and a synthesis of different perspectives and creative emphases, film may be better able to exhibit sets of socially resonant dynamics and values than other forms or media that are less collaborative: "in film making we see society in a microcosm [in and through the group which makes the film]. . . . This perhaps explains why the mass media can sometimes develop an extraordinary resonance with a contemporary mood—quite different from that ever achieved by a single creative artist working by himself."[90]

Throughout this book we will, therefore, insist on the interconnections between movies and society. We will assume that movies may reflect and refract important aspects of social reality but that they do not do this in any straightforward way. It is worth making this point explicit because some contemporary methodologies in film studies employ a postmodern or poststructural framework that views social reality as a set of textual systems. In this perspective one does not get beyond or "outside" the text. Since one is always already inside language, everywhere one looks are signs and the systems they form. Not only is the "real" not knowable, it is viewed as a fictive or textual construct. The modernist movement in art was tied to a belief in the critical or emancipatory power of aesthetic representations, and that was founded on the conviction that critical art—as practiced, for example, by Pablo Picasso or Luis Buñuel—might help open up the repressive spaces of dominant society by pointing to important realities—political or sexual—willfully ignored by the culture to which the artist wished to speak. On the postmodern landscape, by contrast, this kind of criticality and its associated politics have collapsed: "it [postmodernism] implies the collapse of a by now true and tried (even establishment) sense of criticality, namely, that of anti-establishment modernist (avant-garde) criticality. It suggests that there is no replacement concept of criticality in sight."[91] Postmodernism points to a crisis of politics and representations in which the sign and its relative and relational nature have overwhelmed and replaced the hitherto more durable and enduring categories of history, society, and politics. In place of critical opposition and a pitched battle, the postmodern artist wages a provisional skirmish, a fleeting contestation of dominant ideologies because s/he can oppose the dominant signs only with additional representations. The circuit of sign and representation, of textual systems, is closed. One cannot move outside textuality or representation.[92] (We will return to these issues in Chapter 5.)

By contrast, Terry Lovell has argued that some commitment to a knowable reality outside language or discourse is fundamental for political art and for theories which seek to examine the interplay of politics and art.[93] In the chapters that follow, we will work from Lovell's position and assume that the economic and political conflicts which animated the Reagan era, while often taking a politically symbolic form, helped to feed and fashion distinct representational forms of the period without being themselves necessarily representational. Despite the plethora of political and ideological energies they unleashed—and the cinematic and cultural forms these assumed—conflict with the domestic poor, with the Soviet Union, Libya, and the Sandinistas was really a struggle over territories and access to markets and resources, even though these conflicts were also waged at the level of sign and symbol in the cultural arena. While the important insights furnished by the postmodern critique of politics and culture cannot be ignored, the Reagan era was not just about symbols and discourse. We need to examine those symbols and that discourse, but we also will do well to recall the very real spaces outside symbolic politics where—in Latin America, for example—real peasants and priests struggled and died in the region's wars.

In tracing the politics and symbolism of the Reagan period in American films, we are, of course, dealing with a narrative medium whose products are intended to have a wide appeal. These two factors—narrative and broad-based appeal—affect the nature and shape of political material within the films. We will have an opportunity to study this closely in the coming chapters, but it will be helpful to briefly consider now how this occurs. Narrative provides an excellent vehicle for ideological discourse because, by unfolding a plot over time, narrative organization can stress process—that is, it can provide an ideologically based *argument* in which alternative views are contested and finally resolved. As Dana Polan has noted:

Dominant ideology . . . seems to find in narrative structure a promising form for the mediation of social conflicts and their resolution through the enveloping power of narrative and through the generation of specific figures of mediation who take up sides of a contradiction and work to neutralize such contradiction. What seems to be narrative's openness to change, to the ambiguities of a not-yet-written future, can actually turn out to be no more than a governed progression that merely solves issues (both thematic and narrative), in calculated ways.[94]

Depending on the narrative organization of the film, its ideological values may be displayed with great and explicit clarity (e.g., *Rambo III*, *Rocky IV*) or they may be more implicit and of a second-order nature (*E.T*, *Close Encounters of the Third Kind*). The film's discourse may be highly developed and organized, or it may be fractured, splintered, and incoherent. As a temporal structure, narrative provides a framework for organizing and creating interrelationships among diverse social, ethical, and political values, and these may be more or less skillfully integrated, more or less explicit, more or less coherent.[95]

At times, the broad-based appeal that Hollywood films have traditionally sought works against ideological or political coherence. To appeal to diverse racial, ethnic, or generational groups, Hollywood films may sometimes willingly sacrifice strict coherence. In its place may be a more polysemous, multivalent set of images, characters, and narrative situations. The formula narratives of Hollywood films and television frequently operate through a process of ideological agglomeration, taking a little of this, a little of that, a fragment of social reality here, a constellation of values there. Writing on recent Cold War films such as *Rocky IV* and *Aliens*, Christine Holmlund notes the fissured nature of their discourse, the ways in which they "undercut and extend" established ideologies and "construct alternative points of [audience] identification."[96] Gina Marchetti has noted how ambivalence and contradiction are frequently central to television narratives. In a detailed analysis of the presentation of race, authority, violence, gender relations, and the Vietnam war on *The A-Team*, she notes "the astute way [the show] negotiates racial, sexual and economic contradictions for its audience. *The A-Team* presents a world of open contradiction in which angry blacks like Mr. T 'do as they are told,' hunted Vietnam vets continue to 'obey orders' from their superiors, and adventurous females remain on the periphery of the action serving refreshments to a group of very violent mercenaries."[97]

We will have ample occasion to observe this process of ideological agglomeration in the films to be examined in the remainder of this book. For now it is important to grasp this process as a basic mechanism for linking film to a multitextured society from which viewers and profits alike come. The ideological agglomeration of contemporary film offers a rejoinder to the critique of one-dimensional society classically associated with the Frankfurt school and still advanced by some Marxist criticism. The one-dimensional model assumes that ideology is monolithic, as is the discourse of contemporary cultural products which unproblematically reflect dominant social and political perspectives. But contemporary Hollywood is a place in which Gulf and Western Industries, through its subsidiary Paramount Pictures, could distribute Bernardo Bertolucci's Marxist epic *1900* and Warren Beatty's loving portrait of American Communist John Reed in *Reds*. Corporate capitalism could be savaged in *Blade Runner* and *Robocop* while its wares were purveyed through the product tie-ins of *Dick Tracy* and *Teenage Mutant Ninja Turtles*. In a limited but very real way, Hollywood cares less about content than about the continuity of its formal structures (e.g., linear narratives with star performers at their center, unselfconscious and nonreflective visual styles, happy endings). Looking back on his brief Hollywood career in the 1940s, director-screenwriter Abraham Polonsky noted that his attempts to experiment with film style were hotly resisted by studio executives, but not so his attempts to inflect the dramas with a socially critical portrait of 1940s America: "If you came out for socialism in films, the producer might say, 'I think you're going too heavy on that. Change some of those lines.' But if you said, 'Shoot it in this different way,' he would throw you off the (studio) lot and have you run out of town on the grounds of professional incompetence."[98] Little has changed since then. Hollywood films still tend to be formally conservative while being more ideologically diverse. The limited formal experimentation of the late 1960s and early 1970s[99] was contained and reversed by the blockbuster productions and ascendant fantasy formulas of Spielberg and Lucas in the later 1970s and 1980s. With this retrenchment, ideological agglomeration is a basic structural feature of much (but not all) contemporary production because it promotes the promiscuous appeals required by films produced as part of product chains within a diverse but integrated market.

With these considerations in mind, then, we must be cautious about employing terms like "the dominant ideology" lest we create the impression that ideology is monolithic or coterminous with all of society. Contemporary film theories influenced by Althusserian Marxism and the psychoanalytic paradigm of Jacques Lacan tend to stress the pervasiveness of ideology and its importance in furnishing the glue that holds society together. Ideology, in this perspective, is viewed as a set of false beliefs or illusory images of reality that mystify and confuse people, preventing them from seeing where their own best interests lie. Ideological conditioning, mind control, has been the answer offered by contemporary Marxism to the question confronting it in the modern age: Why haven't the workers in a capitalist society revolted? Viewed as an institution that helps perpetuate the dominant ideology, the cinema, like other mass media, is considered by contemporary Althusserian-Lacanian film theory to make irrational appeals to its viewers, confusing them about where their best interests lie. As one of the ideological engines of modern society, the cinema, therefore, acquires in this perspective a great deal of importance in helping to define and maintain a given political order.

In contrast with this view, which we may term the Dominant Ideology Thesis, following Abercrombie, Hill, and Turner, it will be the contention of this book that ideology plays a more limited role in securing the adherence of individuals to given social formations.[100] An explanation in terms of economic compulsion provides a simpler and more compelling account of the failure of individuals to mobilize in opposition to economic constraints than do the elaborate and convoluted models of ideological conditioning proposed by contemporary Marxism. People have to eat and to survive, and social rebellion or rejection can carry a great deal of risk, while society extends material incentives to reward adjustment and conformity. Ideologies exist and circulate through society, but a perspective arguing from economic force need not view ideology as pervasive and as coterminous with society, nor see people as helpless agents in the grips of a mystifying ideology.

During the Reagan era, as we have noted, a great deal of ideological production occurred, elaborating a set of Ur-themes or archmyths, such as the omnipresent danger of terrorism and/or relentless Soviet expansionism, governmental bureaucracy as a threat to individual economic and political freedom, and so on. We will examine a number of these themes in the chapters to come, as well as their relationship with film narratives and images. Since this book is an analysis of symbolic material, questions about the way it clothes, transforms, or translates reality will be central to our purposes. But not all such transformations are ideological, since such operations and translations are basic to the work of representation. As a convenient shorthand formula, we may follow Noel Carroll's discussion of these issues and maintain that a belief is ideological if it is based on a deliberate exclusion, denial, or repression of pertinent information in the interests of expanding or consolidating a position based on social domination.[101] In this respect, not all films are ideological; and when they are, the ideology is often second order and derivative. *Top Gun*, for example, is ideological to the extent that it codes its depicted reality in terms derived from the Cold War. Viewers, however, may construe the political history of their time in different ways. *Top Gun* probably reinforces the anti-Soviet political perceptions of some viewers, whereas others may enjoy the film while remaining skeptical of its heightened, fantasized portrayals. A comprehensive understanding of the political role of the film requires, as one component, an empirical assessment of the audience or audiences and the ways they may construe its messages. Such a massive undertaking is beyond the scope of this book, as it has been for virtually all books dealing with political film.[102] We will, instead, be concerned with some of the ways films have called out to us in the darkened theaters and home television environments of the 1980s, with analyzing and interpreting some of the ways films have framed and discussed a variety of the eras's most compelling political issues. To get at the ideological role of the era's films, we will frequently concentrate on the areas of information they have repressed or denied. But bearing in mind the points developed earlier, we should proceed cautiously, lest we overstress the role of ideology and the efficacy of film as a political medium. By the end of the book, we hope to be in a position to see that the limitations of American film as a medium of political analysis and discourse are not problems of cinema but of politics.

With these discussions of film and politics in the 1980s frame, we should now proceed to take a closer look at the films themselves. We thus end this chapter close to where we began. Hollywood and Washington, American film and Ronald Reagan—these are terms within a common cultural equation, components of cultural and political systems whose logic is directed toward economic and ideological closure but that must survive by appealing to diverse, broad-based, and not always fully coherent interests and groups. In each there is confusion about the status of the image, about the borders between symbolism and reality, between life as it is and as we would like it to be. In each there is recourse to fantasy and mythology when viewing contemporary America. In each there is an attempt to reorganize the ground of our private lives, one through the appeals of commodity-driven fantasies, the other through appeal to a collective symbolic past. Both Hollywood films and Reagan politics work by assembling bits and pieces of the past, of nostalgic memories. By mobilizing frustrations and desires toward an anticipated happy ending, they assemble a synthetic experience out of discrete parts. This is the logic of montage, as Garry Wills noted in his analysis of Reagan's America: "[Reagan's] approach is not discursive, setting up sequences of time or thought, but associative; not a tracking shot, but montage. We make the connections. It is our movie."[103] Let us now penetrate the montages of contemporary film, make the necessary connections, and begin to assemble portions of the movie world of 1980s America.

NOTES

1. Garry Wills, *Reagan's America: Innocents at Home* (New York: Doubleday, 1987), p. 165.
2. Ibid.
3. See Wills's discussion of Reagan's war memories in ibid., pp. 162–170.
4. Ibid., p. 168.
5. See Michael Rogin's *Ronald Reagan: The Movie* (Berkeley: University of California Press, 1988) for an insightful analysis of the relationship between Reagan's bellicose policies as president and the imagery of weakness and injury that runs through his film work and was a mild obsession in private life.
6. Ibid., p. 9.
7. These figures are from "Background Material and Data on Programs Within the Jurisdiction of the Committee on Ways and Means," quoted in "Richest Got

Richer and Poorest Poorer in 1979–87," *New York Times*, March 23, 1989, pp. A1, A24.

8. Sidney Blumenthal, *Our Long National Daydream* (New York: Harper & Row, 1988), p. xvi.

9. Ibid., p. 119.

10. Ibid., p. 107.

11. Alan Wolfe, "Sociology, Liberalism and the Radical Right," *New Left Review* 128 (July–August 1981), p. 20. Peter Steinfels makes a similar point in *The Neo-Conservatives* (New York: Simon and Schuster, 1979), pp. 274–275.

12. For explorations of the relation between Reaganite America and the films of Lucas and Spielberg, see Peter Biskind, "Blockbuster: The Last Crusade," in *Seeing Through Movies*, ed. Mark Crispin Miller (New York: Pantheon, 1990), pp. 112–149; Robert Phillip Kolker, *A Cinema of Loneliness*, 2nd ed. (New York: Oxford University Press, 1988), pp. 237–302.

13. "Homevid: Child of the '80s Seeks Continued Growth in the '90s," *Variety*, January 24, 1990, p. 153.

14. Warner Communications thinks of film production as the creation of "software." See Robert Gustafson, " 'What's Happening to Our Pix Biz?' From Warner Bros. to Warner Communications Inc.", in *The American Film Industry*, ed., Tino Balio, rev. ed. (Madison: University of Wisconsin Press, 1985), p. 584.

15. Ibid., pp. 547–586.

16. For a discussion of this, see Douglas Gomery, "Corporate Ownership and Control in the Contemporary U.S. Film Industry," *Screen* 25, no. 4–5 (1984), pp. 60–69.

17. On the dominance of special effects and the debasing of narrative, see Richard Schickel, "The Crisis in Movie Narrative," *Gannett Center Journal* 3, no. 3 (Summer 1989), pp. 1–15. On the simplistic moral universe of these films, and the political implications thereof, see Kolker, *A Cinema of Loneliness*, pp. 237–302; and Biskind, "Blockbuster: The Last Crusade."

18. "Top 100 All-time Film Rental Champs," *Variety*, January 24, 1990, p. 46.

19. "The Teachings of Chairman Jeff," *Variety*, February 4, 1991, p. 24.

20. "B.O. Blasts off in Year of the Bat," *Variety*, January 3, 1990, p.8.

21. Anne Thompson, "Field of Dreams: 15th Annual 'Grosses Gloss,' " *Film Comment* 26, no. 2 (March–April 1990), p. 59.

22. "Product Pluggola Padding Pic Producers' Budgets," *Variety*, May 9, 1990, p. 22.

23. Ruth A. Inglis, "Self-Regulation in Operation," in *The American Film Industry*, ed. Tino Balio, rev. ed. (Madison: University of Wisconsin Press, 1985).

24. "Product Pluggola," p. 22.

25. Ibid.

26. Ibid.

27. Mark Crispin Miller, "Advertising: End of Story," in *Seeing Through Movies*, ed. Mark Crispin Miller (New York: Pantheon, 1990).

28. For a decade, Hasbro has considered a film for their G.I. Joe toy, but has stipulated that "Joe couldn't smoke, he couldn't curse and there couldn't be gratuitous violence." *Variety*, April 18, 1990, p. 8.

29. "No Toys in Tokyo Puts 'Turtles' in the Soup," *Variety*, April 15, 1991, pp. 1, 227.

30. "Turtles, 'Toons, and Toys 'R' in," *Variety*, April 18, 1990, p. 8.

31. Ibid.

32. "Warner Communications Annual Report 1982," in *The American Film Industry*, ed. Tino Balio, rev. ed. (Madison: University of Wisconsin Press, 1985).

33. I. C. Jarvie, *Movies as Social Criticism: Aspects of Their Social Psychology* (Metuchen, NJ: Scarecrow, 1978), pp. 86–87.

34. Ibid., p. 93. Dana Polan has explored the ideological and political riches of 1940s films in *Power and Paranoia* (New York: Columbia University Press, 1986), emphasizing the contradictory discourses about family life, domestic consumption, and the war found on movie screens of the period.

35. Screenwriter Michael Mahern described the film in these terms. See Thompson, "Field of Dreams," p. 59.

36. The text of the Code is in Leonard J. Leff and Jerold L. Simmons, *The Dame in the Kimono: Hollywood, Censorship, and the Production Code from the 1920s to the 1960s* (New York: Grove Weidenfeld, 1990), pp. 283–292.

37. Hortense Powdermaker, *Hollywood: The Dream Factory* (Boston: Little, Brown, 1950), pp. 77, 78.

38. Quoted in Inglis, "Self-Regulation in Operation," p. 392.

39. Paul W. Facey, *The Legion of Decency* (New York: Arno Press, 1974), p. 98.

40. Ibid., p. 93.

41. A thorough review of this period is in Garth Jowett, *Film: The Democratic Art* (Boston: Little, Brown, 1976).

42. Quoted in Facey, *The Legion of Decency*, p. 87.

43. W. W. Charters, *Motion Pictures and Youth: A Summary* (New York: Macmillan, 1935), p. 43.

44. Ibid., p. 38, 39.

45. The reasons for this are explored in Ian Jarvie, "Mysteries of the Payne Fund Studies Solved," paper presented to the Seventh International Conference on Culture and Communication, Philadelphia, 1989.

46. See, for example, the findings of the *Attorney General's Commission on Pornography, Final Report* (Washington, D.C.: U.S. Government Printing Office, 1986).

47. Ronald Reagan and Richard C. Hubler, *Where's the Rest of Me?* (New York: Dell, 1981), pp. 186–187. Originally published 1965.

48. Quoted in Gordon Kahn, *Hollywood on Trial* (New York: Boni and Gaer, 1948), p. 44.

49. Ibid.

50. Ibid., p. 56.

51. Richard Maltby, "Made for Each Other: The Melodrama of Hollywood and the House Committee on Un-American Activities, 1947," *Cinema, Politics, and Society in America*, ed. Philip Davies and Brian Neve (New York: St. Martin's Press, 1981), p. 77.

52. Richard Maltby, "The Political Economy of Hollywood: The Studio System," in *Cinema, Politics, and Society in America*, ed. Philip Davies and Brian Neve (New York: St. Martin's Press, 1981), p. 56.

53. Walter Wanger, "OWI and Motion Pictures," *Public Opinion Quarterly* 7, no. 1 (Spring 1943), p. 104.

54. Quoted in Alan Crawford, *Thunder on the Right* (New York: Pantheon, 1980), p. 41.

55. Steinfels provides a detailed analysis of this network of former liberals in *The Neo-Conservatives*.

56. Quoted in Mike Davis, "The New Right's Road to Power," *New Left Review* 128 (July–August 1981), p. 39.

57. Crawford, *Thunder on the Right*, p. 51.

58. Elliott Currie, Robert Dunn, and David Fogarty, "The New Immiseration," *Socialist Review* 54 (November–December 1980), quoted in Davis, "New Right's Road to Power," p. 45.

59. James McEvoy III, *Radicals or Conservatives?: The Contemporary American Right* (Chicago: Rand McNally, 1971), p. 151.

60. Steinfels, *The Neo-Conservatives*, pp. 56–65.

61. For a review of this trend, see C. Carr, "War on Art: The Sexual Politics of Censorship," *Village Voice*, June 5, 1990, pp. 25–30.

62. Jeane Kirkpatrick, "Dictatorships and Double Standards," *Commentary* 68, no. 5 (November 1979), p. 45.

63. Ibid., 44.

64. Ronald Reagan, address to the American people on aiding the Nicaraguan Contras, March 16, 1986, in *Vital Speeches of the Day* 52, no. 13, p. 386.

65. Ronald Reagan, address to the American people on peace and national security, March 23, 1983, in *Vital Speeches of the Day* 49, no. 13, p. 388.

66. Ronald Reagan, address to the American people on U.S. economic relations with South Africa, July 22, 1986, in *Vital Speeches of the Day*, 52, no. 21, p. 644.

67. Claire Sterling, *The Terror Network* (New York: Holt, Rinehart and Winston/Reader's Digest Press, 1981).

68. "Terrorism: Russia's Secret Weapon?" *U.S. News & World Report*, May 4, 1981, pp. 27–29.

69. Rogin, *Ronald Reagan: The Movie*, p. xiii.

70. Ronald Reagan, remarks at the Annual Convention of the National Association of Evangelicals, March 8, 1983, reprinted in Ronald Reagan, *Speaking My Mind* (New York: Simon and Schuster, 1989), p. 178.

71. Ibid., p. 171.

72. Wills, *Reagan's America*, p. 386.

73. Lawrence Grossberg provides a useful summary of different schools of ideological analysis in "Strategies of Marxist Cultural Interpretation," *Critical Studies in Mass Communication* 1 (December 1984), pp. 392–421.

74. Richard Maltby also makes this point in *Harmless Entertainment: Hollywood and the Ideology of Consensus* (Metuchen, NJ: Scarecrow, 1983), p. 24.

75. A detailed discussion of this period can be found in Melvin L. DeFleur and Sandra Ball-Rokeach, *Theories of Mass Communication*, 4th ed. (New York: Longman, 1982), pp. 143–165.

76. Paul F. Lazarsfeld, Bernard Berelson, and Hazel Gaudet, *The People's Choice* (New York: Columbia University Press, 1944; repr. 1968), pp. 151.

77. Elihu Katz and Paul F. Lazarsfeld, *Personal Influence* (New York: The Free Press, 1955; repr. 1964), p. 325.

78. Todd Gitlin discusses this point and others in a critique of the Lazarsfeld school, "Media Sociology: The Dominant Paradigm," *Theory and Society* 6, no. 2 (September 1978), pp. 205–253.

79. Robert K. Merton, *Social Theory and Social Structure* (New York: Free Press, 1968), p. 505.

80. C. Wright Mills, *The Sociological Imagination* (New York: Oxford University Press, 1959; repr. 1982), p. 53.

81. Joseph T. Klapper, *The Effects of Mass Communication* (New York: Free Press, 1960).

82. Paul F. Lazarsfeld and Robert K. Merton, "Mass Communication, Popular Taste and Organized Social Action," in *The Process and Effects of Mass Communication,* ed. Wilbur Schramm and Donald F. Roberts (Chicago: University of Illinois Press, 1971), p. 575.

83. Curran et al. point out that on the empirical level, there is no discrepancy between the formulations of the Lazarsfeldian paradigm and Marxist theories which tend to view the media as having a hegemonic social function. James Curran, Michael Gurevitch, and Janet Woollacott, "The Study of the Media: Theoretical Approaches," in *Culture, Society and the Media,* ed. Michael Gurevitch, Tony Bennett, James Curran, and Janet Woollacott (New York: Methuen, 1982), p. 14.

84. Quoted in Martin Jay, *The Dialectical Imagination* (Boston: Little, Brown, 1973), p. 222.

85. J. Denis McQuail, *Mass Communication Theory,* second edition (Beverly Hills: Sage, 1988), p. 254.

86. See, for example, S. J. Ball-Rokeach and M. L. DeFleur, "A Dependency Model of Mass Media Effects," *Communication Research* 3 (1976), pp. 3–21; J. G. Blumler and E. Katz, eds., *The Uses of Mass Communications: Current Perspectives on Gratifications Research* (Beverly Hills, CA: Sage, 1974); M. Cantor, *Prime-Time Television: Content and Control* (Beverly Hills, CA: Sage, 1980); H. Gans, *Deciding What's News* (New York: Pantheon, 1979); G. Gerbner, L. Gross, M. Morgan, and N. Signorielli, "The Mainstreaming of America: Violence Profile No. 11," *Journal of Communication* 30 (1980), pp. 10–29; M. E. McCombs and D. Shaw, "The Agenda-Setting Function of Mass Media," *Public Opinion Quarterly* 36 (1972), pp. 176–187; G. Tuchman, *Making News: A Study in the Construction of Reality* (New York: Russell Sage, 1978).

87. A wide-ranging debate among representatives of the different paradigms is in the special issue "Ferment in the Field" of *Journal of Communication* 33, no. 3 (Summer 1983).

88. V. N. Volosinov, *Marxism and the Philosophy of Language,* trans. Ladislav Matejka and I. R. Titunik (Cambridge, MA: Harvard University Press, 1973), p. 23.

89. A key text here is Stuart Hall, "Encoding/Decoding," in *Culture, Media, Language,* ed. Stuart Hall et al. (London: Hutchinson, 1980), pp. 128–138.

90. Jarvie, *Movies as Social Criticism,* p. 105.

91. Donald Kuspit, "The Contradictory Character of Post Modernism," in *Postmodernism—Philosophy and the Arts,* ed. Hugh J. Silverman (New York: Routledge, 1990), p. 54.

92. These dilemmas are explored in a variety of aesthetic contexts in Hal Foster, ed., *The Anti-Aesthetic: Essays on Postmodern Culture* (Port Townsend, WA: Bay Press, 1983).

93. Terry Lovell, *Pictures of Reality* (London: BFI, 1980), esp. pp. 79–95.

94. Polan, *Power and Paranoia,* p. 18.

95. A classic analysis of the various relations that may prevail between a film and its presentation of social values is Jean-Luc Comolli and Jean Narboni, "Cinema/Ideology/Criticism," in *Movies and Methods,* vol. 1, ed. Bill Nichols

(Berkeley: University of California Press, 1976), pp. 22–30. In his work on recent Hollywood film, Robin Wood has emphasized and found value in the incoherent text. See Wood's *Hollywood from Vietnam to Reagan* (New York: Columbia University Press, 1986).

96. Christine Anne Holmlund, "New Cold War Sequels and Remakes," *Jump Cut* no. 35 (1990), p. 94.

97. Gina Marchetti, "Class, Ideology and Commercial Television: An Analysis of *The A-Team*," *Journal of Film and Video* 39, no. 2 (Spring 1987), p. 19.

98. David Talbot and Barbara Zheutlin, *Creative Differences: Profiles of Hollywood Dissidents* (Boston: South End Press, 1978), p. 82.

99. This experimentation is chronicled in Kolker, *A Cinema of Loneliness.*

100. See Nicholas Abercrombie, Stephen Hill, and Bryan S. Turner, *The Dominant Ideology Thesis* (London: George Allen & Unwin, 1980).

101. See Noel Carroll, *Mystifying Movies: Fads and Fallacies in Contemporary Film Theory* (New York: Columbia University Press, 1988), pp. 73–88.

102. A limited exception is Michael Ryan and Douglas Kellner, *Camera Politica* (Bloomington: Indiana University Press, 1988). They supplement their analysis of ideologies in contemporary Hollywood film with a small sample survey (153 respondents) of audience attitudes toward specific films. Although there were some attitudinal correlations with such basic variables as gender, race, and income level, viewers proved to be quite mixed in political outlook, quite capable of simultaneously holding divergent political views, and idiosyncratic in their perceptions of values they would label liberal or conservative. While these fluid perceptions indicate some of the challenges confronting research of this nature, more work with larger samples is certainly needed.

103. Wills, *Reagan's America*, p. 4.

Chapter Two

Brave Homelands and Evil Empires

The recent changes in Eastern Europe and the breakup of the Soviet empire have begun to rearrange not only the map of Europe but also the shape of contemporary American politics. In a changing international climate, the marked anti-Sovietism that distinguished much of the Reagan period contrasts sharply with the more tolerant and cooperative international relationships that now prevail and that were anticipated by a softening of President Reagan's own stance later in his second term. Prior to this, however, Reagan brought to the presidency a conscious attempt to reverse the perceived mistakes of the Carter years. As Jeane Kirkpatrick had argued in the pages of *Commentary*, Carter's emphasis upon human rights seemed to many in the new administration to be a symptom of a weakened America, a nation no longer able to forcibly defend its needs and its friends throughout the globe. The Right was offended by the ''loss'' of Nicaragua and Iran, and the Soviet invasion of Afghanistan seemed like a deliberately calculated move in light of the apparent erosion of the U.S. position as a world leader and military force.

As the 1970s ended, for many on the Right the United States had lost its stature in the international arena.[1] The scars of defeat in Vietnam lingered, and the United States seemed unwilling to engage in direct military intervention elsewhere. A 20-year campaign of pressure against Castro's Cuba—including clandestine CIA operations, an economic blockade, and an attempted invasion—had not dampened the revolutionary fires in Central America. The revolution had succeeded in Nicaragua, El Salvador seemed about to fall, and fighting between the rebels and the government in Guatemala was growing increasingly bloody. (These developments are examined in Chapter 3.) The protracted hostage drama playing out on a daily basis in Iran seemed to reveal America as a hobbled giant, especially when its elite hostage rescue team and expensive helicopters fell victim to something as mundane and foreseeable as desert sands and winds. In a bipolar world, as it had been since World War II, every American loss was interpreted as a Soviet victory. America's decline automatically entailed a renewal of Soviet strength. A resurgent America (to borrow a term from Robert Tucker's important *Foreign Affairs* article of the period[2]) was the program and the prescription needed to reverse this course of affairs. As Reagan took office, détente and human rights were discarded as the discredited policies of yesterday, and a new Cold War commenced.

As in the old Cold War, the major source of conflict and aggression throughout the world was held to be the Soviet Union, and against it only the military might of the United States was perceived to be poised. Indeed, President Reagan believed that it was America's military force that had kept the peace throughout the world following World War II and that only now, in a time of a declining American military strength, did the Soviet Union feel sufficiently emboldened to launch aggressive moves in Central America, Africa, and the Middle East. At the end of World War II, according to Reagan:

The United States was the only undamaged industrial power in the world. Our military power was at its peak, and we alone had the atomic weapon. But we didn't use this wealth and this power to bully. We used it to rebuild. We raised up the war-ravaged economies, including the economies of those who had fought against us. At first, the peace of the world was unthreatened, because we alone were left with any real power, and we were using it for the good of our fellow man. Any potential enemy was deterred from aggression because the cost would have far outweighed the gain.[3]

The relationship of world peace to U.S. military power, for Reagan, rested on a kind of first principle governing U.S. conduct in international affairs: The United States would never strike first. "The defense policy of the United States is based on a simple premise: the United States does not start fights. We will never be an aggressor. We maintain our strength in order to deter and defend against aggression—to preserve freedom and peace."[4] This rationale links the new Cold War explicitly with the one begun under Truman. In his famous "doctrine" announcing the shape of postwar foreign policy, Truman in 1947 had pledged the United States would defend "free peoples who are resisting attempted subjugation by armed minorities or by outside pressures," thus implying that the United States would never instigate a conflict but only intervene where "free peoples" were already being threatened. That Reagan saw his policies as an explicit continuation of the Truman era is apparent in his use of the Truman Doctrine in a 1983 speech before Congress on the threat posed by revolutionary Nicaragua to U.S. interests. Quoting from the doctrine and remarking that Truman's words were as relevant now as in 1947, Reagan proceeded to describe a scenario in which creeping totalitarianism in Central America threatened the national security of all the Americas and demanded a vigorous U.S. response.[5] In this speech and elsewhere, Reagan's rhetoric borrowed from the earlier Cold War. To justify Truman's pledge to intervene against the Left in Greece, for example, Dean Acheson had offered the "rotten apple" theory of Communist expansion. "Like apples in a barrel infected by one rotten one, the corruption of Greece would infect Iran and all to the East. It would also carry infection to Africa through Asia Minor and Egypt, and to Europe through Italy and France."[6] Many years later, it seemed the barrel was still infected, though no one was speaking of apples. Reagan noted the grave consequences that the "loss" of Nicaragua threatened: "Using Nicaragua as a base, the Soviets and Cubans can become the dominant power in the crucial corridor between North and South America. Established there, they will be in a position to threaten the Panama Canal, interdict our vital Caribbean sea lanes and, ultimately, move against Mexico."[7] Should this happen, "our alliances would crumble, and the safety of our homeland would be put in jeopardy."[8]

The new Cold War, then, would be explicitly linked to the old one, even though, as noted in Chapter 1, a new political construction—terrorism—was added to the arsenal of anticommunism. Both Cold Wars conjured the vision of a world Communist conspiracy headed by a vast, monolithic, extremely powerful, and unremittingly hostile Soviet Union. If U.S. power had formerly maintained peace in the postwar years, the more recent policies of détente and human rights were assisting the world Communist conspiracy by preventing the United States from properly defending its authoritarian Third World friends. More important, the Reagan administration claimed, the fundamental relationship between peace and U.S. power was threatened because the Soviet Union was conducting "the greatest military buildup in the history of man."[9] With the Soviets allegedly spending more on defense and the United States spending less, the global military balance of power had shifted in a dangerous direction.[10] To counter this, defense spending would have to be increased as an investment in peace while other forms of government spending would be slashed. Furthermore, domestic ideological mobilization would be basic to the maintenance of a new Cold War. Americans would be continually reminded throughout the Reagan years of the grave threat to world peace posed by the Soviet Union. The Soviets were portrayed as an outlaw nation, as the locus of evil in the modern world, as a country that refused to abide by standards of civilized behavior and moral law. The Soviet Union was "a society which wantonly disregards

individual rights and the value of human life and seeks constantly to ex-
pand and dominate other nations."[11] In the political imagery of the
period, it seemed that only the Reagan administration stood between the
free world and the forces of communism—and then only because of its
renewed commitment to the importance of strong military power. Looking back on his first term, Reagan proudly announced, "In the four years
before we took office, country after country fell under the Soviet yoke.
Since January 20th, 1981, not one inch of soil has fallen to the Communists."[12] (Toward the end of his second term, of course, President
Reagan began to soften his earlier hard-line anti-Soviet stance and to
cooperate with Mikhail Gorbachev in seeking an end to the new Cold
War. Furthermore, compared with the major military ventures in Panama
and the Middle East conducted by the Bush administration, it must be
acknowledged that the Reagan administration was rather more cautious
in its use of military force than its frequently aggressive rhetoric had led
many to expect.)

This demonization (in political rhetoric) of the Soviet Union and its allies
animated a cycle of films during the 1980s, those which we will study
in this chapter and will call the new Cold War films: *Red Dawn* (1984),
Rocky IV (1985), *Invasion USA* (1985), *Top Gun* (1986), *The Delta Force* (1986),
Heartbreak Ridge (1986), *Iron Eagle I* (1986) and *Iron Eagle II* (1988), and *Rambo
III* (1988). We will be concerned with the cycle's political imagery and
discourse, how the cycle is tied to political currents of the time, and the
ways that the elements of genre either facilitated or limited this discourse.
Most of these films offer a fairly direct and immediate transposition of
the administration's foreign policy projections into narrative terms. As
such, they help illuminate the cultural atmosphere of the time and
demonstrate the affinities between filmic and political rhetoric. Furthermore, just as the new Cold War explicitly defined itself in relation to the
previous one, so the preoccupations of these films are related to an earlier
period of Cold War filmmaking in the 1950s, when Hollywood embarked
on a cycle of anticommunist films to prove its pro-American credentials
to the House Un-American Activities Committee (HUAC). It is worth
taking a brief look at this earlier cycle so that the new Cold War films
may be compared against it and their operations understood in relation
to the problematic place of political representation in the American film
tradition.

According to Thomas Doherty, who has studied this earlier cycle and
calls it "Hollywood agit-prop," the studios released approximately 40
anticommunist films between 1948 and 1954.[13] With titles like *I Was a
Communist for the F.B.I.*, *The Iron Curtain*, *The Woman on Pier 13* (alternate
title, *I Married a Communist*), and *The Red Menace*, these films extolled the
virtues of traditional American life and castigated the foreign-born menace
of left-wing thought, portraying it as a disease eroding the health and

purity of American society. As we have seen in Chapter 1, direct ideological exhortation was not the norm for Hollywood filmmaking. Instead, Hollywood films almost always placed political content within the familiar formulas and conventions of popular narrative forms.[14] Thus, as Doherty points out, some of the more commercially successful anticommunist films, such as *Big Jim McLain* (1952), absorbed their Red-baiting politics within the formulas of an adventure story, while a box-office dud like *My Son John* (1952) dispensed with generic formulas in favor of explicit ideological platitudinizing. This tension in the cycle between apparently nonpolitical narrative formulas and conventions (and the box-office success that they helped to ensure) and the need to offer an explicit political line was difficult to resolve. The historical traditions of the American cinema and the audience expectations they had helped to shape stressed the importance of genre. As Walter Wanger had cautioned the OWI, American audiences were suspicious of propaganda from either Right or Left, and much preferred to see a repetition of the familiar formulas and conventions. Yet the studios' attempts to prove their anticommunist commitment worked toward a displacement of genre by political ideology throughout this cycle, and Doherty suggests this is why many of these films failed to find much acceptance at the box office.

The importance of genres, formulas, and conventions for a film's popular acceptance, however, did not mean that ordinary Hollywood films (outside the anticommunist cycle) entirely avoided presenting political realities or that studio productions could not function as political filmmaking. A number of major studio directors were highly ideological filmmakers, sometimes explicitly (Frank Capra), sometimes implicitly (John Ford). In either case, however, their success was predicated upon a skillful use of Hollywood conventions, although occasionally political ambition would subvert the organization of the generic story line, as occurred in Capra's *Meet John Doe* (1944), where his theme of the rise of fascism in America overwhelmed his ability to provide a coherent narrative resolution (and compelled him to film a series of alternative endings). The production histories of individual films, moreover, often reveal the ways that producers, directors, screenwriters, and studio organizations such as the Production Code Administration (PCA) would negotiate the acceptable range of political and social meaning contained within a given film. During Sam Goldwyn's production of *Dead End* (1937), about urban poverty and delinquency, a great deal of discussion and negotiation occurred between Goldwyn's team and the Breen office regarding the ways the film would be permitted to represent inner city poverty, squalor, crime, and labor organizations.[15] *Dead End*'s presentation of social discord and the way the film avoided a pat solution to the problems of poverty and social conflict were a challenge to the PCA's preference for reassuring narrative solutions in the final reel, yet the PCA accommodated the film's images and characters of social protest, so much so that the trade paper *Variety* felt the film neglected the mandate of entertainment for that of politics, warning that "The picture public which has little regard for propaganda and high respect for entertainment will find in it a reversal of popular values."[16]

As noted in Chapter 1, Hollywood does have a long-standing tradition of social protest filmmaking, and the institutions of studio production could accommodate films that tempered their entertainment with vibrant social or political perspectives. Sometimes an entire cycle or genre would lend itself especially well to this kind of filmmaking. Warner Brothers' gangster films of the early 1930s were extremely popular, dazzling demonstrations of the use of the new sound technology and were trenchant portrayals of economic inequities in depression America. The postwar cycle of film noir, with its low-key lighting that bathed domestic decor with a disquieting gloom, its fatalistic narratives, and visions of violence, greed, and corruption offered a set of narrative formulas and generic images which could become reassuring through their familiarity and repetition in films from the mid-1940s through the early 1950s. But film noir's formulas and images also enabled politically perceptive filmmakers to connect the genre's pessimism and despair with postwar political realities.

In *Kiss Me Deadly* (1955), Robert Aldrich, working at the very end of the film noir cycle, was able to inflect it with a high degree of political self-consciousness. A liberal filmmaker, Aldrich took an icon of 1950s right-wing, anticommunist culture—Mickey Spillane's Mike Hammer—and set out to portray the character as a brutish heel and, moreover, to ground both Hammer's brutality and film noir's atmosphere of fear and paranoia in the Cold War climate itself. Aldrich implies in the film that film noir is a stylistic symptom of the Cold War, that the genre's paranoia and anxiety are rooted in the profound cultural anxieties maintained by postwar politics. One of the forces driving the onset of the Cold War had been the atomic bomb and the attempt to keep the scientific knowledge that had created it in U.S., rather than Russian, hands, The bomb, as well, is at the center of Aldrich's film. It is "the great what's-it," the grand object and metaphor around which the film's narrative of savagery and anxiety, and its pervasive death imagery, is organized. It turns out to be the object of Hammer's quest, and when he finds it, it blows up in his face, turning a section of the California coastline to ground zero. Hammer's encounter with the bomb provides not the resolution of a mystery but the extinction of narrative and culture. As with the Cold War itself, the bomb drives the narrative of *Kiss Me Deadly*, as Aldrich demonstrates how effectively generic materials can be given a political inflection and content.

Hollywood's embrace of politics, then, has traditionally been an ambivalent one in that its first commitment has always been to the proven building blocks of box-office success: genres, formulas, and star-centered narratives. Working within these parameters, studio filmmaking might cohere periodically with traditions of social protest and a strong native American populism. (The populist component of American films, however, is far more typical of the 1930s and 1940s, in the work of Capra and Ford and the average-Joe heroes of the young Jimmy Stewart, Henry Fonda, and Gary Cooper. With the onset of the Cold War, political discourse substituted idealized notions of the nation for the class-based ideal of "the people" that one frequently finds in films of the earlier period.) In addition, individual directors might inflect genre narratives with a social or political content. In this respect, the overt propagandizing of the brief anticommunist cycle of films during the HUAC era is something of an anomaly to the extent that political ideology was permitted to displace narrative and genre formulas. Doherty notes the uniqueness of this brief period of overt sloganeering:

Since the termination of the anti-communist cycle, Hollywood has not marshalled appreciable resources for propagandistic ends. Even during the 1960s, when some segments of the industry discerned a demand for politically engaged films, the result was sometimes vaguely anti-Establishment, but seldom overtly ideological. In its widest sense, all films may indeed be "ideological." In American cinema, however, ideology continues to be concealed beneath the veneer of generic demands.[17]

Doherty is correct about the shortcomings of the late 1960s films produced during the heyday of the rebellious youth culture. The visions of social rebellion found in Sam Peckinpah's *The Wild Bunch* (1969) and Arthur Penn's *Bonnie and Clyde* (1967) are infused with despair and pessimism issuing from a conviction that the film's heroes will fail in their rebellion and that society can no longer be ameliorated or made less corrupt. An inability to find or commit to political alternatives paralyzed the social visions of both filmmakers, and this blockage was as much a product of their own creative personalities as of the traditional limitations inhering within popular genres to which Hollywood film had long subscribed.

Doherty's claim, however, that since the end of the anticommunist cycle in the 1950s Hollywood has avoided overt propagandizing may need to be amended. The new Cold War films are striking, sometimes strident, exceptions to this claim. These films are linked to that earlier cycle by virtue of their explicit support for and defense of state policy, as well as by direct allusion and acknowledgment. While they employ familiar genres and formulas—many take the form of the adventure thriller centered on a charismatic and powerful hero—they do not shrink from direct political advocacy. Stallone's *Rambo III*, for example, wherein Rambo battles the Soviets in Afghanistan, is dedicated in the final credits to "the people of Afghanistan." John Milius's *Red Dawn*, about a Soviet invasion of America, is offered as a primer on Soviet hostility and duplicity and on techniques of American resistance. Stallone's *Rocky IV* opens with boxing gloves emblazoned with the American flag and the hammer and sickle clashing together and exploding, and it pits Rocky against a superhuman Soviet boxer, the characters intended as explicit national emblems. These three films are the most overtly argumentative of the group, but all of the others pursue as well the great themes of Reagan-era foreign policy: the weakness of the United States in the international arena, the viciousness of the Soviet Union and its allies, and the need for resurgent American military power and a Pax Americana. Furthermore, as we shall see, their politics is a direct function of their genre status. Their use of the adventure thriller with its dependence on high-tech weaponry, outré displays of heroics and physical strength, and lightning-fast narrative pacing is an indication of the immediacy with which the new Cold War was being experienced and waged.

One of the most important cinematic documents of the period's politics is John Milius's *Red Dawn*, which draws its narrative from the assumptions of Reagan's anti-Soviet foreign policy yet becomes entangled in contradictions inherent within Cold War thought. Released in 1984 at the beginning of Reagan's second term, the film was cowritten and directed by the self-proclaimed right-wing filmmaker whose previous work had included an homage to martial prowess and the warrior spirit, *Conan the Barbarian* (1982). *Red Dawn* deals with the efforts of a small band of high school students to wage a guerrilla resistance against Soviet occupation in the western United States. While the focus on adolescents is partly a marketing ploy designed to attract the young audience that films of the 1980s incessantly courted, it also allows Milius to make a statement about political administrations symbolized through generational values. It is the youth of today—that is, of the Reagan years—who demonstrate the fortitude and resolve necessary to combat the Soviet invaders, and these young guerrillas are commemorated at the end of the film as great American patriots, alongside earlier heroes of an aggressive America such as Teddy Roosevelt. Early in the film, the spirit of the Rough Riders is invoked when the camera tilts down a statue of Roosevelt and lingers over the inscription: "Far better it is to dare mighty things than to take rank with those poor, timid spirits who know neither victory nor defeat." This is Milius's prescription for America in the 1980s: Discard the timidity of the 1970s and resume the spirit of the Rough Riders.

The reasons for the Soviet invasion are not clarified, and this lack of explanation allows Milius to construct an ideological frame viewing the Soviets as inexplicably hostile and devious (so devious, in fact, that they manage an invasion of the American heartland without triggering a nuclear war). The opening of the film establishes a fictional international political context within which the narrative occurs. A series of title cards provides a catalog of anti-Soviet political fantasies, and they function as a kind of mystical incantation "explaining" the events that precipitated the invasion: "Soviet Union suffers worst wheat harvest in 55 years. Labor and food riots in Poland. Soviet troops invade. Cuba and Nicaragua reach troop strength goals of 500,000. El Salvador and Honduras fall. Green Party gains control of West German parliament. Demands withdrawal of nuclear weapons from European soil. Mexico plunged into revolution. NATO dissolves. United States stands alone." In the narrative that follows, Soviet troops march across the Bering Strait, and tiny Cuba and Nicaragua invade from the south, while all of Europe decides to sit out the conflict. Despite the incoherence of the basic scenario, the film's paranoia is a powerful distillation of the mood of encirclement and threat and the anxieties about U.S. weakness that typified the early Reagan era.

The narrative follows the exploits of the band of adolescent rebels led by Jed (Patrick Swayze), named after Jedediah Smith and raised on the stories of frontiersman Jim Bridger. Through the characters and setting, Milius connects contemporary American resistance to the national mythology of the taming of the West. Jed applies frontier strategies to their battles with the Soviets as Milius attempts to ground their struggles in the new Cold War with an earlier chapter of American history and with the imagery of the Old West that the Reagan presidency revived. The boys ride horses and camp in the hills as if they were gunfighters of old or a contemporary president. By grounding its contemporary politics in earlier American historical and mythological traditions, *Red Dawn* has an uncommon self-consciousness and explicitness, as if Milius had set himself the task of providing a narrative fantasy that would document the political tenor of the mid-1980s. Sometimes this self-consciousness is used for comic effect, which in turn serves to heighten its explicit nature. Following the invasion, three Soviet soldiers go sight-seeing like tourists with cameras in the Arapaho National Forest. One who has studied English translates a plaque in the forest for his friends. This forest, he says, is a memorial to the great 1908 peasant uprising of wild Indians that was put down by Cossack troops, imperialist armies. and cowboys led by Theodore Roosevelt. He poses proudly in front of the plaque while his friends take his picture, as the sequence comments on the ease with which history is translated into political myth, an embodiment of Milius's own concerns in the film.

The film's political self-consciousness is also apparent in a series of cinematic allusions that position Milius' film in relation to earlier propaganda classics. During an early scene, shortly after the Soviets consolidate their hold over Jed's hometown, the camera tracks through the occupied streets (the drab and devastated buildings look like a town

in Nazi-occupied Europe during World War II), and a viewer with a quick
eye can catch a glimpse of the film playing at the local Bijou: *Alexander
Nevsky* (1938), offered in a series of free showings by the Soviets! (This
is not the only instance where Milius incorporates references to classic
political films. He also borrows from the imagery of Leni Riefenstahl's
Triumph of the Will [1935] and Gillo Pontecorvo's *The Battle of Algiers* [1965]).
Nevsky, directed by Sergei Eisenstein on the eve of the Soviet struggle
against the Nazis, dramatized heroic Soviet resistance against an invading
Teutonic army during the Middle Ages. Referencing the film enables
Milius to construct a double-edged political metaphor: He can make fun
of Soviet propaganda (while poking fun at Eisenstein, whose classic film
is shown as a contemporary instrument of oppression) while implying
that he is making, from an anti-Soviet, anti-Marxist position, a kind of
contemporary equivalent, an Americanized version of *Alexander Nevsky*.

These two sequences reveal an interesting ambiguity and ambivalence
within the film. The sequence in the forest humanizes the Soviet invaders,
who are then killed by Jed's group, which is not a particularly effective
propaganda strategy: We are made to feel some sadness over their deaths.
The use of *Alexander Nevsky* points to historic parallels in the Soviet and
American experiences, as both (the Soviets in historical reality, the
Americans in the narrative of the film) valiantly resisted an outside in-
vader. Milius further complicates our responses to the Soviets by including
among the invaders a Cuban officer named Bella who, because of his own
experience aiding Third World rebels in Angola, El Salvador, and
Nicaragua, grows increasingly sympathetic toward Jed's group. He
derisively refers to himself as a policeman, and he lashes out at his Soviet
superior's penchant for firing squads: ''Every time you shoot, the revolution grows.'' In the film's climactic sequence, he permits the wounded
Jed to escape with his brother and then symbolically throws down his gun.

Because of his understanding and compassion for the American rebels,
Bella becomes a sympathetic figure, but it is precisely because of his Marxist politics and commitment to national revolution and independence that
he is able to feel this compassion. By designing the narrative as a story
of American revolution and resistance, Milius is unable to completely
disentangle his film from the Marxian tradition promoting revolution and
resistance. In a deeply ironic maneuver, considering the political
framework that undergirds the film, Milius is maneuvered into invoking
some of the imagery and language of the Marxian heritage in *Red Dawn*.
While this certainly does not subvert the film's intense commitment to
Cold War perspectives, the use of the Bella character does raise lingering
and unanswered (and within the logic of the film, unanswerable) questions about the similarities of the American, Cuban, and Nicaraguan
revolutions. The film cannot answer these questions for the very reason
that the issue of revolution is so troublesome for Cold War perspectives.

Ever since Truman proclaimed his doctrine as an explicitly counterrevolutionary manifesto, pledging the United States to resist insurrections by "armed minorities," America's own revolutionary heritage and its implication that the United States might take the side of revolution throughout the world necessarily became one of the great unexamined topics within Cold War thought. With the character of Bella, the film comes dangerously close to asking this question but cannot, finally, pose it without transcending its own ideological boundaries.

These ambiguities, the self-conscious use of political humor, and the references to the classics of political cinema provide *Red Dawn* with a measure of sophistication (however small) that enables the film to engage the ideology it promotes rather than being merely its handmaiden. Cold War thought became accessible to the conventions of popular genres to the extent that it had already assumed a pervasive cultural presence inside American society, its bipolar moral and political coordinates internalized by generations of postwar Americans as requisites for political thought and analysis. A second reason for its accessibility to popular genre conventions is due to shared principles for coding information operative in film genre and Cold War ideology. A word here on restricted coding will help us to understand the structural affinities between film genre and political projections like Cold War thinking. The term (and its opposite, elaborated coding) is drawn from the work of sociolinguist Basil Bernstein, who developed them as a way of analyzing the speech patterns of different social classes.[18] Our purpose here is not to suggest that linguistic models can or should furnish a basis for analyzing film structure. Film lacks the syntactic rules that establish such linguistic features as tense, a propositional structure, negatives, and so on (although much contemporary film theory has been influenced by linguistic models). However, in this limited case, an understanding of restricted coding techniques can help us to see the way that genre films typically communicate. (Bernstein's own usage of the terms applied to nonverbal behavior as well as to aspects of syntax.)

With restricted coding, content is drawn from a narrow range of material. The structural rules governing the presentation of this content are rigidly applied and generally intolerant of significant variations from the norms. Meanings are condensed and implicit, deriving from common expectations shared by communicator and audience. By contrast, elaborated coding features greater flexibility in the application of structural rules, and content is drawn from a larger range of referents. Meanings are often elaborated at length and made explicit. Elaborated coding strategies often arise in situations where the intention of a communicator cannot be assumed or taken for granted or where shared expectations do not prevail. Restricted coding, on the other hand, permits efficient and rapid communication. In a Western, for example, it suffices merely to show at the film's beginning a gunfighter riding into an isolated town from the distant mountains to immediately reference and set in motion a restricted but potent set of narrative situations and conflicts, arousing specific expectations in the minds of fans of the genre. Much can be said very quickly using methods of restricted coding, and such coding provides the basic communicational structure of genre films.

Cold War thought, with its rigid conventions and its mapping of the world into polarized social, economic, and moral oppositions, depends upon a form of restricted coding. Political and cultural developments in the United States following World War II worked to stigmatize the broad-based, ecumenical Left that had been such an important part of American politics and society during the 1930s and through the war. In changing postwar circumstances, following Churchill's "Iron Curtain" speech at Fulton, Missouri, and Truman's doctrine, the ascension to power of Mao Tse-tung in China and the detonation of the first Soviet nuclear bomb, the cinctures of Cold War thought operated to reduce an ecumenical Left to the status of a univocal, despised political-cultural sign—"Communist"—that excluded alternative forms of conceptualizing, of coding, postwar history and culture. Henceforth, conflicts throughout the world were reduced to rigid moral and teleological terms, as the struggle of good and evil, manifestations of the U.S.-Soviet opposition. The structure of Cold War thought—reductive, rigid, conventionalized, and familiar—thus lent itself quite well to an articulation by the narratives of genre films, bonding ideology with visual-narrative form, following the principles of restrictive coding operative in each.

The extent to which the new Cold War ideology had become a kind of free-floating political and conceptual framework by the mid-1980s, available for assimilation and propagation by genre images and narratives, is illustrated by a film made the year after *Red Dawn*. Produced as a Chuck Norris vehicle and cowritten by Norris, *Invasion USA* repeats and reinforces the narrative and thematic material of the Milius film by dealing with an army of thugs led by a renegade Soviet officer that spreads terror throughout the United States. The army is racially and ethnically heterogeneous, composed of blacks, Latins, Asians, a catalog of groups excluded from the New Right's America, so that their depradations become a kind of nightmare vision of the return of the repressed. With calculated outrageousness, they blow up churches, shopping malls, and families at home celebrating Christmas. Evidently, they hope (though this is never terribly clear) to precipitate a civil war that will erode American democracy.

As a Chuck Norris vehicle, the generic elements are much stronger here than in *Red Dawn*, but their fusion with a Cold War framework demonstrates how serviceable the ideology is and how compatible it is with certain contemporary genres. Since the ideology and the genre narratives play upon a reductive repertoire of conventionalized expectations, they readily bond with each other as content and form, the vigilante, superhero narratives of action and violence providing the formal framework necessary for absorbing the incipient violence and paranoia operating within Cold War thought. This structural fusion of ideology and genre helps make these films potent vehicles for ideological expression. Genre is an especially effective and efficient vehicle for ideology because it works on an intimate level with its audience, playing upon sets of shared expectations that naturalize the political discourse to the extent that it becomes part of the structural rules that define the narrative operations of the genre. Of all the films examined in this book, these invasion-and-rescue films exhibit the most complete structural integration of political and narrative meaning and function.

Chuck Norris began his career making martial arts films and gradually evolved into an action hero who sometimes used martial arts. Like Sylvester Stallone, though not as self-consciously, Norris evidently sensed the way the prevailing winds were blowing in the mid-1980s, and he followed in Stallone's path by fashioning himself as an action hero of the Right, here as well as in his *Missing in Action* films (examined in Chapter 4). The partnership was a profitable one. The Soviets had become, in the political discourse of the period, such figures of melodrama, such outsized caricatures of evil, that they could generate equally outsized heroes to oppose them. The superhuman, over-the-top stature and power of the Chuck Norris-Sylvester Stallone vigilante heroes were thus necessitated by the extreme, almost cartoonish terms in which the evil of the Soviet Union was drawn in the period's discourse. The Cold War imagery that preexisted the films, and from which they drew in fashioning their narratives, structurally necessitated such disproportionate heroes and battles. Besides, and illustrating again the cohesion of ideology and genre, these were good for the box office.

The film begins by evoking the worst fears of the HUAC period and the anticommunist films it inspired: that the Soviets are already here, disguised and lurking among us, working to subvert the country. The opening scene tracks a boatload of refugees escaping (inevitably) from Cuba. They are greeted by what appears to be the U.S. Coast Guard. An American naval officer waves and says, "Welcome to the United States," but his men abruptly machine-gun the refugees. The officer is not American but Soviet. It is Rostov, the renegade officer who will lead the invasion. Rostov's men have some drugs stashed in the refugees' boat, which they retrieve and use to purchase weapons. (Richard Lynch, the actor who plays Rostov, also appeared as a crazed Soviet agent on a murderous rampage in *Little Nikita* [1988], a film dealing with deep-cover Soviet spies operating in the United States.)

From this bloody opening with its calculated savagery (and its implication that the institutions of U.S. authority have been undermined by the
Communists), the narrative draws on familiar generic formulas as Rostov
and his army perpetrate a series of outrages that only Norris, an-ex CIA
agent, can stop. But the action formulas are inflected with the anxieties,
phobias, and aggressions that course through new Cold War thought.
Why has U.S. authority been undermined? Because the country has
grown soft and because freedom itself has become the problem. In an
explicitly political sequence, Rostov makes clear how much he counts on
this softness. He tells his associate Nikko, "America has not been invaded
by a foreign enemy in nearly 200 years. Look at them, Nikko, soft,
spineless decadence. They don't even understand the nature of their own
freedom. How we can use it against them. They are their own worst
enemy, but they don't know it." The film cuts from this speech to its
illustration. A young couple make love on the beach, engaging in sen-
sual pleasure and ignoring a mysterious flare just offshore. While they
make love, a portable TV on their blanket carries a talk show featuring
Phyllis Diller, and the blare of the TV and their own infatuation with each
other conceal the approach of Nikko. He executes them as Rostov's army
storms ashore, rushing over and crushing the television and the bodies
of the lovers. A nation addicted to sex and television is no match for this
ruthless foreign enemy. The country has been weakened by an excess
of freedom and democracy, which (as the attempts of Oliver North to
circumvent the law would demonstrate a few years later) could be considered as much an enemy as the Soviets.

To counter this turn of affairs, Hunter (Chuck Norris) personifies the
kind of old frontier, cowboy heroism that had become a staple of Reagan-
era folklore. Norris has an Indian friend who is killed by Rostov. In an
image culled from countless Westerns, Norris torches the cabin with his
friend's body inside before setting out to track Rostov. A reporter who
follows Hunter dubs him "Cowboy." Eventually, Hunter catches Rostov
and dispatches him in grand fashion, and the U.S. army defeats Rostov's
band. Order and calm are restored, but the narrative has employed its
formulas to stimulate and work up anxieties about foreign affairs and
domestic social institutions. The worst thing about Rostov's terrorist
group, an FBI man says, is that they're turning people against authority.
As the Cold War films of the 1950s had done, *Invasion USA* works to certify the validity of the security apparatus: police, army, FBI, CIA, those
groups which work together to stop Rostov and which form the infrastructure of a militarized Cold War state. The FBI character's fear, that authority
is being subverted by alien Leftists, is precisely the anxiety to which the
films in this cycle respond with their dramas of American society protected and guarded by the institutions of local and national security. *Invasion USA*'s affirmation of the vigilance needed by police, army, and FBI

in guarding domestic society links the film with the political vigilance counseled by the earlier cycle of Cold War productions during the HUAC era, which had warned Americans, in the closing lines of one of the most famous films of the group, to "keep watching the skies." In fact, a politically and cinematically self-conscious sequence explicitly links the film with its Cold War precursors. Hunter and Rostov, in separate hotel rooms, watch the same film on television: *Earth vs. the Flying Saucers* (1956), a classic Cold War science fiction film about American society under attack by alien invaders. As spaceships crash into the Capitol dome and terrorize the United States in the earlier film, matched cuts show us Rostov's men on their rampage and the response of the police and U.S. Army in the present film. "Reality" (the narrative of *Invasion USA*) is linked to fantasy (*Earth vs. the Flying Saucers*) as the Norris film self-consciously acknowledges both its own identity and its roots in the cinematic and historical past.

Not all films of the period, of course, assumed the worst-case scenario of Cold War nightmares by presenting narratives of Soviet invasions. A more common type of narrative focused on the drama of U.S. hostages being held in inhuman conditions by the Soviets or their proxies and a daring military rescue by the United States. These films represent a kind of wish-fulfilling fantasy because the realities of the time were that U.S. hostages languished without rescue. These films develop out of, and skillfully exploit, widespread national feelings of helplessness and anger coupled with a failure to look very closely at the regional complexities and the U.S. role therein. By contrast with the tangled geopolitical alliances and civil wars within which the phenomenon of hostage-taking developed, the films dealing with these issues present them within a simplistic framework, as a struggle of civilization (the United States) against barbarity (the Soviets and their Middle Eastern allies), and as a problem that is rather simply solved by the intervention of an invincible hero. Relying on an individual hero both secures the films to powerful and profitable conventions of popular cinema and solves the problem of how to stage U.S. military strikes during a period when no official war had been declared. It is dramatically easier, and it raises fewer narrative problems, to send Rambo rather than the U.S. Army into Afghanistan.

Rambo III, one of the most important and ideologically potent films of the group, scores a number of political points by marrying its hostage drama to a propagandistic narrative about the need to support the Afghan rebels, who are portrayed as a group of "freedom fighters" resisting Communist aggression. As the film opens, in an amazing feat of ideological agglomeration, John Rambo (Sylvester Stallone) is discovered living in Thailand in a Buddhist monastery, having renounced his professional soldiering but engaging in brutal and bloody stick-fighting in Bangkok for money (which he promptly turns over to the Buddhist priests with whom he lives). The film does not acknowledge the paradox that Rambo can be both a Buddhist and a violent fighter at the same time. Colonel Trautman (Richard Crenna), with whom he has served and who is a kind of father figure, visits to try to persuade Rambo to accompany him into Afghanistan to gather intelligence on an especially brutal Soviet officer. When Rambo refuses, Trautman says his going will make a difference. "Not like last time?" Rambo asks, referring to Vietnam, which he believes was "lost" because the officials in Washington wouldn't permit the United States to win. Trautman tells him he has to come "full circle," that he'll always be tearing at himself until he comes to terms with what he is: a full-blooded combat soldier, a fighting machine. Trautman's prescription is a directive for the country, which, like Rambo, is felt to be mired in a wrongheaded reluctance to use its military power. The ridiculous images of the muscular, warlike Rambo living among Buddhist monks become a satiric symbol for the recent past, a metaphor for the U.S. stance of international disengagement during the Carter period. (Another popular hostage-rescue film of the period, *The Delta Force* [1986], begins with the failed mission to rescue the Iranian hostages launched by President Carter. The film then explicitly links this failure to defeat in Vietnam; both are examples of an ignominious heritage that must be overcome.)

Rambo embraces his martial prowess only when Trautman is captured inside Afghanistan by the brutal Soviet officer. As he arranges for supplies with a weapons dealer in Pakistan, the dealer tells Rambo he doesn't look like he has much combat experience; perhaps he should go home and think over his commitment. The Third World doubts American resolve, but Rambo wins the admiration of a band of Afghan rebels who witness his superhuman fighting abilities. Having rescued Trautman, Rambo rampages through Afghanistan, wreaking a maelstrom of death and destruction. Rambo is such a supremely (and impossibly) powerful warrior that he becomes a charged national emblem, a creature of mythology and symbolism embodying the strength not of an individual but of an entire nation (thus, President Reagan would invoke him when making real threats against Middle Eastern hostage takers). The Soviet troops don't stand a chance against him because his primal power overwhelms their high-tech weaponry. He shoots helicopters out of the sky with explosive arrows. He overpowers a squad of armed men with a bow and arrow. He can see so well in the dark that he can ambush and destroy a group of Russians equipped with night-vision goggles. Driving a tank straight into an onrushing helicopter, Rambo survives the explosion of both. He knows how to withstand suffering, too. When a piece of shrapnel lodges in his side, he pulls the metal spike all the way through, pours gunpowder in the wound and ignites it to cauterize the bloody hole, then promptly (in the next scene) climbs a mountain to ambush the Soviets.

Rambo's glistening, rippling muscles lovingly dwelt on by the camera, his eager embrace of Trautman's designation as a fighting machine, the detailed sadomasochism of the violence, the spectacular Götterdämmerung of the battles—all this is uncomfortably close to the virile posing and celebration of death that Susan Sontag has argued is central to a fascist aesthetic.[19] The elaborate ritual of suffering, killing, and purgation that Stallone has designed for his hero, and that he enacts with a narcissistic intensity, has so inflated the potential abilities of normal human accomplishment and the symbolic stakes of the battle that the film's orgy of violence becomes comical and tinged with an unpleasantly oppressive quality. Enacting idealized scenarios of pain and death, Rambo becomes the übermensch, something Stallone himself apparently realized and tried to back away from, remarking, "This man can't be defeated. I feel sorry for the guy who's fighting him. In *Rambo I [First Blood]* he was always running, always scared. But now, there's no jeopardy. That's what turns people off."[20]

Trautman also gets to demonstrate his iron will and resolve by bearing up under Soviet torture. The Soviet commander wants to know where the rebels will be receiving a new shipment of missiles and threatens him with an array of tortures: beating, hanging, electric shock, acetylene torch. But none of this can shake Trautman's ability to take a historical view of things. When the commander tells him that it's only a matter of time before the Soviets win, Trautman gives him a history lesson:

You know there won't be a victory. Every day your war machines lose ground to a group of poorly armed, poorly equipped freedom fighters. The fact is that you underestimated your competition. If you'd studied your history, you'd know these people have never given up to anyone. They'd rather die than be slaves to an invading army. You can't defeat a people like that. We tried. We already had our Vietnam. Now you're gonna have yours.

This amazing speech is a classic example of ideological agglomeration. Note how a leftist analysis of the U.S. role in Vietnam, with the United States as an invading force stomping on an indigenous people's desire for freedom, has been placed in service of Cold War perceptions of the Soviet presence in Afghanistan, employing the political terminology of the Reagan administration (the Afghan rebels as "freedom fighters"). While this does produce a conceptual mishmash in which the political discourse short-circuits and breaks down, the contradictory appeals of the speech aim to attract disparate audience members, both liberal and conservative. The passage portrays the United States as both an imperial aggressor and a staunch defender of Third World freedom and democracy. In this case, Cold War ideology accommodates to the needs of the marketplace and the desire to manufacture a blockbuster film that will appeal to diverse audience groups.

Rambo III, however, did not turn out to be a phenomenally successful blockbuster (at least in the United States). While the filmmakers obviously hoped that the genre formulas of the ultraviolent adventure thriller would suffice to carry the political messages of the film to a wide audience, in this case history simply overwhelmed ideology. By the time the film was released, the Russians were withdrawing from Afghanistan, and Gorbachev's policies and presence were changing the international climate, helping to lay the Cold War (temporarily, at least) to rest. In the process, the dramaturgical premises of films like *Rambo III* were demolished. Stallone has remarked that Gorbachev destroyed his film, and he faced a crisis over how best to use his cold warrior.[21] Stallone reportedly considered making Rambo into an ecologist by having him, in some future film, fight on behalf of the whales. It may be, however, that a cold warrior without a cause simply fades away. On the other hand, the recent war against Iraq may provide Stallone with a violent new international arena for his hymns to brawn and blood; and if economic and political chaos in the Soviet Union helps to renew the Cold War, then Rambo will almost certainly leap back into popular culture, grunting, flexing, and shooting. He is too potent a political icon not to remain visible on the cultural landscape, especially since, as the Iraq war demonstrated, the United States remains committed to maintaining the capability for a global projection of its military power. As the cinematic emissary and symbol of this power, we should not expect Rambo to return soon to his Buddhist monastery.

The Cold War drama of *Rambo III*, like that of many other films examined in this chapter, is inseparable from a crisis of paternal authority.[22] This crisis symbolically encodes the anxieties about the state of the nation that have already been described. Father figures in these films are threatened with capture and torture, or else their authority is placed in jeopardy when questions surround their honor. The narratives collectively provide a vindication of the honor of the father. Jed's father in *Red Dawn* had shouted from the concentration camp where he was interned, "Avenge me!" Rambo's heroics are directed toward saving Trautman, his mentor and boss. The patriarchal aspects of Trautman's relationship with his "fighting machine" are conveyed in their modes of address. Rambo refers to Trautman as "Colonel" or "sir," whereas Trautman consistently uses Rambo's familiar name, "John," much as one would do with a child or social subordinate. We need to consider this symbolic encoding of paternal authority more closely because it is a major facet of the political meaning of this film cycle.

In *Iron Eagle*, a very popular film of the period, the narrative centers on the drama of the absent father and the son's despair over the disrupted family. With the rescue of the father, the narrative acquires its political force through images of the family reconstituted (a symbol for a nation healed). Doug Masters's father has been shot down by Soviet Migs over an unnamed Middle Eastern country, although the narrative clearly implies that the country is Libya, which Reagan had designated, along with the USSR, Iran, Cuba, and Nicaragua, as a sponsor of international terrorism. As the film sends Doug on the rescue mission, *Iron Eagle* becomes a potent ideological register of its time as well as an anticipation and reflection of real events.

A dispute over territorial limits has precipitated the capture of the father. The unnamed enemy claims a 200-mile territorial limit, whereas the United States recognizes only 12 miles. Flying inside the 200-mile limit, Doug's father is captured and put on trial as a means of exacting revenge against the United States. Just as U.S. officials would not permit Rambo to win the Vietnam war and would refuse to mount a rescue mission for the captured Trautman, Washington officials rule out a rescue mission for Doug's father. "The suits up in the White House have our hands tied on this," a friend tells him. With the U.S. government reluctant to use its military force, things are once again up to the individual hero, whose behavior stands as an example for the nation. Enlisting the help of a scrappy combat pilot named Chappy Sinclair (Louis Gossett, Jr.), Doug plots a rescue mission; and as he does so, the film demonstrates how domesticated, how interwoven with the apparatus of consumer culture, the Cold War and advanced weapons technologies had become in the mid-1980s.

In the film, electronic weapons and supersonic aerial combat merge with the consumer culture of rock and roll and video games. Doug learns aerial combat by practicing for hours on an Air Force simulator, and he can relate instinctually to the blips on the screen because they are just like the blips on arcade video games. Moreover, he can hit the targets only when he listens to rock and roll! On a test run, when Chappy tells him to turn off the rock music, Doug can't hit a thing. When he does it his way, with pop rock blaring in the cockpit, he destroys all of his targets. The video game imagery and the rock music help to make the Cold War political framework of the film familiar and accessible to a teen audience. The film is aimed at the adolescent market, and it features many of the generic staples of teen films, including an extended sequence during which the teens on the air force base outwit their parents by smuggling intelligence information from classified areas to help Doug pinpoint his father's location. With generic Cold War politics a cultural given by mid decade, it could be used to invigorate the formulas of Chuck Norris action films as easily as it could pump up the conventions of the teen comedy-drama. Understanding Cold War politics as a genre helps to explicate the ease with which it bonded with popular filmmaking. Formulaic imagery is essential to both, and a consequence of this is the loss of the real geopolitical world.

The outlaw country in the film is mysterious and unnamed, generating a kind of medieval geographic projection dividing the world into regions of civilization and regions of darkness and the unknown. (*Top Gun* also partakes of this medieval geography, staging its climactic aerial duel with the forces of an unnamed country over vaguely located hostile waters.) The vague geographical and political specifications accruing to the national and cultural conflicts expressed in the narrative render them in strongly ideological terms, in which the enemy occupies no terrain specifiable on a map's coordinates but is, rather, a nebulous, threatening Other, a projection of political and cultural anxieties poorly understood and assignable to regions of the world only in general and superficial terms. The international arena and the political maps that contain the conflicts in films like *Top Gun* and *Iron Eagle* are not fixed according to the physical coordinates of real time and space. They are surveyed by an emotional logic fixed in stereotyped and caricatured terms that require, in the logic of the films, no further justification or elaboration.

In this geopolitics of the mind, fantasy is master of the world, and wishing is sufficient to make things come true. Doug has an instinctual talent with fighter planes, and Chappy becomes a kind of Obi Kenobi telling Doug to trust the force. Chappy is shot down and apparently killed during the rescue, but he leaves a tape with Doug so his spiritual presence (like Obi Kenobi in *Star Wars*) is there to guide him:

God doesn't give people things he doesn't want them to use, and he gave you the touch. It's a power you have inside you, down there where you keep your guts, boy. It's all you need to blast your way in and get back what they took from you. Your dad's just sitting there waiting for a miracle, and if you fly your heart out, you can give him one. It's up to you. . . . First thing you gotta do is convince yourself that nothing can stop you. You've gotta believe that plane you're in is like a suit of armor, an iron eagle nothing can penetrate.

Believing he can do it, Doug is able to fly deep inside the enemy's airspace, locate his father, survive attacks by Migs and antiaircraft guns on the ground, blow up the air depot and an oil refinery (''Looks like they'll be importing oil this year,'' he gloats, offering the audience a wish-fulfilling fantasy of revenge against OPEC's perceived economic hostage-taking of America), and free his father. In this patriarchal geopolitics of the mind, fathers are never lost and, best of all, friends and mentors do not die. Chappy is not really dead. He waits at home for Doug to return, thus enabling the film to climax with a vindication of once-threatened institutions.

As the enemies of America are defeated, as family and friendship are restored, so is the honor of the nation. The Reagan era, the film assures us, is truly different from the wimpish administration that preceded it. Earlier, one of Doug's friends has assured him that ''Everything'll turn out. Those dudes won't mess with us. The Air Force'll kick ass if they do.''

"Like in Iran?" Doug asks, alluding to the Carter hostage rescue mission. "Oh, no, that was different," another friend replies. "Mr. Peanut was in charge back then. Now we got this guy in the Oval Office who don't take shit from no gimpy little countries. Why do you think they call him Ronnie Ray-Gun?" This overtly political moment evokes the emotional displays of resurgent America and explicitly aligns the film with the foreign policy attitudes of the period. As in the enormously popular films of Steven Spielberg, narrative resolution hinges on familial reunification and, as in the New Right agendas of the period, this carries a political charge.

The problem of the missing father also inflects the drama of one of the biggest hits of the period, *Top Gun*, wherein cocky U.S. Navy pilot "Maverick" Mitchell (Tom Cruise) is tormented by the mystery surrounding his father's disappearance and death, the circumstances of which have been classified. His father crashed while flying one of the navy's most advanced planes, and Maverick is haunted by the possibility that his father failed as a pilot, committed some error that resulted in the loss of plane and life. When, through no fault of his own, he loses control of his plane and his friend and copilot Goose is killed while ejecting, Maverick blames himself and begins to suspect he is following the possibly disgraced path of his father. But he learns from one of his superiors that his father died a hero, saving his comrades in an aerial dogfight with a group of Soviet Migs. Newly fortified with filial pride, Maverick at the climax of the film is able to repeat his father's heroic feats, is able to become his father, to revisit and reclaim his familial past. He rescues a comrade from a cluster of attacking Soviet Migs and, by surviving, does what the father could not do and transcends the older man's remarkable heroism.

Threats to the father and anxieties about his health, reputation, or continued power riddle these new Cold War films because in the guise of the father, and through narratives elaborating threats to his safety, a discourse about the country and national politics is developed. Reagan projected himself as a new commander at the helm of the ship of state, and his paternalism made him seem a benevolent, kindly patriarch to Americans but a steely foe to the enemies of freedom. As he succeeded discredited leaders like Carter, a drama of the father played itself out in the national arena, and films of the period are acutely sensitive to this development. Partly, of course, it was a matter of imitating successful cinematic conventions. Hollywood films had always centered on the family, and Spielberg revived this interest with his sentimental dramas of adolescent innocence and absent fathers, such as *Close Encounters of the Third Kind* (1977) and *E.T.* (1982). The Spielbergian influence in the cinema of the 1980s has been enormous, and the drama of the father that runs through the films examined in this chapter certainly has one of its roots there. But the saliency of the imagery is responsive to domestic political and ideological currents, which Spielberg's films themselves reflect. As we saw in Chapter 1, the conservative agenda that Reagan carried to the level of national politics was deeply concerned with preserving the authority of traditional social institutions—family, school, church, law enforcement, the military—which were perceived to have been weakened or whose authority was believed to have been eroded as a result of social changes originating in the 1960s and 1970s. The new Cold War films translate these anxieties into narrative patterns. Narratives centering on searches for the honorable father provided a means of picturing this emotional and political climate. As the popularity of many of these films suggests, this ideological grounding of visual and narrative form resonated with the interests and desires of the public. If Reagan had been politically successful by playing on these anxieties, why couldn't films do the same?

It is worth returning for a moment to *Top Gun* because, like *Iron Eagle*, it vividly shows how internalized and how much a part of the domestic landscape the Cold War had become by the mid-1980s. By definition, "Cold War" refers to the waging of war by means other than hard weaponry and battlefield clashes. It extends military antagonisms to the field of culture and to the psyches of those who inhabit that culture so that by living their daily lives and absorbing the cultural forms that surround them, they come to internalize and enact the political frameworks which help to sustain a global state of military tension. Following World War II, the Cold War was absorbed into the lived texture of daily life. It was no longer experienced as such but became part of the air people breathed and the language people spoke, and was equally invisible and intangible. Only now that it has briefly subsided is an understanding emerging of how much it was like an invisible black box into which many people unknowingly walked.[23] By looking again at *Top Gun*, we can see clearly how the imagery and rhetoric, the very forms and objects, of real-world consumer culture and leisure pursuits were fused with the psychological and emotional dynamics of the Cold War (as they were in *Iron Eagle* via Doug's penchant for rock music and video games in his cockpit). The film's political messages are rarely propounded through dialogue or explicit statement. Instead, they emerge through the film's audiovisual design, its "look," and through the camera's presentation of the characters.

This "look" extends beyond the film itself. The videotape release of *Top Gun* broke new marketing ground by including an advertisement for Diet Pepsi preceding the film. The ad, however, is a stylistic and thematic twin of the film. It features a group of jet pilots returning to base after maneuvers, is edited with quick, aggressive cutting, and employs a rock music soundtrack like the film's. In the ad, "Mustang" (a thematic call-sign name, like the film's characters who are known as "Viper," "Iceman," and "Jester") has difficulty pouring his bottle of Diet Pepsi while flying, prompting one of the other pilots to ask, "Trouble with your refreshment system?" Mustang loops around, executing the kind of flashy stunts Maverick does in the film, flying upside down, enabling the bottle to pour its contents into his mug. Satisfied at last, Mustang and the other pilots streak home. The paraphernalia of war—the camouflage markings on the planes, the evasive maneuvering, the macho bantering of the pilots—is deployed in this case to open a bottle of Pepsi, is absorbed within and by a thoroughly domestic context and function. And the Pepsi, in turn, is redeployed as a "refreshment system" within the automated cockpit of the plane. An emblem of consumer culture—Diet Pepsi—and the pleasures of leisure-time pursuits that it stereotypically represents are fused with the military apparatus at a seamless audiovisual level as the ad makes the kind of connections between political ideology and domestic life which are the essence and function of the Cold War. (In Chapter 4, we will study a similar advertisement placed on the videotape of *Platoon*.)

It is convenient to begin with the ad rather than the film because, in many ways, the film is like a longer advertisement. The U.S. Navy admitted it regarded the film as a recruiting ad, and the movie's structure employs the montage editing, minimal dialogue, and pervasive use of rock music to establish mood and theme that have become staples of MTV and that producers Jerry Bruckheimer and Don Simpson had perfected in their earlier work. Much of the film's strategy in this regard is to use these cinematic elements to eroticize the planes and weaponry and the bodies of the students and teachers at the "Top Gun" school of aerial combat that Maverick and Goose attend. An extended montage sequence, for example, lingers on the rippling muscles of the bare-chested fliers as they play a heated game of volleyball. They flex and pose for the camera while the rock lyrics proclaim the passions of "bodies working overtime." One of the pilots remarks that flying against Soviet Migs gives him a "hard-on," and the pilots' banter is incessantly sexual, especially that between Maverick and "Charlie" Blackwood, a female astrophysicist who wears black, seamed stockings and heels to class. She and Maverick talk about "thrust-to-weight ratios," "negative G pushovers," "rolling reversals," and "going to hard guns," ostensibly referring to flying but completing the film's sexualization of weaponry and combat. In *Dr. Strangelove* (1964), Stanley Kubrick satirically castigated the "merkwürdigliebe" (love of death) that sustained the arms race, the love of death symbolized by the title character's German name, and by the eroticized weaponry that fascinates all the characters in the film. *Top Gun*, by contrast, gives us the merkwürdigliebe itself, without the critical and humane moral perspectives of Kubrick's Cold War satire.

The drama of the father's redemption and the sexualizing of flying and fighting work to domesticate and make pleasurable the elite weaponry of war which the film depicts and to mythologize that weaponry by shifting its locus of action to an ill-defined geography, an ideological battle-field where, as in *Iron Eagle*, the enemy is mysterious and unknowable, and military aggression is not fraught with irreversible, real-world con-sequences. As in *Iron Eagle*, the result is a politics of the mind, a psychological projection of international relations and combat. In the film's climax, one of the navy's ships is disabled and helplessly drifts into undefined, hostile foreign waters, and Maverick is sent to provide air sup-port for the ship's rescue. He encounters and shoots down a group of Soviet Migs, whose pilots wear Darth Vader-like dark helmets that con-ceal their faces and render them inhuman. In the real world, a violent clash between the U.S. and Soviet air forces could, potentially, render international tensions red-hot, if not trigger wider hostilities, possibly even nuclear war. But in the film there are no consequences. The Soviets deny the combat ever took place, and nothing further happens. In the fantasy world of Cold War wish fulfillment that *Top Gun* elaborates, the United States can act with impunity and without regard for consequences because none exist and the enemy dares not retaliate.

In concluding this discussion of *Top Gun*, we should note once again the ambiguities that surround the linkages between film and society. The film's jaunty reassertion of a martial national will was clearly a response to domestic political currents advocating a resurgent American military power. The influences, though, may also move in the other direction, from film to society. Video footage of the early phases of the real-world air war against Iraq, showing "smart" bombs seeking out targeted buildings and bridges, rather than people, had the same clean, thrilling, bloodless qualities as the aerial dogfights and bombings in *Iron Eagle* and *Top Gun*, especially because of the virtual absence of Iraqi retaliation. Because of the extraordinary control exercised by the Defense Depart-ment over journalists' access to information, the popular understanding of the air war was based on images that had a disquieting resemblance to Hollywood products. It was no longer simply a question of films imitating reality (or of helping to mobilize popular support for a foreign war) but of reality becoming the simulacrum of cinema due to policies of censorship and information control. The imagery provided by films like *Top Gun* and *Iron Eagle* accordingly may have helped to furnish the public with an experiential basis for responding to and evaluating the war in the Persian Gulf and its resulting censored news footage. To this ex-tent, films in the resurgent America cycle, combining political advocacy with box-office success, help extend and deepen the political desires and cultural anxieties to which they were originally responses.

The ideological material that inflected the genre conventions of these war films reached a climax in Sylvester Stallone's other contribution to the Cold War, *Rocky IV*, which proved to be nearly as popular as *Top Gun*. While the film is not an explicit war film treating ground or aerial combat, or a rescue of the father, it is quite interesting for the way it draws upon the cycle's narrative themes and imagery of national weakness, invasion, and politically charged physical combat. In the film, Rocky has unofficially retired from the ring to enjoy his wealthy, comfortable life, and he spends his time washing his expensive cars and loving his wife and son. But the Soviets launch an invasion of the United States via athletics. A cover of *Sports Illustrated* proclaims "Russians Invade U.S. Sports" and presents their fearsome boxer, Drago (Dolph Lundgren), whom the Soviets have made a merciless fighting machine through the use of genetic engineering, drugs, and exercise science. They bring him to the United States for what they announce as a goodwill exhibition match.

Apollo Creed (Carl Weathers), Rocky's former nemesis and current friend, is stirred by national feeling to accept the Soviet challenge. More politically sensitive than Rocky, Apollo sees the match as a symbolic opportunity for the United States to regain lost esteem. He says he doesn't want the Soviets making the United States look bad again (implying that they have done so repeatedly in the past): "They've tried every other way. Now we can make them look bad for a change." It's us against them, he tells Rocky, succinctly summarizing the national symbolism Stallone has built into the film. Apollo's complaint that the Soviets have made the United States look bad implicitly articulates the basic premise of the resurgent America ideology—that a decade of national political and military weakness throughout the 1970s has made possible a series of Soviet triumphs in the global political arena.

The film demonstrates why and how the Soviets are not to be trusted. Their delegation is all smiles, and they insist on the goodwill they wish the match to generate between the countries, but they are really launching a vicious propaganda offensive. Drago is an inhuman, unfeeling Soviet enemy who is disgusted by the decadence of American society and confident of his victory over American weakness. This weakness is visualized in the Las Vegas production number that introduces Apollo during the exhibition match. Sequined showgirls dance with Apollo, who wears the flag on his trunks, while James Brown sings a funky pro-America song. It's all empty razzle-dazzle, and Drago watches with silent and lethal disgust.

Drago's cold, robotic qualities place him in the same cinematic family as Rostov and the villains of *Red Dawn* and *Rambo III*. He also, however, connects with another lineage present in films of the period: the Nazis. Spielberg had revived satanic Nazi villains in *Raiders of the Lost Ark* (1981) and *Indiana Jones and the Last Crusade* (1989), partly because they were suited to the Manichaean morality of the films, and he presented them in a culturally and historically nonspecific manner. His Nazis were not rooted in the European politics of the 1930s but were, instead, anti-historical icons used as a kind of visual shorthand for signifying evil.

For a similar purpose, Stallone merges Nazi imagery with Cold War attitudes in the presentation of Drago, whose huge, blond physique suggests an Aryan superman, the first of a new race, a product of eugenics and drug therapy. As both Nazi and Soviet, Drago is doubly evil, doubly aggressive, a villain of both the past and the present.

The Soviet overtures of friendship, therefore, are presented in the film as lies. In a Cold War context, friendship initiated by the Soviets is merely a stratagem in a larger offensive. Ludmilla, Drago's wife, tells Apollo's wife, "I hope we can be friends after this. After all, they're sportsmen, not soldiers." But they *are* soldiers, because in the Cold War all of culture is militarized, and Drago gives the lie to Ludmilla's words by beating Apollo to death. "The Soviet strength is incredible," an announcer exclaims as Drago pummels Apollo to the ground, obviously a reference to more than boxing abilities. With Apollo's death, Rocky realizes how wrong he had been in his earlier political indifference, when he was uninterested in the exhibition match and said it didn't mean anything. Now, committed to beating Drago and avenging Apollo, Rocky journeys to the USSR to train for his match, as the narrative subtly reworks the invasion themes common in the period's war films. Rocky now invades Russia with his inspiring example of underdog individualism. Drago's coach proclaims that the defeat of Rocky, this little man, "will be an example of how pathetically weak your society has become," but Rocky brings a different and compelling model to the Soviets: American heart versus state engineering. While Drago trains with his engineers and scientists and high-tech machinery, an elaborate montage intercuts Rocky's more primitive methods. Rocky jogs through snow, hoists rocks, saws wood, chops down trees, climbs mountains as Stallone elaborates the same primitive machismo he developed in *Rambo III*, demonstrating that American spirit is more than a match for Soviet technology. (The cultural irony, however, is that to demonstrate this, Rocky has to live and work like a Russian peasant.)

During the match, Rocky sustains an incredible pummeling from Drago but stays on his feet and manages to fight back. Drago grows anxious over his inability to pound Rocky into the mat, and the crowd, which booed the American when he arrived, begins to chant his name. Gorbachev and the Politburo watch this turnaround in the crowd's sympathies with growing concern. Drago, too, eventually succumbs to Rocky's inspiring example and displays his own rebellious individualism, declaring to his trainers that he now fights to win for himself, not the state. As he says this, a cut returns us to a worried Gorbachev who, it is clear, is now presiding over a mini revolution in the sports arena as American individualism awakens the passions of the dormant Soviet masses. Rocky, of course, wins the match, and he wraps himself (literally) in an American flag while giving a speech that is a masterpiece of ideological agglomeration. While the entire logic of the film has pointed toward the inevitability of U.S.-Soviet conflict and the need for the United States to hone its martial spirit, Rocky now preaches the need for peace, brotherhood, and cooperation between the two nations:

I came here tonight, and I didn't know what to expect. I've seen a lot of people hating me. I didn't know what to feel about that, so I guess I didn't like you much none either. During this fight I've seen a lot of changing, the way you felt about me and the way I felt about you. In here there were two guys killing each other, but I guess that's better than twenty million. What I'm trying to say is that if I can change and you can change, [then] everybody can change.

Overcome by these words, the crowds chants rapturously, in love with Rocky and the flag that he wears. Even Gorbachev slowly stands and begins to applaud, at first hesitantly and reflectively, then more passionately. Although it was released in 1985, the film thus seems to anticipate some of the thawing of U.S.-Soviet relations that would occur later in the decade. Within the ideological system of the film, however, this thawing is entirely the result of American effort and example, to which the Russians merely respond. *Rocky IV* is thus a bifurcated film, for the most part content to recycle Cold War clichés about the Soviets but at the very last moment able dimly to glimpse alternatives.

The shifting tides of the Cold War are much more vividly illustrated by the sequel to *Iron Eagle*, released in 1988, at the close of the Reagan period. This time around, Chappy Sinclair leads a joint strike force of U.S. and Soviet personnel against an unnamed Middle Eastern state that has constructed a nuclear weapons launching facility which threatens both the United States and the Soviet Union. The narrative is sheer fantasy, and while it celebrates the needs and privileges of empire—the U.S.-Soviet air strike is justified, according to the film, because the enemy is an "outlaw" nation—it clearly anticipates a new era of U.S.-Soviet peace and cooperation. The American and Soviet pilots learn to work with and to respect one another, and the film ends with a plea for both governments and peoples to work for a day when their flags will no longer separate them. Even more tellingly, the film opens with a dogfight between Doug Masters (the hero of *Iron Eagle I*), another American pilot named Cooper, and some Soviet Migs. Cooper and Masters have been horsing around in the skies and have strayed into Soviet airspace. The Soviets destroy Masters and his plane while Cooper escapes, but the narrative doesn't generate much propaganda from this. Instead, Cooper and the Soviet pilots involved come to see how both sides were at fault, and they are able to forgive each other!

As *Iron Eagle II* clearly indicates, and as the ending of *Rocky IV* seemed to wish, the intensity of cinematic Cold War visions of the early and mid-1980s began to diminish toward the end of the decade, as the Soviets came to seem less inevitably an enemy. With a changing international political relationship and slow adjustments in U.S. foreign policy and the political perceptions underlying those changes, popular culture began to make its own set of readjustments. A film like *Red Heat* (1988) was possible, whereas four or five years earlier it would not have been made (or, at least, not in quite the same way). The film is about a Soviet policeman who comes to the United States tracking a ruthless criminal whose violent activities are part of a rising crime wave in the USSR. Methodically precise, he teams with a sloppy U.S. cop, and while the film is a routine collection of shoot-outs and car chases, it does demonstrate a newfound compatibility between the Soviet presence and the urban police thriller. An incipient sympathy for Soviet society is demonstrated as both cops realize they are very much alike, coping with rising crime in their respective countries. Indeed, the sequences portraying criminal organizations in the USSR pitted against local police forces enable the American viewer to identify more closely with the Soviet policeman because he is seen as responding to the same problems that have plagued American society. Even though it is not a Cold War thriller, the film is nevertheless able to absorb the Soviet character and incorporate him within the action formulas, demonstrating new possibilities for the formulas of popular film. Interestingly, and an indicator of the uncertain, transitional time in which the film was made, the Soviet cop remains rather mysterious and unknowable, unlike his familiar and predictable American counterpart. The casting of Arnold Schwarzenegger as the Soviet ensures that he remains somewhat alien, even though presented as a decent and heroic fellow.

No Way Out, released in 1987, also departs somewhat from the Cold War clichés in its presentation of naval intelligence officer Tom Farrell (Kevin Costner), who is in reality a deep-cover Soviet spy. Throughout the film, however, Farrell remains a sympathetic and, at the end, somewhat tragic figure, enmeshed within the web of deceit and treachery spun by Cold War conflicts. In its vision of U.S. governmental conspiracy and impossibly convoluted avenues of corruption, the film is much closer in spirit to the paranoia thrillers of the 1970s than to the Cold War thrillers we have been examining in this chapter. Furthermore, with its reference to U.S. support of the death squads in El Salvador, the film briefly acknowledges a political viewpoint incompatible with the Manichaean politics of those films.

Another prominent film of the period, Clint Eastwood's *Heartbreak Ridge* (1986), deals explicitly with the Grenada invasion but presents that event, and its view of military and civilian society in the mid-1980s, with considerable ambiguity and irony. Eastwood plays Sgt. ''Gunny'' Highway, a veteran of Korea and Vietnam, a tough soldier whose gung-ho patriotism is out of place in peacetime and ill-suited to the new Marine Corps, whose officers frequently lack combat experience. Gunny is a relic, an anachronism from an earlier era of empire. An officer tells him he "should be sealed in a glass cage that says 'break glass in the event of war.'" On the one hand, consistent with Cold War perspectives, Gunny's languishing spirit and career are emblematic of the wasting of the U.S. martial spirit. On the other hand, however, Eastwood really does play Gunny as a relic, as a man who can no longer relate to the world around him. The focus of the film is a microscopic one, detailing the emotional currents of Gunny's daily relationships rather than focusing on overtly symbolic portrayals of international great power relations as *Red Dawn*, *Iron Eagle* and *Top Gun* do. When it comes, the Grenada invasion is not presented as the kind of daring, heroic military operation that redeems the honor of the nation, as are the rescues in the other films. Eastwood's squad encounters a few skirmishes on the island, and that's about all. The film clearly implies that Grenada was no Heartbreak Ridge, the bloody battle in Korea that earned Gunny his Congressional Medal of Honor. Rather than a plea for resurgent America, *Heartbreak Ridge* is a restrained elegy for the passing of empire. At the end, Gunny glances at the flag and then walks away, into retirement and into the past where he feels he truly belongs.

As *Heartbreak Ridge*, *Red Heat*, and *No Way Out* indicate, popular films in the latter half of the decade could find ways of negotiating a mild critical distance from the politics and Cold War ideology of the period. But more instructive, perhaps, are those films examined in the bulk of this chapter which heartily embraced the foreign policy framework of Reagan-era politics. These films clearly demonstrate the responsiveness and sensitivity of Hollywood film to the political frameworks of the time. In part, this sensitivity was due to the extraordinary ideological intensity and self-consciousness of the Reagan years. Always eager to tap the national pulse in the interests of box-office success, Hollywood obviously targeted the new nationalism as a compelling basis for potentially resonant images and narratives, and many of our films swelled with portraits of brave homelands and evil empires. In doing this, American film stayed within the boundaries of its stylistic traditions. By and large, these were generic films that incorporated this newly explicit nationalism, and many of them aimed to be blockbuster productions, some succeeding (*Top Gun*, *Rocky IV*).

The absorption of dominant political frameworks by these films shows clearly how promiscuous the conventions of genre are, how they are able to couple with extraneous ideological content and to internalize it so that it seems, in turn, to drive the narrative. *Invasion USA*, for example, is both a Chuck Norris action film and a statement of extreme right-wing politics. As the former, it illustrates Walter Wanger's maxim that politics had best be internalized by the familiar trappings of genre narratives and characters. As the latter, however, the film is aligned with the anticommunist films of the HUAC period and tries to enforce a similar exclusivity of ideological choice upon the viewer. This chapter has been suggesting that despite their generic nature, the ideological explicitness of these Cold War films, and their simplistic conflicts of good and evil, tie them more closely to traditions of propaganda than Hollywood generally has permitted in the past, except during the HUAC period. The foreign policy pronouncements of the Reagan years produced two major ideological tracts—*Red Dawn* and *Rocky IV*—and the other rescue/invasion films in the cycle work to extend and deepen the Cold War. As cultural products, they help to create and sustain a psychology of threat, of containment, of narrowed social discourse and diminished political choice requisite for a heavily militarized society. In this respect, the conventions of genre may actually further this process of psychological and political closure. As previously noted, genre communicates quickly and intensely because it is so familiar, and the repetition of easily assimilable narrative formulas may lend the political frameworks embedded within them a perceived inevitability. Since the anti-Sovietism of the period was so strong and so pervasive, these genre formulas could link up with, and be verified by, much larger, extracinematic currents of anxiety and mistrust.

This Cold War cycle really had nowhere to go from a narrative standpoint, beyond a repetition in future films of what would become increasingly familiar and dull scenarios of invasion, subversion, and rescue. (The rescue formula also figures in the cycle of films about American MIAs in Vietnam; see Chapter 4.) The ideology that informed and generated the films was already in full flower when the cycle commenced and, as a nondialectical structure of thought, could not admit subtlety, distinction, or alternatives. Perhaps as a measure of this exhaustion, *Rambo III* had elevated the heroes and villains and the stakes of the conflict to an impossibly superhuman level of caricature. Thus it is quite likely that this cycle would have become even more redundant and repetitious had the international political situation not dramatically changed. But we should be glad that it did. Many of these films are implicitly, sometimes explicitly, apocalyptic. Had the Cold War not subsided, these genre fantasies might ultimately have become unpleasant historical realities. It's a world much to be preferred where Rambo is not slaughtering entire continents of Communists but need only fight to rescue whales and trees. It is, however, inappropriate to pronounce the arrival of the new world order. The Persian Gulf war revived calls for increased investments in weapons research and a general cultural fascina- tion with "smart" weapons, and the war itself showed that political differences are being resolved in the old familiar ways. The Soviet Union has not found its way out of a process of economic and political disintegration,

and dictatorship may again return. The new world order eagerly anticipated before the Gulf war accordingly seems increasingly elusive.

Furthermore, the nationalism these films mobilize, and that in turn feeds
them, is an extremely powerful tradition in American culture. As such,
it remains a potent force in American society and in the American psyche,
despite the apparent erosion of the Cold War. The diminishing tensions
between the United States and the Soviet Union have not entailed a
lessening of U.S. military involvement in regional conflicts. Despite the
bellicosity of the Reagan administration's political rhetoric, no major
military ventures occurred during his tenure in office. By contrast, in the
first three years of the Bush presidency, the United States launched two
major military offensives, in Panama and Iraq. Thus, despite the rhetoric
of a new world order that was voiced while the Soviets lost their grip
on Eastern Europe, the United States continues to define its role in international affairs in familiar ways. For this reason, and especially because
of the tidal wave of nationalism aroused by the war with Iraq, there seems
to be no reason to believe that the rescue-and-invasion cycle has really
played itself out. As noted, the reflex emotions it arouses are extremely
deep-seated in the culture and, as the demonization of Saddam Hussein
in the popular press attests, other evil empires can be found. Expansive,
nationalist, imperial ideologies will be likely, therefore, to inflect popular
narratives in the American cinema for a long time to come. In this respect
the substitute gratifications of film need not be true to life. Real-world
decline of U.S. economic power can, paradoxically, elicit defiant
ideological celebrations of national glory, as the films in this chapter indicate. While the United States had to go hat in hand to other nations
to foot the bill for the war against Iraq, Rambo and the Delta Force can
continue to act unilaterally and imperiously on film, at no cost to the tax-
payer and proudly scorning the largess and patronage of other nations.

The cycle of invasion-and-rescue films diligently celebrates and promotes the frameworks of ideology and foreign policy that supported the
new Cold War. Was there room in the Hollywood film industry of the
1980s for alternative political perspectives, for films that sought to critique
and question aspects of U.S. foreign policy and their corresponding
political assumptions and military imperatives? To explore this question,
in Chapter 3, we need to consider the decade's rapidly escalating conflicts in the Caribbean basin.

NOTES

1. Noam Chomsky analyzes the new Cold War as a response to a perceived
context of U.S. weakness and defeat in *Towards a New Cold War* (New York: Pantheon, 1982).

2. See Robert W. Tucker, "The Purposes of American Power," *Foreign Affairs*
59, no. 2 (Winter 1980/1981), pp. 241–274. It should be noted that Tucker counseled
caution in implementing such a policy.

3. Ronald Reagan, address to the nation on arms control, November 22, 1982, in *Vital Speeches of the Day* 49, no. 5, p. 130.

4. Ronald Reagan, address to the nation on peace and national security, March 23, 1983, in *Vital Speeches of the Day* 49, no. 13, p. 387.

5. Ronald Reagan, address on Central America, April 27, 1983, in Ronald Reagan, *Speaking My Mind* (New York: Simon and Schuster, 1989), pp. 145–160.

6. Dean Acheson, *Present at the Creation* (New York: Norton, 1969), p. 219.

7. Ronald Reagan, address to the nation on aiding the Contras, March 16, 1986, in *Vital Speeches of the Day* 52, no. 13, p. 386.

8. Reagan, address on Central America, in *Speaking My Mind*, p. 160.

9. Ronald Reagan, Inauguration Address, January 21, 1985, in *Vital Speeches of the Day* 51, no. 8, p. 228.

10. Reagan, address to the nation on arms control, in *Vital Speeches of the Day* 49, no. 5, p. 131.

11. Ronald Reagan, address to the nation on the downing of a Korean airliner, September 5, 1983, in *Vital Speeches of the Day* 49, no. 24, p. 739.

12. Ronald Reagan, remarks on accepting the GOP presidential nomination, August 23, 1984, in *Speaking My Mind*, p. 204.

13. Thomas Doherty, "Hollywood Agit-Prop: The Anti-Communist Cycle, 1948–1954," *Journal of Film and Video* 40, no. 4 (Fall 1988), pp. 15–27.

14. For a more detailed exploration of this phenomenon, see Robert Ray, *A Certain Tendency of the Hollywood Cinema, 1930–1980* (Princeton: Princeton University Press, 1985); and Richard Maltby, *Harmless Entertainment: Hollywood and the Ideology of Consensus* (Metuchen, NJ: Scarecrow, 1983).

15. See, for example, the discussion of the production of *Dead End* in Leonard J. Leff and Jerold L. Simmons, *The Dame in the Kimono: Hollywood, Censorship, and the Production Code from the 1920s to the 1960s* (New York: Grove Weidenfeld, 1990), pp. 57–78.

16. Quoted in ibid., p. 76.

17. Doherty, "Hollywood Agit-Prop," p. 26.

18. See Basil Bernstein, "A Sociolinguistic Approach to Socialization, with Some Reference to Educability," in *Directions in Sociolinguistics*, ed. John J. Gumperz and Dell Hymes (New York: Holt, Rinehart and Winston, 1972), pp. 465–497.

19. Sontag's classic essay "Fascinating Fascism" is in *Movies and Methods*, vol. 1, ed. Bill Nichols (Berkeley: University of California Press, 1976), pp. 31–43.

20. Cameron Stauth, "Requiem for a Heavyweight," *American Film* 15 (January 1990), p. 24.

21. Ibid.

22. The father figure in Reagan-era films is also explored in Robert Phillip Kolker, *A Cinema of Loneliness*, 2nd ed. (New York: Oxford University Press, 1988), p. 255.

23. This imagery of the black box was used by Daikichi Irokawa to describe the effects on Japan of the emperor worship that helped to undergird the nation's role in World War II. He likened it to an enormous black box into which the nation unknowingly walked. Daikichi Irokawa, *The Culture of the Meiji Period*, trans. Marius B. Jansen (Princeton: Princeton University Press, 1985), pp. 245–246.

Chapter Three

The Fires of Rebellion

As Ronald Reagan assumed the presidency, rebellion and revolution swept through Central America, threatening to remake the region's political and economic history and to challenge the imperial prerogatives of the United States in an area traditionally regarded as its "backyard." The administration's tendency to see a Communist menace behind indigenous political rebellions in the Third World led it to attribute the political firestorms in Central America to the machinations of the Soviet Union and Cuba. The countries of the region became a line of dominoes, whose toppling would allegedly disrupt Mexico and, beyond that, the United States itself. "The goal of the professional guerrilla movements in Central America is as simple as it is sinister: to destabilize the entire region from the Panama Canal to Mexico," Reagan assured a joint session of Congress in 1983.[1] "The national security of all the Americas is at stake in Central America. If we cannot defend ourselves there, we cannot expect to prevail elsewhere. Our credibility would collapse, our alliances would crumble, and the safety of our homeland would be put in jeopardy."[2] In response to this perceived threat, the administration maintained or increased military assistance to El Salvador, Honduras, and Guatemala while launching an economic boycott and covert programs of military and economic sabotage against Nicaragua.

What lay behind these policies? As Reagan came to office, storm clouds of change seemed to be sweeping through the Caribbean basin. In 1979, Maurice Bishop's New Jewel Movement overthrew the government of Eric Gairy in Grenada, which was backed by the United States and Great Britain. Also in 1979, and perceived as a more significant threat, the Sandinista National Liberation Front succeeded in toppling the corrupt

Somoza dynasty that had ruled Nicaragua since it was installed by the U.S. Marines in 1933. The Marines had occupied the country since 1912. In addition, armed resistance to the Guatemalan government had intensified in the early 1980s, and the Farabundo Martí National Liberation Front posed an increasingly powerful military challenge to the Salvadoran government. The conflicts erupting in Guatemala and El Salvador were long-standing and indigenous to the region, despite the Reagan administration's claims about outside intervention. In El Salvador, Guatemala, and Somoza's Nicaragua, where economies were geared to the export market and constrained to produce a narrow range of products (frequently coffee); where vast inequities in the distribution of wealth and landownership prevailed, and where military governments steadfastly resisted any real land reforms and used the police and National Guard to repress dissent, the stage was set for the political explosions that had begun to rock the region as Reagan took office.

Perhaps in no other area of the Reagan administration's political agenda was there such a gulf between ideological projection and the root causes of social conflict. Since so many people in Central America died or were subject to lasting misery during the period, some review of these root causes is in order. As noted, the administration diagnosed the region's problems as the result of outside interference. Cuba and the Soviet Union were allegedly fomenting discord and had a new ally in Nicaragua. However, this framework of analysis ignored the crushing poverty and exploitation under which the bulk of the region's citizens lived. In Guatemala, for example, in the 1970s one-quarter of the population earned 67 percent of the nation's wealth, while the bottom quarter earned only 7 percent; 90 percent of the rural work force either owned no land or was unable to subsist on the tiny parcels it did own.[3] In El Salvador, 2 percent of the population owned 60 percent of the land and earned one-third of the nation's income;[4] and agricultural production and export had been dominated for decades by the "Fourteen Families," an oligarchy that absolutely refused to countenance any reforms in the economy. In 1975, more than 45 percent of the rural population were estimated to be unemployed.[5]

In both countries, the governments were run by or closely allied with the military, which received large amounts of U.S. aid and training. With no external enemies threatening the region with invasion, the function of the military became internal repression; and during the 1970s and early 1980s, the citizenry of both countries was subjected to an especially bloody slaughter by the police, the National Guard, and death squads with names like White Hand and White Warrior's Union. Thousands died, and the complicity and participation of the Salvadoran and Guatemalan governments in the slaughter is quite clear. In its 1984 report on El Salvador, Amnesty International noted "the continued involvement of all branches of the security and military forces in a systematic and widespread program of torture, mutilation, 'disappearance,' and the individual and mass extrajudicial execution of men, women and children from all sectors of Salvadoran society.'' The group had reached similar conclusions regarding Guatemala.[6] Unspeakable tortures were a routine part of the terror and helped to make the region a chamber of horrors reminiscent of what the Nazis had done in Europe. This is no exaggeration; abundant evidence exists of the cruelties perpetrated by the security forces whose operations helped to create a new climate of fascism in these states during the early 1980s. Before being killed, victims were beaten, electrocuted, burned with fire or acid, dismembered, or sexually mutilated; their disfigured corpses were left on public display to terrorize the population. The reign of terror was directed at peasants, teachers, priests, journalists, trade unionists— any and all sectors of society where protest against the current system might be found.

Land reforms, when instituted, were accompanied by more killing by the military and the death squads. President Reagan praised the land reform program in El Salvador as an example of the kind of democratic reform for which his administration had pressed. While noting that El Salvador was progressing toward ''an orderly and democratic society'' (this was during the period when Amnesty International was protesting the system of torture and murder carried out by the government's security forces), Reagan claimed that the land reform program was making thousands of farm tenants into farm owners by redistributing parcels of land. In fact, in El Salvador, while the land reform was being administered, the military and the death squads executed radical peasants. As the reforms progressed, the murders increased and the number of terrorized refugees fleeing the areas increased. Amnesty International noted that ''Internal refugees or displaced persons fleeing areas where the government's agrarian reform program had been violently imposed and confiscated lands handed over to ORDEN supporters [a right-wing vigilante organization linked with the military] have been removed from church-run relief centres and summarily executed.''[7] The infamous Sumpul River massacre resulted when a large group of refugees tried to cross the river into Honduras but were blocked by Honduran troops, who turned them back to waiting Salvadoran troops and ORDEN members who slaughtered hundreds, mainly women and children.[8]

This state-sponsored terror and policy of systematic extermination in the early 1980s did not figure in President Reagan's report to Congress, perhaps because it constituted a clear and compelling reason for cutting off support to the Salvadoran government. That government, however, was an authoritarian but friendly regime (in Kirkpatrick's terms of analysis) that would be supported because it was anticommunist. The administration therefore promoted the view that the Duarte government represented a viable middle ground between the extremes of the Left and the Right, and that no evidence linked the death squads with the military, despite a contrary conclusion by Amnesty International that the death squads were indeed operated by the security apparatus. Moreover, the scale of the killings, in the words of Socorro Jurídico, the legal aid service of the archdiocese of San Salvador, qualified as a program of "genocide": "We can no longer speak of the mere violation of human rights in El Salvador. The statistics prove that in quantitative and qualitative terms, a policy of systematic extermination is being carried out against a wide sector of the Salvadoran people, and to achieve this an apparatus of extermination has been designed and is constantly up-dated."[9] Socorro Jurídico noted that the United States shared responsibility not only for the planning of the program but also for the technical and political assistance needed to implement it. As for the notion that the Duarte government represented a viable political center, this was belied by the scale of the government-sponsored slaughter. The killings by the state, and armed resistance to its policies, testified to the absence of viable political institutions that could mediate between the needs of the poor and the interests of the landed oligarchy. Indeed, it was the collapse of the electoral and politically centrist institutions under the onslaught of state terror in El Salvador and Guatemala that signaled the demise of the center. An analyst of U.S. policy in the region noted:

By the late 1970s there was no viable "centre" position left in Central America. The electoral process, nearly always fraudulent and inevitably carried out in a climate of repression and corruption, had proved a totally inadequate vehicle for change. The political initiative passed to those who advocated direct forms of political action including armed struggle. It was no longer a question of small guerrilla bands trying to "create the conditions for revolution" as in the 1960s; the political-military movements which emerged in the 1970s were based on a genuine mobilization of the people as peasants, urban workers and sectors of the middle classes saw they had no option but to fight for social justice. The intransigence of the dictatorships was partly due to an awareness that any relaxation in their iron rule would result in an explosion of this mass movement.[10]

This perspective, however, was inadmissible in official American political discourse, which could not conceive that substantial sectors of the people of a state supported by the United States might willingly take revolutionary action. Unable to acknowledge this, the Reagan administration's rhetoric of dominoes and Soviet-directed Communist subversion spread like a heavy, dark cloud over public discussions of Central America. The thorn in the administration's side, and the source of its anxiety, was Nicaragua, where a popular insurrection, born of poverty and state corruption, did topple a dictatorship and institute a revolutionary government. Not since Cuba in 1959 had a popular, armed revolution succeeded in dethroning a client state in America's backyard, where the United States has traditionally felt free to force in and out of power governments of its choosing. (An under secretary of state had noted as far back as 1927 that "Central America has always understood that governments which we [the U.S.] recognize and support stay in power, while those we do not recognize and support fail."[11]) Assuming an explicitly counterrevolutionary posture and policy, the Reagan administration pledged to destroy Nicaragua and prevent it from being an example to the insurrections in Guatemala and El Salvador, lest America's backyard begin to wrest itself free of the string of military regimes that ensured its docility. This destruction would be a dual one, both of Nicaraguan society and of the Nicaraguan government, and it was achieved through policies of economic destabilization, military assault, and disinformation campaigns carried out by the mass media.

Given the extraordinary amount of press coverage and public discussion of these conflicts in Central America during the 1980s, it should not surprise us that a modest cycle of films emerged which dramatized the political and social issues of dictatorship and revolution. In numbers, this was a far more limited cycle than those productions which were faithful to Cold War perceptions. As we saw in Chapter 2, Cold War ideology and preoccupations were manifest across a wide spectrum of films, including not only overtly militaristic entries like *Invasion U.S.A.*, *Rambo III*, and *Top Gun* but also the Spielberg and Lucas science fiction and adventure fantasies. The Latin America films, by contrast, tend to diverge from Cold War assumptions. They question and criticize the foreign policy framework applied by the Reagan administration. As such, these films push at the formal, thematic, and narrative limits governing the American film tradition. As we have seen, American film has generally shied away from an overt foregrounding of social or political issues, preferring instead to absorb those issues within the confines of the genre film. This was the strategy of the Cold War films. They offered familiar narratives of adventure and heroic action but inflected those formulas with the politics of resurgent America.

If the Latin America films, then, are not, strictly speaking, genre pieces, what kind of films are they, and in what sense can we define them as political films? How are they related to traditions of political filmmaking, not just domestically but also in the international cinema? A convenient way of grouping these traditions is by reference to a distinction between instrumentalist and transformative functions.[12] Instrumentalist models of political art tend to locate their political messages within a naturalistic style. The political message, for example, typically would be absorbed within a dominant emphasis upon narrative, character, and naturalistic visual style. Characters remain "in character." Their actions are plausibly and naturalistically motivated, and the narrative is organized in a predominantly linear direction, building toward a single climax that resolves all of the narrative threads in a fairly tidy way. This is the general approach of the American cinema.

The transformative approach, by contrast, has been far more typical of European and Third World cinema. This approach aims to locate politics within formal structure—within the visual and aural texture of the film— and not merely as a matter of content pointed to by the characters through their dialogue and behavior. Filmmakers working within the transformative approach include Jean-Luc Godard, Nagisa Oshima, Bernardo Bertolucci, and Glauber Rocha, to name just a few of the best known. The influence of the German playwright Bertolt Brecht has been particularly strong in this tradition. Brecht insisted that the emotional spell of the theater, of the narrative, of the artwork, must be broken—that is, must be reorganized and restructured in such a way that the spectator will come to see the relationship of the artwork to the real social and political world rather than submitting to the artwork as a mere reflection of reality. Brecht's goal, and the goal of all of the filmmakers who have worked within the transformative tradition, is to restructure not just the artistic fiction but also the spectator's perceptions and relationships with reality. Glauber Rocha, the father of Brazil's Cinema Novo movement, pointed out the importance of using film to stimulate discussion and criticism: "We do not want to patronize the public; we want the public to participate a great deal in our films, to debate among themselves. . . . This is why we feel that film should have a dialectical relationship to its audience, meaning that the issues should be openly posed to the public in a way that allows for debate between the audience and the film."[13]

Filmmakers in Latin America, and other practitioners of what is now referred to as the Third Cinema, have drawn upon indigenous, regional forms of theater, song, dance, and costuming and a visual style different from the Hollywood norms in order to develop the socially transformative function of their art. In this respect, works by Latin American filmmakers are substantially different, in their narrative, visual, and political design, from Hollywood films about the region. In his essay on the aesthetics of Third Cinema, Teshome Gabriel points out the centrality of "activist aesthetics" and "critical spectatorship."[14] He notes that the centrality of the hero in Western film narratives tends to displace this critical activism: "the aesthetic form of the narrative in Western film culture is the aesthetic of the hero—it starts with a hero, develops with a hero, and ends with a hero. This is as natural a style as breathing." But, he adds, "This kind of cultural identity, of separateness and of isolation, privileges the individual over the social and the collective."[15]

As we shall see, Hollywood films about the wars in Latin America have had inordinate trouble identifying the collective and class forces at work in the conflicts; have been unable, for the most part, to identify by name the key figures and political organizations involved in the conflicts; and have tended to situate the conflicts as background to the exploits of a charismatic protagonist. By contrast, the subjects of Third Cinema are the wretched of the earth, the collectives "who still inhabit the ghettos and the barrios, the shanty towns and the madinas, the factories and working districts."[16] Validating their experience and the memory and legacy of their struggle takes such films far from the Hollywood style and outlook: "Third Cinema . . . serves not only to rescue memories, but rather, and more significantly, to give history a push and popular memory a future."[17]

With its emphasis on giving history a push, the transformative approach has been virtually nonexistent within American filmmaking. If we recall Abraham Polonsky's remark about how difficult he found it to depart from the conventions of American film style and, by contrast, how comparatively easy he found it to insert political and social messages removed from the norms of American political discourse inside the dialogue and narrative, so long as those narratives conformed to the stylistic norms of the studios, we have an explanation of how and why the transformative approach has been so foreign to the Hollywood cinema. Quite simply, as Polonsky pointed out, American film producers were extremely suspicious of departures from the formal norms of American film while sometimes, and to a surprising degree, being tolerant of alternative social viewpoints within a film. In its most explicit guise, politics has always been more a matter of content than of form for Hollywood films. As we have seen in Chapter 2, the Cold War films were quite successful in this respect, as their action and adventure formulas absorbed a newly salient dimension of right-wing political meaning during the 1980s.

The cycle of films dealing with the conflicts in Latin America, then, had to face a double set of aesthetic challenges. These films had to find ways of presenting a level of analysis appropriate to the region's historical, economic, and political transformations that would, at the same time, be congruent with the stylistic traditions of Hollywood film narratives. Throughout these films—*Missing* (1982), *Under Fire* (1983), *El Norte* (1984), *Latino* (1985), *Salvador* (1986), and *Romero* (1989)—is a range of strategies for achieving an accommodation between a socially critical view of the role of the United States in the region's conflicts and the need to reach a mass audience and achieve commercial acceptance. The dilemma here for the filmmaker who wishes to depart from, and perhaps to challenge, basic assumptions of American foreign policy is the difficulty of doing this while working within a commercial film industry. As the films examined in Chapter 2 demonstrate, reinforcing the political and ideological status quo can be very profitable. Furthermore, the industry imposes limits on the degree to which a filmmaker can depart from popular stylistic conventions, and if a director strays too far outside those boundaries, box-office failure will likely result. Expressing a critical politics with critical cinematic forms has always been very difficult in the American cinema. With this problem in mind, it is somewhat surprising to realize that this cycle of films generally avoided the blandishments and seductions of genre in favor of constructing narratives which, while full of the melodrama, the action, and the adventure that one might find in typical genre films, still managed to venture forth in rather new directions. To the extent that genre formulas can work toward ideological closure, as the films discussed in Chapter 2 demonstrate, the modest departure from genre in the Latin America film cycle can be understood as a means of creating the critical space necessary for an interrogation of U.S. foreign policy in the region. But these remain Hollywood films and, as we shall see, genre and formula are never far away.

We need, then, to take a closer look at the visual and narrative strategies of these films and to see how they portray and explain the sources and shape of the region's problems. A useful comparison can be struck by contrasting the space available for political analysis within these films with the achievements of a European film produced some years earlier that examines many of the same issues. *Burn!* (1968), directed by Gillo Pontecorvo, focused on a popular revolution and the ensuing counter-insurgency warfare on an island in the Caribbean, controlled first by the Portuguese and then by the British in the late nineteenth century. *Burn!* employs a Marxist perspective and analysis at the same time that it uses conventions of the Hollywood cinema, such as a linear narrative emphasizing visual spectacle with a star (Marlon Brando) at its center. Because of its political perspective, *Burn!* is able to treat social forces— class conflict and colonialism—as the causal agents of the narrative, despite the presence of a big Hollywood star. In Hollywood films, by contrast, social forces and issues are typically personified and sometimes deflected by scenarios of individual struggle, melodrama, and personal conflict. Individual characters are typically the causal agents here. These differences do not just distinguish between films like *Salvador, Under Fire*, and *Romero*, on the one hand, and *Burn!*, on the other. They also underscore the important differences between the American cinema and the European and Third World cinemas, between the instrumentalist approach to visual and narrative form and approaches that we have labeled transformative, between using film to portray historical events and employing the medium to intervene in them. As we will see, films in the Latin America cycle occupy an ambivalent middle ground between these oppositions, produced as part of the Hollywood film industry yet inclined toward the interventionist aesthetics and politics of a committed, partisan cinema. The ambiguities of this position between opposing cinematic traditions are responsible for the distinctive features of image, narrative design, and political analysis that characterize this film cycle.

The collective focus of *El Norte, Salvador, Missing, Under Fire, Latino*, and *Romero* is truly regional, in that their narratives deal with Guatemala, El Salvador, Nicaragua, and Chile. Taken collectively, these films attempt to offer a dialogue on and an analysis of political conflicts throughout Latin America. The earliest major film in the cycle is *Missing*, directed by veteran political filmmaker Costa-Gavras and released in 1982. The film deals with the aftermath of the 1973 military coup in Chile, which overthrew the democratically elected government of socialist President Salvador Allende. Allende claimed the allegiance and support of a wide sector of the Chilean working class. His Popular Unity government, however, did not control the Chilean Congress or the military, which was to prove decisive in the class conflicts and the violent events that soon followed his 1970 election. Allende began a program of economic reorganization that alienated large sectors of the middle and upper classes. It has always been risky for a national leader in Central or South America to risk such changes because they are often viewed by the United States as threats to its political or economic interests. Allende's efforts to nationalize the Chilean copper industry, for example, helped to precipitate the military coup supported by the United States. Allende learned the same lesson that Jacobo Arbenz learned in Guatemala when he expropriated a large amount of land from United Fruit, precipitating a U.S.-sponsored invasion of the country during which Arbenz was overthrown. U.S. companies whose operations had been nationalized by Allende began to boycott Chilean copper in the world market, an especially effective economic threat because copper brought Chile 80 percent of its foreign exchange. The United States also moved to embargo spare parts, food, and consumer goods, thus preventing these items from reaching Chilean markets, while increasing the amount of assistance it was providing to the Chilean military and police forces. Despite the embargo, Allende's popular support did not significantly waiver, so in September 1973, the Chilean armed forces staged a coup. Allende was killed during the fighting, and the presidential palace was bombed. General Augusto Pinochet seized power and rounded up, tortured, and executed hundreds of Allende supporters as well as large sectors of the Chilean population who were accused of being Communist or socialist agitators. In all, approximately 10,000 people died in the aftermath of the coup.

These events form the narrative background of *Missing*. As the film begins, the Allende government has fallen and Pinochet's troops are in the streets burning books, assaulting civilians, and spreading terror. The film is extremely effective in evoking the fear, paranoia, and mass hysteria attendant upon a violent military coup, and with exceptional dramatic force it delineates the extraordinary brutality of a fascist police state. The narrative focuses on the efforts of American businessman Ed Horman, played by Jack Lemmon, to locate his son, Charles, who has mysteriously disappeared during the chaos of the coup. Ed enlists the aid of Charles's wife, Beth (Sissy Spacek), and as the two search the city, their differing political perspectives begin to clash. Ed's complacent trust in the virtue of American foreign policy is gradually undermined by Beth's skepticism. She suspects that the United States is complicit in the coup. She is openly hostile to the U.S. embassy officials and military officers in Chile and greets their ostensible efforts to find Charles with bitterness. Ed finds her apparent anti-Americanism very disturbing. He tells her that if she and Charles had stayed in the United States and looked after what he calls ''the basics,'' Charles would not be in trouble. Ed's initial political naiveté enables the film to address the geographic isolation and complacency of North Americans. Ed has come to Chile only because of his son's disappearance, and one of the ironies the film emphasizes is that his complacency and isolationism are not shared by the military and corporate sectors of North America. In congressional hearings that were conducted in the mid-1970s, for example, the role of the CIA in mounting a disinformation campaign in the Chilean media with the assistance of U.S. media and advertising companies was revealed.[18]

Ed's initial defense of the United States is crucial to the film's political strategy. Ed tells Beth that the American way of life is a very good one, ''no matter how much people like you and Charles try to tear it down with your sloppy idealism. I can no longer abide the young people of our country who live off their parents and the fat of the land, and then they find nothing better to do than whine and complain.'' Ed has accused Beth and Charles of playing poor, which he believes is easy to do because both of their families have money. He criticizes the youth of the late 1960s and mocks what he terms Beth's political paranoia. By detailing Ed's eventual conversion to Beth's realpolitik perspective, the film argues that the reaction against a Left-leaning political analysis of U.S. antagonism toward Third World revolutions itself may be naive.

The transformation of Ed Horman, then, becomes the central political and social symbol of the film, as well as its most important dramatic stratagem. Jack Lemmon's empathic and quite sensitive performance as the American father provides the central emotional hook for the audience— a North American audience. There are no Chilean protagonists who are offered as figures of identification. The film is designed to play to a North American viewer, and this is both its strength and its limitation. *Missing* undoubtedly alerted many uninformed Americans to the brutality of the Pinochet dictatorship. On the other hand, the film presents these events as a North American tragedy, the tragedy of a father bereft of his only son. Interestingly, the opening shot of the film seems to acknowledge this restriction of its focus. After the credits, we see a close-up of Charles Horman as he sits inside a car, looking through its side window. Reflected on that window overtop his face are images of children playing in the street and, a moment later, the arrival of tanks and soldiers. As it does in the film itself, the imagery in this shot of military occupation and oppression becomes a projection superimposed (against the car window) on this American character, whereas the real emotional drama involves the disappearance and death of this charismatic and idealistic young American, the focal point and center of the shot as of the film itself. The American will be presented to us in close-up, as social and political events become refections laid over that American character, dilemma, and drama.

This does not mean that the film fails to develop a sophisticated presentation of the events surrounding the overthrow of Allende, nor that it is incapable of offering powerful images and political metaphors. One of the finest moments in the film, and a very cinematic one because it is so visual, occurs near the beginning. Charles and his friend, Terry, are stuck in the Viña del Mar region, spending a night at a hotel because the airports are closed. The coup is under way and, as Charles looks out his window, he sees a line of troops and trucks going down the street. As they pass the hotel, a large group of the Chilean bourgeoisie who have been partying, dining, and dancing rush to the balcony to greet the soldiers. The troops salute them, and the party goers applaud the soldiers. The film cuts from them to Charles looking out the window. He says, ''I just keep thinking about what Patrick said about bodies everywhere.'' This compact and powerful series of shots offers an eloquent description and illustration of the class allegiances driving the military coup and of the almost surreal juxtaposition of the wealth and complacency of the upper class with the death and destruction wrought by the coup.

The strength of the film as a political and cinematic document lies in its ability to render complicated political relationships in terms of concrete and powerful imagery. We have already noted the degree to which the film evokes a climate of incipient violence as the Chilean military roams the streets, looting, burning, and accosting civilians. In addition, the narrative is grounded in a fairly detailed presentation of the events that were manipulated to bring down the Allende government. The film mentions the U.S. trade embargo against Chile, as well as the series of strikes led by truckers organized by the CIA, which crippled the Chilean economy and helped sow dissension about the Allende government. Early in the film, when Ed arrives in Chile, he gives Beth some toilet articles because Charles had said these things were hard to get. Beth replies, ''Not any more,'' referring to the fact that the embargo has been lifted now that the coup has succeeded.

The truckers' strike was responsible for stranding Charles and Terry in Viña del Mar, where they witnessed the massing of tanks and troops for the coup and where Charles discovered too much to be permitted to live. In the hotel, he met U.S. military officers. Questioning them, he became convinced that the United States was providing the leadership

to facilitate and coordinate the coup. One of the American officers tells
Charles that the truck drivers "are the real heroes here." It happens that
this particular officer has a long history of covert action in the Third World.
He tells Charles that he had helped coordinate the Bay of Pigs invasion
in the early 1960s and complains that if President Kennedy had provided
decent air cover and military support there, "we wouldn't be having these
problems here." For him, Chile is another Vietnam, and he remarks that
the military here is conducting search-and-destroy missions just like in
Vietnam, with "bodies everywhere." These remarks link the events
depicted in the film to a larger pattern and legacy of U.S. intervention.
The Chilean coup is presented not as an isolated tragedy but as part of
the ongoing history of such events in the Third World where the United
States has acted with force to install client regimes.

There is a major difference here between *Missing* and the Cold War films
studied in Chapter 2. The events of the narrative are integrated within
a fairly detailed historical context, as opposed to the vague and anxiety-
laden framework that positions the narratives of the Cold War films.
Geopolitical conflicts in *Top Gun* and *Iron Eagle* occur within an imaginary
geography where enemy countries and the role of the United States in
regional conflicts are not identified. The difference between this strategy
for portraying historical and geographical context and that employed by
Missing discloses the different social functions to which these films aspire:
providing ideological reinforcement, on the one hand, and political
critique, on the other. In *Missing* the emotional climax of the film, and
its thematic point, lies in Ed Horman's recognition that the United States
has supported the coup. Growing increasingly frustrated with the apparent inability of the American embassy to locate his son, Ed confronts
the ambassador and tries to force him to admit that the United States
operates a police assistance program for the Chilean security forces. The
ambassador denies that any such operation exists, and he is filmed in
close-up with a portrait of President Nixon hanging prominently on the
wall behind him. Both he and Nixon almost face the camera, so that the
composition offers us a nearly direct address by American authorities.
Unfortunately, the ambassador is lying. Between 1950 and 1975, the
United States helped to train more than 6,000 military personnel in Chile,
and between 1946 and 1975 it provided nearly $217 million in military
aid.[19] As the narrative develops, it is implied that American authorities
cosigned a kill order with Chilean security officials to eliminate Charles
because of what he saw and learned.

By the end of the film, Ed has been disabused of his political complacency, but neither he nor the audience is allowed to escape moral cen-
sure. Before leaving the country after learning that his son has been executed, Ed is reminded by the ambassador and a U.S. naval officer of
the role they all play in helping to administer an international economic

alliance. The ambassador says that but for his son, Ed would still be at home, pleasantly ignorant of the events he has seen: "We're here to protect American interests. Over 3,000 U.S. firms do business here and that is your, our, interest. . . . I'm concerned with the preservation of a way of life." "And a damn good one," Captain Tower adds, echoing Ed's earlier words. "You can't have it both ways," the ambassador concludes. This scene is a brief but very important one because it sets out the material rationale for the overthrow of the Allende government. Indeed, by calling attention to the economic imperatives behind the brutality the film has depicted, *Missing* goes farther than many other American films of the period in delineating what Chomsky and Herman have referred to as the Washington connection in Third World fascism.

There are limits, however, to the clarity and specificity with which the film can present these relationships. As noted, this scene is brief and the 3,000 U.S. firms and the "way of life" the ambassador says the United States is pledged to protect do not receive further elaboration. Moreover, the film's narrative does not explicitly identify the country in which it is set. In one brief background shot, the name Chile appears on a sign, but neither General Pinochet nor Salvador Allende is mentioned by name. This does not mean that *Missing* creates the slippery and vague political geography typical of the Cold War films. The film develops its critique by way of implication and allusion, although this is probably an insufficient strategy for communicating with the uninformed viewer. (Some critics have charged that the film's politics are too overt and blatant, although such criticism is probably influenced by the generally muted political focus of the American film tradition.) With respect to the politically uninformed viewer, the inability of the film to identify the country and the stakes of the issue more clearly than it does limits its efficacy as a political document. But such a limitation is structurally connected with the tradition of instrumentalist filmmaking, wherein the filmmaker will attempt to use the formulas and narrative conventions of popular cinema while infusing them with a new, more liberal, and at times politically radical content.

The other films discussed in this chapter confront similar problems because they proceed by a linear narrative centered on individual characters and by grounding their political analysis, as background material, in the relationships and emotional tribulations of these characters. This tension between political analysis and character-centered psychological dramas defines the ambiguous middle ground staked out by this film cycle between Hollywood formulas and a more partisan and analytic use of political cinema. Inclining too much toward the latter mode would probably entail failure at the box office because clear ideological commitment and politically partisan filmmaking are quite foreign to the American cinema, and the tolerance for the political Left that informs many of these films is too far removed from the norms of American political discourse. Inclining too much in the other direction, however, could extinguish the modestly critical ground these films seek to occupy. It is a real dilemma and, given the market at which these films aim, probably an irresolvable one.

What these films can do successfully is to take narrative material and conventions frequently utilized in another ideological context and give them a different political inflection. In this respect, we should note the deceptive, apparent affinity of the narrative of *Missing* with a central preoccupation of the Cold War films, the disintegration of the American family. As noted in Chapter 2, many of the Cold War rescue scenarios hinged upon the efforts of a son to rehabilitate or otherwise redeem his father or father figure. In an apparently similar manner, *Missing* focuses on generational ruptures within the family. Charles and Ed are estranged when the film begins because of Charles's leanings toward the political Left and Ed's inability to understand why and how Charles could be critical of what Ed perceives as an abundant and beneficent way of life. At the end of the film, when Charles's body is returned in an unmarked wooden casket, it bears the marks of mutilation by the Chilean military. This is more than a simple bodily corruption; it is, as well, symbolic of political stigmata that afflict Ed as he returns to the United States, burdened with his new knowledge about the role his country assumes in foreign affairs. Rather than a rescue of the father figure, we have here the failure of a complacent father to redeem his son, and that failure becomes a political metaphor for the sacrifice of naive American idealism by a corrupt and corrupting world. Rather than offering a spectacle of the triumph of resurgent patriarchal authority, as the Cold War films do, *Missing* offers a cautionary tale about the collapse of uninformed complacency and the sacrifice of the sons by the fathers. *Missing* inverts the narrative patterns of the Cold War films, replacing right-wing anxieties with the socially committed analysis of the political Left.

Missing was produced nearly ten years after the overthrow of Allende and the assumption of power by the Pinochet government. There is, thus, a quality of looking back within the film, an attempt to survey from a historical distance the cost in political terms and in human suffering of the destruction of Chilean democracy. By contrast, Oliver Stone's *Salvador* was produced in 1985 and dramatizes events that had occurred only a few years earlier. The film is set in 1980 and 1981, at the time of the election of Ronald Reagan to the presidency, and it dramatizes the impact of Reagan's victory upon the political process in El Salvador and the disintegration of civil society. Given the traditions of American political filmmaking that we have been describing, Oliver Stone's film is a quite remarkable document for its intense political commitment and the clarity with which it portrays the contending factions in the Salvadoran civil war.

(Of all the Hollywood directors whose work is discussed in this book, Stone is the most consistently committed to a political and topical use of the cinema, but his work is not always as politically focused as it is in *Salvador*. See, for example, the discussion of *Platoon* in Chapter 4.)

The film occupies an interesting middle ground, somewhere between the documentary and the fictional narrative. Stone employs his protagonist, based on real-life journalist Richard Boyle, as a vehicle for portraying the central events of those years. Much of the power of the film, and much of its persuasive credibility, lies in Stone's ability to create a richly textured narrative organized around the period's most notorious acts of terror and violence. The film portrays the assassination of Archbishop Oscar Romero during Mass, as well as the rape and execution of four American churchwomen. In addition, there are references to the "Soccer War" with Honduras, to the infamous Sumpul River massacre, the Matanza of 1932 (the massacre of thirty thousand peasants during a rebellion against the oligarchy), and a harrowing presentation of a massive open-air grave site where the Salvadoran death squads dump their mutilated victims. At this grave site, fellow journalist John Cassady tells Boyle that the greatness of World War II photographer Robert Capa lay in his talent for illuminating the nobility of human suffering, his ability to portray the reasons why people died or were killed during times of violent political upheavals. Cassady aspires to something of the same, as does Oliver Stone. Stone is not content to portray the events in El Salvador as a chaotic and inexplicable series of clashes between the political Right and the Left, as mainstream media have tended to do. He avoids presenting the civil war as a struggle between equally corrupt factions.

In order to capture the dignity of human suffering and the reasons for the killing, Stone orients his narrative with a carefully specified series of historical and political referents. In a practice that is unusual for the American cinema, Stone identifies left-wing political organizations by name. Thus, we meet a character who acts as a spokesman for the Democratic Revolutionary Front, one of the umbrella organizations of the Left in El Salvador, and we see the flags and the insignia of the Farabundo Martí National Liberation Front (FMLN). Some characters, however, are given fictionalized names, although they are clearly meant as representatives of well-known figures. One of the leaders of ARENA (National Republican Alliance), Roberto D'Aubuisson, is portrayed in the film as Maj. Maximiliano Casanova (played by Tony Plana, who hopped to the other side of the Salvadoran political fence with his portrayal of a radical priest sympathizing with the guerrillas in *Romero*), and the film's U.S. Ambassador Kelly is clearly a stand-in for Ambassador Robert White, who had been identified with the human rights policies of the Carter years and was promptly discharged from his post by the Reagan administration.

In the candor of these portrayals, Stone's film goes far beyond the norms of American political filmmaking. For example, D'Aubuisson is widely suspected of complicity in the assassination of Archbishop Romero, and the film clearly portrays his fictionalized equivalent, General Max, as the instigator of the assassination. The plan is, furthermore, shown as having been inspired by the recent electoral victory of Ronald Reagan. The film cuts from an announcer telling a crowd of the Salvadoran middle class and U.S. officials that ABC projections indicate a Reagan victory to a nighttime scene of paramilitary groups shooting into the air as they ride through the streets. The film then cuts to a scene between General Max and members of the death squads. Surveying the death squad members gathered about the table, General Max says, "These fucking priests who are poisoning the minds of our Salvadoran youth are going to be the first to bleed. They are pig shit, and this Romero is the biggest pig shit of all, a shit-faced desecration of an archbishop, and with this bullet, he will be the first to die." General Max assigns one of the death squad members the task of assassinating Archbishop Romero. The next sequence presents General Max posing on television with his family as he announces to the public, "I stand for nationalism, law and order, and economic prosperity, church, family, and a peaceful El Salvador."

The editing of these scenes links the assassination of Archbishop Romero with domestic right-wing reaction to Reagan's election and counterpoints the private truth of this reaction (the conspiracy to kill Romero) with publicly presented bourgeois ethics (respect for the church, the family, and private property). Later in the film, after the four American churchwomen have been raped and murdered, and the evidence implicates the Salvadoran military, an outraged Ambassador Kelly tells Colonel Bentley-Hyde, the senior U.S. military adviser, that he is in favor of cutting off all military aid to the country and that he knows about the attempt by the Reagan campaign team to coordinate with the political Right by sending a secret transition team to El Salvador to meet with General Max. This is a remarkable statement for an American film to make, but a basis exists for the portrayals. Robert D'Aubuisson visited the United States in 1980 and 1981 and had meetings with several conservative congressmen and senators. The film clearly implies that a signal was sent by the Reagan administration that death squad activities in El Salvador would be tolerated in the name of anticommunism.

This is precisely what Richard Boyle (James Woods) tells Colonel Bentley-Hyde and Jack Morgan, the U.S. State Department analyst, in one of the film's most politically passionate scenes. Boyle cuts through the rhetoric about foreign subversion and intervention in El Salvador, telling Hyde, "You guys have been lying about that from the beginning. You haven't presented one shred of proof to the American public that this is anything but a legitimate peasant revolution." Boyle castigates the alliance between the U.S. military and General Max, who was trained at the Washington, D.C. Police Academy, and notes that the death squads are the brainchild of the CIA. "You let them shut down the universities, wipe out the best minds in the country. You let them kill whoever they want, let them wipe out the Catholic Church, and all because they're not Communists." American money, Boyle argues, has funded a murderous regime in El Salvador and has helped turn the country into one giant military zone. These are remarkable denunciations for an American film to offer. *Salvador* is politically sharp and passionate, committed to one side of the struggle rather than the other, and is able to sustain this commitment with clarity throughout much of its length. Stone embeds the political perspectives within an emotionally powerful narrative that is visualized by using sophisticated, politically informed cinematic techniques, as when he cuts from a sequence showing children mutilated by the Salvadoran military to a shot of Ronald Reagan on television proclaiming the need to stop Communist subversion and intervention in Central America. As Reagan speaks about the inevitable Communist march from Central America to the United States, the images of the wounded children contextualize the abstract political rhetoric in a way that condemns the ideology by showing the terrible price it exacts.

We have been noting how difficult it is for American films to construct a coherent political perspective in opposition to dominant political and foreign policy frameworks. The remarkable qualities of *Salvador* lie in its intense commitment to such an alternative but, not surprisingly and at the last moment, indicative of the ambiguities that characterize this film cycle, Stone includes a sequence that subverts the film's hitherto rigorous point of view. Late in the film, as the rebels mount a major offensive in an attempt to take the country before Reagan assumes office, the government launches a counterattack. Facing an onslaught of army tanks and helicopters, the rebels execute some prisoners before retreating. Seeing this, Boyle screams at them, "You've become just like them," meaning that the brutality of the rebels is indistinguishable from that of the military and the death squads. As he screams this denunciation repeatedly, the distinction between the violence of the Left and the Right that the film has been carefully maintaining collapses. In the subsequent battle scenes, all coherence vanishes, and all political reference points are lost. In the killing that follows the government's attack on the rebels, hell and chaos seem to be everywhere, and the film evokes these qualities as apolitical attributes. In other words, following Boyle's denunciation, the film substitutes for its earlier perspective a more mainstream view of El Salvador as a country torn apart by indiscriminate killing. The film's analysis pivots on this scene, and it is nearly enough to overwhelm all that has gone before. At the end of the film, Boyle escapes El Salvador with his girlfriend, Maria, and her children, only to be stopped by the

U.S. Immigration and Naturalization Service, which returns Maria to El Salvador and probable death. Boyle is led away handcuffed. In despair, he shouts at the immigration officers, "You don't know what it's like in El Salvador. You can't send her back there." It is finally a godless world that Stone portrays in the film. Earlier, Boyle said that if God were to give him Maria, then indeed there must be a God. Now that she is taken away, the landscape seems devoid of hope. *Salvador*, in some ways, is really two films: a historical portrait of a civil war unfolding as the film was being made, and a grim evocation of hopelessness, horror, and despair situated within what is finally an apolitical context eliciting only futility and defeat. As Boyle is led away in handcuffs, so is the political heart of the film.

The events dramatized in *Salvador* occurred in the early 1980s during a period of intensified repression and heightened death squad activity, when hundreds of Salvadorans were being murdered each month. Another film dealing with approximately the same period is *Romero*, an independent production financed by a number of Catholic organizations, including the Paulist Fathers, which portrays the life of Salvadoran Archbishop Oscar Romero (Raul Julia) from his appointment as archbishop in 1977 to his assassination while saying Mass in 1980. During those three years, Romero had become an outspoken critic of the Salvadoran government and its unwillingness to institute serious economic reforms. A key moment in Romero's growing social and political engagement came only a few months after he was appointed archbishop. In April 1977, a Jesuit priest named Rutilio Grande was assassinated on his way to Mass in the Aguilares region. The army then occupied the town, conducting house-to-house searches and beating the occupants.[20] Flyers announcing "Be a patriot, kill a priest" were turning up in the streets, distributed by the White Warriors' Union, one of the Salvadoran death squads. The assassination of Grande seemed to mark a new and darker chapter in Salvadoran politics, one in which priests were now targeted by the army and the National Guard. Ultimately, Romero became such a victim. But before that, he was a strikingly articulate and visible spokesman for the poor and discontented. He delivered weekly radio homilies during which he read the names of those who had disappeared or had been murdered the previous week, and he discussed the circumstances surrounding their fate. Furthermore, he openly proclaimed his belief that economic problems were at the root of the turmoil in Salvador and declared, "These are insurrectional times. The morality of the church permits insurrection when all other paths have been exhausted."[21] About a month before his death, Romero sent President Carter a letter calling on him to suspend military assistance to the Salvadoran government, on the grounds that it was using the funds and the weaponry to repress and murder its own citizens. By the time of his death, Romero had become, for many, an embodiment of the tenets of liberation theology, a growing social and political radicalization among the Central American clergy, developed from a conviction that the Bible contains a social and political message that is revolutionary in its implications and counsels clergy to stand with and to defend the interests of the poor.

Through its compassionate portrait of Romero's growing social commitment, the film dramatizes the conditions that underlie liberation theology. In a climate of pervasive state violence, where all legal avenues of political protest had been closed and popular organization prohibited, the church remained one of the few institutional centers capable of providing political and spiritual protection for the peasantry and the urban poor. For this reason, the church was potentially an enemy of the state and came to be regarded so partly because of the efforts of priests like Father Grande and Oscar Romero. While not as graphically violent as *Salvador*, *Romero* motivates its central character's growing activism by presenting particularly egregious examples of government repression. While Father Grande is saying Mass, for example, the National Guard surrounds the square and opens fire on the parishioners, killing several. The work of the death squads is portrayed as well, most powerfully during the climax of the film when Romero makes a passionate plea to the military to lay down its arms and stop the repression, saying that no soldier is compelled to obey an order that is counter to God's commandment not to kill. As he speaks, the film intercuts photographs of real death squad victims, showing their unspeakable mutilation and lending a special poignancy to his words. Unlike *Salvador*, however, *Romero* limits its portrayal of the political machinery of the Salvadoran state. The death squads are never explicitly described as extensions of the security apparatus, nor does the film mention any of the relevant political parties, such as ARENA. This lack of specificity about the political structure of the Salvadoran state and the contending factions in the civil war gives the film a political vagueness. But it may be hagiography and not politics that organizes the narrative. The film constructs a generic portrait of a saint with the narrative organized to describe the requisite stages of suffering and commitment that elevate an ordinary man to sainthood.[22]

Certainly a major omission in the film is an acknowledgment of the role played by the United States in the civil war. Except for one scene, an uninformed viewer would have no idea that the Salvadoran government remained in power through the support and financial assistance of the United States. That scene follows the assassination of Father Grande, when the army occupies Grande's church and turns it into a barracks. Archbishop Romero returns to the church to remove the Eucharist, but is prevented from doing so by an American soldier who is apparently a military adviser to the security forces. The soldier blocks Romero from approaching the Eucharist and machine-guns the altar in a shocking display of contempt for the church and for Romero's symbolic authority. Except for this brief scene, the U.S. presence is virtually invisible. In a similar way the film fails to deal with the radical revolutionary organizations that were becoming quite powerful in the rural areas. The Salvadoran guerrillas appear in only three brief scenes, and the narrative does not acknowledge their institutional or political organization. They remain a shadowy presence in the film.

In addition, the film is very uncomfortable with the relationship among the Left, the armed struggle, and liberation theology. Late in the film, Romero chastises Father Morantes (Tony Plana), a priest who is sympathetic to the guerrillas and who joins their struggle. Morantes tells Romero, "I am a priest who sees Marxists and Christians struggling to liberate the same people," but Romero accuses him of losing God and waging class warfare just like the rich and the military. Morantes replies that he has no real choice because all the people he loves and is sworn as a priest to protect are being slaughtered. Although the film allows Morantes to state his case with dignity, until the moment of his death Romero remains quite uneasy with the implications of Morantes's position. Although the film is clearly committed to Romero's vibrant example of the protective power of the church for the poor, it refrains from offering a clear endorsement of Father Morantes and his brand of political activism.

This inability to come to terms with the political Left is a major feature of these productions. *Missing* fails to identify Allende's government by name or with reference to its policies or programs. In *Salvador*, although revolutionary groups appear by name in the film, their platforms and plans for reorganizing Salvadoran society are not acknowledged. Although *Under Fire* deals with the triumph of the revolution in Nicaragua, the guerrillas there, too, remain a kind of abstract and nebulous presence lurking outside the capital and the major cities. As we will see in a later chapter, a similar visual and dramatic strategy prevails in the films dealing with Vietnam, which have consistently failed to come to terms with the social and political nature of Vietnamese opposition to the American presence. It wasn't until *Good Morning, Vietnam* (1987) that an American film permitted a South Vietnamese guerrilla to offer an explanation for his political opposition, but even then the character, although sympathetic, was a minor one. The political Left has traditionally eluded the representational conventions of the American cinema. As we have seen, there is a historical reason for this: the hearings of the House Un-American Activities Committee during the late 1940s and early 1950s, which helped to chill the climate of political filmmaking. Given this aesthetic, cultural, and political legacy, the films dealing with the conflicts in Latin America can go only so far. They can adopt a liberal perspective and be quite critical of the Reagan administration's regional policies. They cannot, however, engage the Left as a viable organizational and institutional presence within the region.

What these films do, instead, is elaborate a visual and narrative language of metaphor that is used to imply or portray the region's class conflicts. Typically receiving metaphorical treatment are the instruments of culture common to the aristocracy, including music, food, and clothing. These are carefully situated within a narrative context where they become political signs charged with oppositional meaning. In *Romero*, just after the National Guard opens fire on the outdoor Mass, killing a number of its participants, a cut takes us to a party held by the business class to celebrate Romero's appointment as archbishop. A string quartet plays classical music on the lawn while tuxedo-clad men talk about the danger of the trade unions, and the student and worker organizations, to "our whole way of life." Romero's presence at the party reveals his initial class allegiances. At the time of his appointment as archbishop, his congregation is composed mainly of members of the military and wealthy Salvadoran families. Accepting the appointment, he cautions that the church must steer clear of priests clamoring for radical action and must keep to the center. As he says this, cuts to shots of the generals and the businessmen in the audience show them nodding, smiling, and applauding. Afterward, they offer him their homes for his personal use, extend invitations to lunch, and introduce him to the president-elect of the country. At the lawn party held to celebrate his appointment, several elegantly dressed young men are revealed to be members of the military. In addition, the juxtaposition of the lawn party and the string quartet with the sequence of the massacre during Mass implicates the wealthy aristocracy and its cultural world in the ongoing repression.

In the classic *Battleship Potemkin* (1925), director Sergei Eisenstein emphasized the political function of instruments of culture as the sailors on board the Potemkin staged a mutiny and overthrew the czarist officers. Eisenstein used objects such as the piano, the candelabra, and the potted plants inside the officers' cabin, which were smashed by the mutinying sailors. In the classical Marxist terms of Eisenstein's film, overthrowing the authority of the czarist class entailed destroying its cultural forms. *Romero* is not situated within this classical tradition, but the lawn party sequence does display an analogous sensitivity to the social exclusivity of the implements of aristocratic culture and the way this exclusivity may become a partner in repression. Similar patterns of cutting prevail in *Salvador* and *Under Fire*, where sequences alternate between violent struggle in the countryside and decadent celebrations held by the aristocracy in posh urban centers. Furthermore, in *Missing*, as we have noted previously, one of the film's finest visual metaphors occurs as the wealthy party goers applaud the passing troops during the bloody coup.

A common cinematic rhetoric extends to the use of sound. The noise of approaching helicopters, in particular, signifies repression because they are used by the governments in power to wage war on the peasantry and the guerrillas. As *Romero* opens, the sound of a whirling helicopter blade is briefly heard under the main credits, and it recurs in an unmotivated, almost expressionistic fashion several times later in the film, most notably during a sequence where Romero is having a nightmare about the civil strife in his country. In *Under Fire*, the military attack helicopter assumes a dominant visual and acoustical presence with the sound of its rotor blades emphasized through amplification on the soundtrack. It is worth noting that this symbology is also employed by the Nicaraguan film *Alsino and the Condor*, directed by Miguel Littin (1983), which deals with the Sandinista rebellion prior to 1979. That film opens with an identical cue as the distinctive thumping of a whirling helicopter blade is heard against a dark screen. The condor of the title refers to the surveillance and attack helicopter flown by a U.S. military adviser. Throughout these films, the sound of the chopper signifies not just the U.S. presence but also the pervasive climate of fear and the threat of violence deforming life in these countries.

An additional rhetorical device shared by a number of these films is the figure of the itinerant American mercenary whose presence symbolizes the counterinsurgency role of the United States. In *Missing*, Charles Horman meets the mysterious retired naval officer Babcock (Richard Bradford), who is in Chile to help coordinate the coup and who tells Charles that he is going next to Bolivia, where, we infer, he will do more of the same. In *Under Fire*, the American mercenary (Ed Harris) first appears in Chad, then in Nicaragua, and, with the success of the revolution there, he announces to his journalist friends, "See you in Thailand." An antecedent of these characters appears in *Burn!*, where the British imperialist William Walker (Marlon Brando) is sent to foment revolution on the Caribbean island of Quemada. With the success of the revolution, Britain steps in to take control of the island from the Portuguese, and Walker cheerfully announces that he is now off to Indochina. Although the Walker character in the film is British, in historical reality William Walker was an American adventurer who briefly invaded Nicaragua and set up his own government before being overthrown.

This common visual, aural, and narrative rhetoric is evidence of the liberal politics unifying this cycle of films and also shows how quickly cinematic material becomes codified, conventionalized, and established as a formula. Within the space of a few years, this cycle had begun to articulate its own peculiar stock of characters, images, and narrative devices that it found useful for characterizing the political turmoil addressed by the narratives.

The other major political flashpoint in the region during the 1980s was Nicaragua. The success of the revolution in 1979 was a major irritant to the Reagan administration, and it moved quickly to contain the Nicaraguan example by trying to overthrow its government. The United States cut off aid, exerted pressure on international lending agencies to block loans and investments, instituted a trade embargo, and recruited, trained, and financed the Contra army to launch attacks into Nicaragua from bases in Honduras. As with Vietnam, when Hollywood films refused to deal with that debacle while it was transpiring, very few American films portrayed the Nicaraguan revolution or the Contra war during the 1980s. A notable exception, especially since it was released by a major studio, was *Under Fire* (1982), a film that explicitly differed with official administration policy. The film is a romantic and idealized portrait of the triumph of the revolution, as witnessed by three American journalists covering the fighting. As in *Missing* and *Salvador*, Third Word revolutionary struggle is mediated here by the presence of American characters. The hero and heroine, journalists Russell Price (Nick Nolte) and Claire (Joanna Cassidy), move from being detached, "objective" reporters to sympathetic participants aiding the cause of the revolution. *Under Fire* is a more straightforward genre piece than the other films examined in this chapter. It derives from a category of journalistic adventure stories wherein heroic American reporters travel to exotic countries to cover romantic and dangerous events. Furthermore, the political turmoil takes a back seat for much of the film to the developing love interest between Russell and Claire. The Nicaraguan revolution is thereby domesticated for North American cinema audiences by being integrated into a love story and a drama about journalistic ethics. The plot hinges upon the question of whether Russell was ethically correct in faking a photograph of a dead Nicaraguan guerrilla leader to make him seem alive and thereby give the revolution the momentum it needs for victory. As many commentators have pointed out, this plot device falsifies the historical reality of the revolution. It was a broad-based uprising that was not dominated by a charismatic leader, contrary to the implications of the film. While the fictional guerrilla leader, Rafael, may be a convenient screenwriter's crutch employed to simplify and condense broader currents of social turmoil by providing a colorful handle with which to grasp them, the use of this character nevertheless indicates the difficulties North American films have in understanding and representing popular Third World revolutions.

This is not to minimize the political importance of *Under Fire*. As a major studio production, it was virtually alone during the early 1980s in offering a note of caution and criticism regarding Washington's policies in Nicaragua. The generic forms the filmmakers employ, however, place severe limits on the analysis the film can offer. *Under Fire*, for example, fails to portray the unique feature of the revolution: the alliance between the political Left and disaffected sectors of the middle class and business elite who had been alienated by the corruption of the Somoza regime.

In other words, the film does not acknowledge the alliances crossing class and political lines that carried the revolution to victory. As in *Romero* and *Salvador*, the guerrillas in *Under Fire*, while idealized, nevertheless remain a remote and undifferentiated presence in the countryside until the moment they overwhelm Managua and march through the streets in triumph. A commitment to linear narrative and generic formulas prevents the emergence of the dialectical, self-referential structure commonly used by political filmmakers in Europe and the Third World, where a reflexive cinematic style is used to comment upon the narrative and the characters even as they are being offered to the viewer. Dialectical political films do not "naturalize" their narratives and characters but instead, by using self-reflective forms, break these characters and narratives apart so that the films are able to construct a metacommentary upon the social and political issues raised by the narrative. Films in this tradition, such as Humberto Solas's *Lucia* (1969), include a melodramatic narrative but contain this narrative and its emotional appeals by socially contextualizing the melodramatic response as a fundamentally apolitical and ahistorical one.[23]

The operations of this tradition are quite foreign to *Under Fire*. It is, however, necessary to point to a remarkable scene where something analogous does occur. After the American journalist Alex (Gene Hackman) is killed by the Nicaraguan army, Claire sees television footage of his execution. She breaks down and begins to cry because they had been lovers. A Nicaraguan nurse sees her weeping and asks if she knew that reporter. Claire says a tearful yes, and the sequence seems about to offer a full-bodied emotional endorsement of her grief. Instead, the Nicaraguan nurse points out that over the decades thousands of Nicaraguans had been killed by the Somoza regime. The nurse adds, "Maybe we should have killed an American journalist 50 years ago." Sobered by these words, Claire stops weeping, and the sequence ends. The melodramatic discourse has been absorbed and neutralized by the application of historical perspective. The generic formulas, which mandate that the North American's death be foregrounded as a center of dramatic and emotional interest, are broken apart by a larger frame of reference applied by the Nicaraguan nurse. Historical consciousness deflects the melodrama as the film deftly switches from one discourse to another. This is very nearly a dialectical moment, but it is, unfortunately, unique. The analytic clarity and the intellectual power of this moment are poignant reminders of the firm limits that constrain and confine American filmmaking.

A more recent film that did try to overcome some of these representational limits by incorporating the antirealist style of transformative political filmmaking was Alex Cox's *Walker* (1988), which dealt with the nineteenth-century American adventurer William Walker and his ill-fated attempt to invade Nicaragua. Cox attempted to establish parallels between Walker's behavior and the contemporary political presence of the United States in Central America by including in his period setting such temporally inappropriate objects as Coca-Cola bottles and army helicopters. Unfortunately, however, the film lacks both the artistic and the political discipline necessary to be fully coherent. In particular, Cox was so intent on imitating the grandiose and excessive film styles of directors Sam Peckinpah and Sergio Leone that his film became little more than an operatic bloodbath. The excessive gore overwhelms the film's political discourse and nullifies its relevance for the present period.

A difficulty acknowledging the Left as an organizational and political presence in the region and a tendency to subordinate political issues to a story line emphasizing the melodramatic fates of individual characters were characteristic of the major studio productions but also typify a film like *El Norte* (1983), independently filmed and financed by Chicano director Gregory Nava. Filmed in Spanish, *El Norte* tells a story of two young Guatemalan teenagers fleeing the poverty and repression of their country. Enrique and Rosa journey north to the United States, which they have always heard about as a kind of mythological place of abundance, wealth, and eternal happiness. What they find, however, is quite different. Policies of cultural segregation confine them to a Spanish section of Los Angeles, where a succession of menial jobs and further impoverishment becomes their future.

Director and cowriter Nava has noted that he deliberately sought to avoid a political presentation in the film, favoring instead a personal and psychological focus upon the struggle and drama of the two main characters. Nava was concerned that an excessively political focus might offend or estrange large sectors of his potential audience. Consequently, the conditions that drive Enrique and Rosa from Guatemala are only sketched. Their father, Arturo, has been meeting clandestinely with a group of fellow plantation workers who are angry over their treatment by the landowner. One night their meeting is broken up by the army. Arturo is killed, and soldiers return to the village the following day to arrest everyone. The details of Arturo's activism remain vague and have no real political content beyond the general references he makes to the way the rich steal land from the peasants. The narrative does not connect Arturo's protest to the guerrilla struggle being waged in Guatemala, nor is the violent response of the soldiers connected with the program of total war then being applied by the Rios Montt regime against the rebels and their Indian supporters. As Amnesty International and other human rights organizations have documented, this was a particularly ruthless counterinsurgency campaign carried out in the name of anticommunism, resulting in the deaths of thousands of Guatemalans. These omissions help to produce a narrative that is not fundamentally different from a studio production. The emphasis is upon the personal fates and emotional relationships of the characters, and sociopolitical issues form a background for personal drama. While it is a visually striking film and a heartfelt one, *El Norte* remains caught in some of the same contradictions and challenges that beset the major studio productions.[24]

Another nonstudio production, Haskell Wexler's *Latino* (1985), dramatizes the Contra war against Nicaragua from a more committed left-wing perspective, although here, too, an emphasis upon a naturalistic style tends to impede the potential for political analysis, and an analytic stance, in some degree, is probably necessary if the filmmakers wish to avoid creating a film that performs the function of simple reinforcement of Cold War ideology. This was Hollywood cameraman Wexler's first return to feature-film directing since his 1969 classic *Medium Cool*. *Latino* deals with the efforts of U.S. military forces to train and assist the Contras in their attacks against Nicaraguan civilians, peasants, and cooperative farm laborers. The film is set in 1982 and follows the efforts of two Hispanic Green Berets, who had served in Vietnam, to mold the Contras into effective combat units. One of the Green Berets, Ruben (played by the ever-present Tony Plana), remarks that the Contra bases in Honduras remind him of Na Trang, and other references to Vietnam link the Contra war with that earlier effort at counterrevolutionary warfare. The other Green Beret, Eddie (Robert Beltran), begins to have second thoughts about aiding the Contras after he falls in love with a Nicaraguan agronomist working in Honduras and he begins to recognize the racism of white officers who are contemptuous of "the spics" in Nicaragua, even of the Contra soldiers. "We're the niggers of this war," Eddie tells Ruben after being ordered by his white commander to accompany the Contras on a raid deep inside Nicaragua. Eddie is ordered to go without wearing a U.S. uniform or dog tags because the United States needs to maintain plausible deniability about there being no direct U.S. military involvement in Contra operations inside Nicaragua. Eddie goes on the raid, though he is by now soured on his role in helping the Contras, and he is captured by Nicaraguans defending their cooperative farm. As he is led away, the narrative ends.

Latino is an earnest effort to dramatize the heavy costs inflicted on Nicaraguan society by the U.S.-funded and -trained proxy army, but Wexler unfortunately permits the co-op farmers to speak in political slogans, and Eddie's romance with the beautiful agronomist is not convincing. The result is that for all its good intentions, the political perspectives seem superimposed upon the formula romance and action scenes, rather than fusing with them as in films like *Rambo* or *Invasion USA*, which are far less intelligent but probably more effective political films due to their shrewd and emotionally powerful use of Hollywood conventions.

Missing, Salvador, Romero, Under Fire, El Norte and *Latino* position themselves outside the framework of Cold War ideology. But dominant political culture during the 1980s regarded the problems in Latin America as a local manifestation of the global struggle between the United States and the Soviet Union. Given this, it is not surprising that at least one Hollywood film reconstructed the Latin American conflicts in a Cold War package. *Predator* (1988) offers a strikingly literal manifestation of Cold War anxieties, albeit in science fiction terms. In the film, a team of commandos is recruited by the CIA to go into an unidentified Central American country where guerrilla fighters are holding American hostages. The rebels' political movement remains unspecified, thus enabling the film to construct the guerrillas as a kind of generic political and military menace. Furthermore, by employing a hostage scenario, the film's anxieties are linked with those of the invasion-and-rescue cycle examined in Chapter 2. As things transpire, however, a far deadlier menace than Marxist political revolutionaries is found. An alien predator from another world awaits the Americans, and it will hunt them down and methodically eliminate them one by one. The mercenaries, however, are alarmed long before they meet the guerrillas or the predator. The encounter with the forests proves to be a disquieting and anxiety-provoking experience. The density of the foliage and the forbidding terrain gradually and steadily unsettle the Americans' nerve. Though it is a generic film, *Predator* is charged with political metaphor. The forests are rendered as a jungle much as Joseph Conrad described the jungles of Africa in his classic *Heart of Darkness*. There, in the colonialist perspective, the jungle became a place of terror and unspeakable mystery. In *Predator*, the forests are viewed in these terms. They contain not only the guerrillas but also the ruthless alien hunter, a projection of political anxiety. Astonishingly, the hunter does not bother the guerrillas. They are able to set up base camps and establish political networks without being attacked by the alien. The creature quickly focuses on the Americans, however, and identifies them as targets.

Central America, then, is portrayed in the grip of an alien subversive presence. The rhetoric of the Reagan administration about outside intervention by alien powers is rendered in starkly concrete, if highly fanciful, terms. In light of Vietnam, where American firepower could not prevail against a poorly armed peasant army, *Predator* offers a discourse on the waging of counterinsurgency warfare. The American commandos in the film are armed to the teeth with high-tech weaponry but, as in Vietnam, it proves ineffective against the enemy. Only when the commandos fight as wily guerrillas with homemade weapons can they beat their opponent. The anxieties of the film seem to have been mobilized by a general cultural fear in the first half of the decade that an American invasion of Central America, particularly of Nicaragua, might be a real possibility. While its vision of the dangers lurking in a hostile terrain seems to caution against such an eventuality, the concluding images of the film nevertheless resonate powerfully with the darkest impulses of the Cold War. At the end, the forests have been leveled and burned, the environment and the local region destroyed in the struggle. They are a fiery wasteland, but the enemy is defeated and the surviving American is airlifted to safety. The Central American threat has been eradicated. The land has been destroyed in order to save it.

The region's problems could be given a Cold War twist, but they were also capable of serving as the pretext for comedy. Paul Mazursky's *Moon Over Parador* (1988) is set in the mythical country of Parador, whose dictator suffers a heart attack and is replaced by an American actor. The actor stands in for the dictator long enough for the state machinery to reconstitute itself and prevent a victory by the guerrillas. The film is curiously ambivalent. On the one hand, it is capable of making jokes about torture and the Nazis who serve in the dictator's household, and it shows the American actor (played by Richard Dreyfuss) being seduced by the thrill of wielding power. On the other hand, the actor Jack Noah learns to sympathize with the poor and dispossessed, and he engineers a complicated plot that brings a populist regime, headed by Jack's Paradorian paramour, to power. Remaining completely in the realm of fantasy, *Moon Over Parador* offers a political vision in which all contending oppositions are reconcilable. Jack's lover heads a new, presumably more tolerant government, and the CIA representative on the island, along with the aristocracy, makes no fuss when she dedicates herself to a restoration of the privileges and power of the underclass. At the end, the film opts for what Richard Maltby has termed an ideology of consensus, wherein narrative structure and plot resolution function to reconcile divisive and contending positions. By the end, the CIA, the aristocracy, and the guerrillas have joined hands under the new moon of Parador.[25]

Neither *Predator* nor *Moon Over Parador* shares the political commitment that largely characterizes the Latin America film cycle. These two films are essentially commercial properties, rather than films that explicitly address real political and historical situations. When compared with the other films in this cycle, these two productions, distant cousins, demonstrate once again the relatively wide ideological range of the American cinema. In films employing Latin America as a setting, comedy and suspense coexist with a political engagement that, at times, approaches the partisan. In assessing the importance of the limited cycle of productions dealing with Latin America, it must be noted that they were far less successful commercially than the Cold War films. By 1989, *Top Gun* had returned $79 million to its distributor. *Rocky IV* had returned $76 million, *Rambo III* $28 million, and *Red Dawn*, a comparative piker, had returned $17 million. *Red Dawn's* figures, among the smallest in the group, are considerably higher than the highest of the Latin America films (excluding *Predator*). *Missing*, for example, returned only $7.8 million to its distributor by 1989. One has to be careful in generalizing from box-office returns, however, because in the age of video, films that failed to perform at the box office frequently have an extended life on videocassette, reaching a multitude of viewers who failed to go to the theaters. Nevertheless, these figures help to indicate that the Cold War fantasies had greater resonance with the theatergoing audience in the 1980s than did the generally more critical group of Latin America films. *Predator*, for example, which placed Central American conflicts in a generic Cold War frame, returned $31 million to its distributor by 1989.

Although the Latin America films were by no means box-office blockbusters, their existence clearly demonstrates the heterodox nature of cultural discourse. While official ideology clearly inspired the popular Cold War films, it did not represent the universe of discourse. The cinema of the 1980s was not univocal. It did not speak with a unified ideological voice, nor was it inevitably reflective of the contours of a core ideology. The Latin America films demonstrate that filmmakers working either independently or for the major studios could step outside the Cold War framework, depart from the assumptions held by the Reagan administration, and attempt to criticize them while constructing commercially appealing narratives. If Cold War thought is a genre possessing its own familiar conventions and formulas, as was suggested in Chapter 2, it may not be coincidental that the Latin America films operated outside the confines of generic filmmaking in the construction of their images and narratives. Rejecting the assumptions of Cold War thought may have compelled a rejection of genre. They did, however, stay firmly within the American film tradition of linear, character-centered narratives and naturalistic imagery rather than employing the dialectical, self-conscious, and analytic cinematic forms of politically committed European and Third World filmmakers. This stylistic commitment, in turn, imposed limitations upon the political discourse these films could offer. Those limitations, however, derived as well from the anxieties and ambivalence within the American political tradition regarding revolution and the political Left. These films acknowledge and accept the Left as a force in Latin America while, in general, being unable to fully engage the terms of a leftist analysis of the region's conflicts.

As the decade ended, major changes continued to sweep the region. Most important in strengthening the political presence of the United States, the Sandinistas were voted out of office in Nicaragua in February 1990. The National Opposition Union (UNO), a coalition of 14 political parties, received 55 percent of the vote. The Sandinistas, however, received 40 percent of the vote, making them still the largest and perhaps the most powerful unified political party in Nicaragua. The election outcome was clearly the result of a deteriorating economy; inflation in 1988 was running over 30,000 percent and nearly 35 percent of the population was either unemployed or underemployed. The economic collapse was due to ten years of war and economic sabotage carried out by the Contra army, as well as to accumulating political contradictions inherent within the Sandinistas' political and economic programs.[26] While the Nicaraguan elections seem to reflect the ongoing collapse of the international socialist world, in El Salvador, the region's other flashpoint, the protracted civil war continued. In March 1989, ARENA's candidate for the presidency was victorious, and the party also won the majority of the mayoralties, gaining leverage in national as well as local government. The FMLN had gone underground between 1984 and 1988 when it realized its military offensives earlier in the decade were unable to spark a general insurrection. After four years devoted to strengthening its political network and reevaluating its military strategies, the FMLN resumed military and political offensives in 1990.[27] In the following year, the FMLN, while not renouncing its military offensive, entered into negotiations with the government on ending the civil war, and the Left won nine seats in the country's National Assembly, giving it a modest political voice in Salvadoran institutions that it had not had for many years.

The political futures of both Nicaragua and El Salvador remain far from clear. The underlying problems in the region that sparked rebellion and insurrection throughout the 1980s remain unaltered. Poverty and immiseration remain the norm for great numbers of people. Export economies prevent the development of national economic self-sufficiency, and crushing national debts owed to Western banks and lending agencies drain scarce resources and help to perpetuate relationships of subordination and dependency with the West. Social reforms, when attempted, have not changed the extraordinary concentration of landownership and wealth that has been a flashpoint in the region. Although the 1980s have ended and the wave of revolution that seemed imminent earlier in the decade failed to sweep through the region, changing its coordinates, the social tinder needed to ignite a revolutionary fire remains in ample supply.

To what extent will our films continue to reflect and report upon changes in this region? Unfortunately, unless the area threatens to explode again, as it did throughout the first half of the decade, it is likely that very few films will address the problems of the Caribbean basin. As we have seen, the phenomenon of revolution has been extraordinarily troubling and disturbing for U.S. political perceptions, and most American films accordingly choose to look the other way. Even when political fires were burning the brightest throughout Latin America, comparatively few North American film productions were interested in looking south of the border, but the imagery of those few films remains to haunt the political conscience. Despite the ambivalence about revolution that is an indelible part of U.S. culture, this small group of films about Latin America earnestly attempted to understand and portray the conditions breeding insurrection so that North American viewers might be exposed to alternative accounts of the region's turmoil. The Reagan administration's account of Communist subversion and falling dominoes was consistent with a maintenance of the claims of empire, that is, with traditional attitudes regarding Central America as the backyard, or the property, of the United States. In suggesting that the roots of insurrection lay in indigenous, oppressive socioeconomic conditions, rather than in a power projection by Moscow, these films explicitly challenge imperial prerogatives by endorsing regional claims to free government, an end to dictatorship and the immiseration it has helped create. These films passionately engage the controversies and exigencies of their historical moment and try to envision the shape of an alternative and more humane political future. This ambition is probably the finest and the most significant to which political film can aspire.

In *Romero*, the archbishop tells his parishioners before his death that if he is killed, he will arise in the Salvadoran people because their pain and suffering will contribute to El Salvador's redemption and liberation. In the final shot of the film, stirred by his death, a large crowd of peasants and urban poor walks toward the camera and engulfs it. Though the 1980s have ended, the struggles in Central America go on, offering a continuing set of political, dramatic, and representational challenges to the North American cinema. That our films might honestly attempt to meet these challenges may seem unlikely, but the effort could help to rejuvenate a cinema grown moribund pursuing inflationary budgets and special effects.

To the extent that the forces of revolution and regional unrest persist throughout Latin America, they will continue to elicit the potential for U.S. intervention—if not directly, then through proxy armies such as the Contras that intensify regional suffering. In the early 1980s, the prospects of direct U.S. intervention were inhibited by the lingering scars of Vietnam and the challenges that debacle posed to policies of regional military intervention. As the 1990s commence, nearly 20 years after the Vietnam war, that disaster remains sharply etched in the national memory. But social memory is selective, idiosyncratic in the ways it recalls and transmits the historical past to new generations. Symbolic cultural mythologies frequently come to replace the historically unbearable. Throughout the 1980s, Hollywood film participated in this process of codifying social memory and mythology by elaborating contemporary accounts of the Vietnam war. As a means of gauging the strength of continuing claims to empire, it is to those celluloid visions of Vietnam that we now turn.

NOTES

1. Ronald Reagan, congressional address on Central America, April 27, 1983, in Ronald Reagan, *Speaking My Mind* (New York: Simon & Schuster, 1989), pp. 152–153.

2. Ibid., p. 160.

3. Statistics compiled by the World Bank, quoted in Edelberto Torres-Rivas, "Guatemala—Crisis and Political Violence," *NACLA Report on the Americas* 14, no. 1 (January–February 1980), pp. 17, 20.

4. Quoted in Robert Armstrong and Janet Shenk, "El Salvador—A Revolution Brews," *NACLA Report on the Americas* 14, no. 4 (July–August 1980), p. 3, and in Jenny Pearce, *Under the Eagle* (Boston: South End Press, 1982), p. 210.

5. Pearce, *Under the Eagle*, p. 209.

6. *Amnesty International Report 1984* (London: Amnesty International Publications, 1984), p. 148.

7. *Amnesty International Report 1981* (London: Amnesty International Publications, 1981), pp. 140–141.

8. For details, see ibid., p. 140.

9. Quoted in Pearce, *Under the Eagle*, p. 228.

10. Ibid., p. 134.

11. Ibid., p. 19.

12. This distinction between instrumentalist and transformative views of art and political film is developed in detail by Sylvia Harvey in *May 68 and Film Culture* (London: BFI, 1980), pp. 45–86. Discussions of political filmmaking in Europe and the Third World are in Robert Phillip Kolker, *The Altering Eye* (New York: Oxford University Press, 1983); and in Michael Chanan, *The Cuban Image* (London: BFI, 1985).

13. "Glauber Rocha: Cinema Novo and the Dialectics of Popular Culture," in *Cinema and Social Change in Latin America: Conversations with Filmmakers*, ed. Julianne Burton (Austin: University of Texas Press, 1986), pp. 108–109.

14. Teshome H. Gabriel, "Third Cinema as Guardian of Popular Memory: Towards a Third Aesthetics," in *Questions of Third Cinema*, ed. Jim Pines and Paul Willemen (London: BFI, 1989), p. 60.

15. Ibid.

16. Ibid., p. 63.

17. Ibid., p. 64.

18. Essays on the role of multinational corporations and the role of mass communications in Third World political struggles are in Armand Mattelart's *Multi-National Corporations and the Control of Culture*, trans. Michael Chanan (Atlantic Highlands, NJ: Humanities Press, 1979), and *Mass Media, Ideologies and the Revolutionary Movement*, trans. Malcolm Coad (Atlantic Highlands, NJ: Humanities Press, 1980).

19. These figures are in Noam Chomsky and Edward S. Herman, *The Political Economy of Human Rights*, vol. 1 (Boston: South End Press, 1979), frontispiece.

20. Robert Armstrong and Janet Shenk, "El Salvador—Why Revolution?" *NACLA Report on the Americas* 14, no. 2 (March–April 1980), p. 24.

21. Ibid., p. 25.

22. These hagiographic aspects of the film are discussed by Dennis West and Joan West in their review of the film, which appears in *Cinéaste* 17, no. 4 (1990), pp. 46–47.

23. See, for example, the discussion in Kolker's *The Altering Eye*, pp. 287–298.

24. The limitations of the linear narrative and the melodramatic form are explored in more detail by Chris List, "El Norte: Ideology and Immigration," *Jump Cut* no. 34 (1989), pp. 27–31.

25. The argument is developed in Richard Maltby, *Harmless Entertainment: Hollywood and the Ideology of Consensus* (Metuchen, NJ: Scarecrow, 1983).

26. Discussion of the significance of the elections for Nicaragua and the causes of the electoral surprise are in "Nicaragua: Haunted by the Past," *NACLA Report on the Americas* 24, no. 1 (June 1990), pp. 10–39.

27. A useful analysis of El Salvador's current political situation is in Sara Miles and Bob Ostertag, "D'Aubuisson's New ARENA," *NACLA Report on the Americas* 23, no. 2 (July, 1989), pp. 14–39, and "FMLN: New Thinking," *NACLA Report on the Americas* 23, no. 3 (September, 1989), pp. 15–38.

Chapter Four

Hearts and Minds

Although the direct U.S. military role in Vietnam officially ended in 1973 with the withdrawal of the last U.S. troops, the aftershocks of that war continued to reverberate on the political landscape of the 1980s. The war remained an open wound on the body politic, healing slowly at best and generating wildly differing diagnoses of its origins. The war has proved to be an especially slippery event for historians and politicians to grasp, and even though nearly a generation has passed since the withdrawal of the last American troops, political and ideological consensus has not yet emerged—and may never emerge. The war cut too deeply for that, exposed too many contradictions, and unleashed a profound sense of political betrayal nationwide. Although the war's trauma was intensely felt during the 1960s and 1970s, its relevance for the 1980s must also be emphasized. Commentators on both the political Right and the political Left agree that the politics of resurgent America in the Reagan period were, in part, an attempt to overcome the lingering effects of the Vietnam war, effects that were construed as operating to inhibit an aggressive U.S. military presence throughout the world.

On the Left, Noam Chomsky analyzed the movement toward a new Cold War in the late 1970s and early 1980s as an effort to overcome what he termed the "Vietnam syndrome," understood as damaging to the doctrines supporting military intervention in the internal affairs of other nations.[1] On the Right, political and military strategists deplored cuts in the armed forces, reductions in the CIA, and cuts in security assistance to friendly military governments that followed the Vietnam period. With the defeat in Southeast Asia, policy strategists of the Right argued, the U.S.S.R. and its proxies seem increasingly predisposed to act openly against formerly neutral or pro-American countries; regional powers are far from awed by the United States; and internal insurrections—especially those with a strong Marxist-Leninist component or leadership—pursue their own objectives with the foreknowledge that, in an earlier "revolutionary war," the U.S. military machine was fought to a standstill by a far weaker nation with a greater degree of "cost tolerance."[2]

Jeane Kirkpatrick's piece in *Commentary*, as we have seen, offered a similar analysis in its recommendation that the United States be ready to assume a more interventionist global posture and cast off what she termed a Vietnam-induced sense of helplessness and political resignation.

The legacy of Vietnam, then, was felt very deeply during the Reagan period. This legacy was construed negatively, as a national shame contributing to a failure by the United States to exercise its rightful global prerogatives, a veritable breach in the empire, rather than as an opportunity for rethinking international relationships. Accordingly, America resurgent sought to close that breach, giving rise to the ideological operations and cultural manifestations studied in previous chapters. But scars lingered, and the specter of Vietnam continued to haunt the contemporary political landscape. It was animate, for example, throughout Central America during the early 1980s, when a U.S. invasion seemed a real possibility. Nicaragua and El Salvador, it was often said, were the new Vietnam; and Central America, it was feared, might become the new political quagmire.

By exploring the cinematic representations of the Vietnam war during this period, then, we can measure both the historical adequacy of the representations and the ways they were tailored to respond to contemporary needs. Furthermore, by focusing on narrative films, the constraints upon the American film tradition as a mode of political discourse will become most apparent. Fiction films, whether produced in old Hollywood or new, generally lack the analytic and dialectical modes of address that are routinely found in the documentary. The documentary tradition has produced a number of films about Vietnam—*Hearts and Minds* (1974), *In the Year of the Pig* (1969)—whose social and political analysis is richer and lies far outside the ideological boundaries of their fictional counterparts. At the same time, other documentaries, like their fictional counterparts, have sought to avoid a political presentation of the war. *Dear America* (1987), for example, which reconstructs the war through the letters of U.S. troops stationed in Vietnam, views the conflict from the personal, experiential level of the letter writers. In an analysis of this film, Barry Dornfeld discusses how the letters read by actors in the film were sometimes edited to omit the writer's political remarks and observations. Dornfeld concludes, "[the film] works within the conventions of transparent dramatic documentary form, operating effectively, for some audiences, on an experiential, affective level, but occupying a conservative authorial position that avoids critical political issues."[3] In brief, we shall see that the Vietnam war has proved to be too complex an event for easy capture within the confines of a narrative film. As the French director Jean-Luc Godard knew, the characters and plot complications of a fiction film can overwhelm, simplify, and even distort the historical referents from which the narrative is drawn. It may be that only the analytic voice of the documentary or a dialectical and self-referential cinematic style can do justice to a debacle as immense as Vietnam. Lacking these and often confined to the production of lean, efficient narratives, Hollywood directors have frequently resorted to metaphor as a mechanism of historical representation and understanding. We will want, therefore, to consider some of the metaphors employed during three periods of production: the late 1970s, the early and mid-1980s, and the late 1980s.

Hollywood was very slow to address Vietnam. The only major studio production during the war was John Wayne's *The Green Berets*, released in 1968. This is not to imply, however, that Vietnam had few effects on American films before the 1980s. Indeed, throughout the 1970s, an unfortunate convention presented the Vietnam veteran as a crazed homicidal vigilante in such films as *Magnum Force* (1973), *The Stone Killer* (1973), *Taxi Driver* (1976), and *Rolling Thunder* (1977). Furthermore, Vietnam had a profound but indirect effect upon the social vision of American filmmakers contemporary with the war. During the war American films became far more explicitly violent than ever before in works by contemporary socially critical filmmakers. Slow-motion and multi-camera techniques used to film scenes of bloody carnage were introduced into the American cinema by Arthur Penn in *Bonnie and Clyde* (1967) and Sam Peckinpah in *The Wild Bunch* (1969). Penn and Peckinpah used the formulas of the gangster film and the Western as a means of exploring contemporary issues of social rebellion and state violence that resonated with the Vietnam conflict. Peckinpah's *The Wild Bunch*, in particular, has sometimes been interpreted as an allegory about the American presence in Vietnam.[4]

Why was Hollywood so slow to address Vietnam directly while being comparatively eager to make melodramatic use of the crazed veteran stereotype? Several scholars have suggested that the conventions of the war film genre were not suited to capture the realities of Vietnam. Albert Auster and Leonard Quart, for example, note that "Hollywood could neither fit the Vietnam war into any of its old formulas nor create new ones for it."[5] There is certainly some truth to this suggestion. In contrast with World War II, in Vietnam the enemy did not wear a uniform and was often indistinguishable from the ostensibly friendly forces that the United States was there to assist. Both hostile guerrilla and friendly villager might appear as a farmer working his rice paddy. The crucial visual distinctions that conventional war films relied upon in distinguishing, at the most basic level, friend from foe were not available for representing the conflict in Vietnam. Furthermore, the Vietnam war was not a war fought by seizing territory. It was a conflict whose successes were measured by the number of hearts and minds converted and the number of bodies counted.

On the other hand, if conventions limited the representation of the war, it is not clear why Hollywood did not simply develop new conventions. In earlier chapters, we have seen how quickly cinematic conventions can evolve as the social realities they address undergo transformation. Furthermore, an oppositional tradition within the war film genre was potentially available for critical filmmakers to utilize in addressing Vietnam. Stanley Kubrick's *Paths of Glory* (1957) and *Dr. Strangelove* (1964) illustrate the deployment of new narrative and visual conventions to capture a critical view of modern warfare; and the bleak, existential violence of such genre pieces as Don Siegel's *Hell Is for Heroes* (1962) was available as a potential model for new Vietnam films. In *Cross of Iron* (1977), in fact, Sam Peckinpah treated World War II as a grim, existential stage on which political abstractions and ideas lost their force. Displaying relevance to the subsequent phenomenon of fragging in Vietnam, Robert Aldrich's World War II film, *Attack!* (1956), climaxes with a group of American soldiers collectively executing their commanding officer. While the Vietnam war undoubtedly presented novel realities to challenge the visual and narrative conventions of American cinema, it is not clear, if we confine our attention strictly to the matter of cinematic form, why filmmakers should have failed to adjust these novel realities to the available conventions or, failing that, to invent new conventions. To explain Hollywood's reluctance to engage the Vietnam experience solely in terms of the lack of available formulas is insufficient because it omits the very real ideological blockages operating inside the political discourse of the culture that surrounded the films. Hollywood's failure to respond to Vietnam is not so much a question of cinema as it is a question of political perception.

The war in Vietnam had been presented to the American public by a succession of presidents and political officials as a war of Communist aggression by North Vietnam against South Vietnam, and the American role as one of assisting the people of South Vietnam in defense of their freedom. In a 1961 Chicago address, for example, President Kennedy described the United States as a chief defender of freedom, assisting South Vietnam against ''a small army of guerrillas, organized and sustained by the Communist Viet Minh in the north.'' In a 1962 news conference, Kennedy noted, ''We are out there on training and on transportation, and we are assisting in every way we properly can the people of South Vietnam, who with the greatest courage and under danger are attempting to maintain their freedom."[6] As Frances FitzGerald noted in her study of the war, American officials tended to ignore the strong national differences among the nations of Southeast Asia while simultaneously giving the impression that South Vietnam was a nation distinct from North Vietnam.[7] This tradition has persisted after the war. In a radio address in 1978, for example, Ronald Reagan remarked, "There were two Vietnams, north and south. They had been separate nations for centuries."[8] The idea, however, that South Vietnam was a separate, democratic nation fighting aggression by North Vietnam is not supported by the Defense Department's own history of the war. The partitioning of Vietnam along the seventeenth parallel in 1954 was intended as a temporary division pending reunification elections. Backed by the United States, the leader of South Vietnam, Ngo Dinh Diem, refused to hold the elections and was supported by U.S. aid and assistance.

South Vietnam, however, remained a weakened, client state unable to sustain itself either politically or militarily. As a Defense Department analyst admitted, it "was essentially the creation of the United States."[9] As for the aggression of Communist North Vietnam, the Defense Department's history acknowledges that Ho Chi Minh and the Viet Minh were sufficiently popular as the main repository of Vietnamese nationalism to become an effective Vietnam-wide government after World War II, except for the reassertion of French colonial power and, following that, the U.S. presence.[10] As *The Pentagon Papers* acknowledge, U.S. perceptions of Vietnamese politics were unduly influenced by notions of dominoes and monolithic communism. These prevented a perception of the possibility of an alliance with Ho Chi Minh, and constrained officials from portraying the Vietnamese war against the French as an anticolonial struggle into which the United States might step only at its own peril. Pentagon analysts noted that "when the U.S. was faced with an unambiguous choice between a policy of anti-colonialism and a policy of anti-communism, it chose the latter."[11] The Pentagon's history stresses that the nationalist and anticolonial sentiments in South Vietnam were very strong and that those who took up arms against Diem fought for causes which "were by no means contrived in North Vietnam."[12]

The official U.S. position that North Vietnam manipulated the entire war is not wholly compelling, conclude the Defense Department's analysts, especially for the years 1955 to 1959:

As far as most Cochinchinese peasants were concerned, Diem was linked to Bao Dai, and to the corrupt, French dominated government he headed. Studies of peasant attitudes conducted in recent years have demonstrated that for many, the struggle which began in 1945 against colonialism continued uninterrupted throughout Diem's regime: in 1954, the foes of nationalists were transformed from France and Bao Dai, to Diem and the U.S.[13]

Stepping into the breach left by the French following their evacuation from Southeast Asia in the mid-1950s, the United States attracted all of the animus the French had heretofore aroused: "In the eyes of many Vietnamese of no particular political persuasion, the United States was reprehensible as a modernizing force in a thoroughly traditional society, as the provider of arms and money for a detested government, and as an alien, disruptive influence upon hopes they held for the Geneva Settlement."[14] The Pentagon's history also admits that the Diem regime remained a one-party, highly centralized familial oligarchy which was not democratic and lacked the foundations for developing democracy.[15]

In light of these assessments, the pronouncements of public officials about the territorial integrity and the defense of democracy in South Vietnam are examples of what, in the 1960s and 1970s, helped generate the "credibility gap." What Americans knew of the war as relayed to them by their elected officials was at variance with what the intelligence analysts were saying. Moreover, when the war became a visible and controversial issue in the middle to late 1960s, the roots of U.S intervention already stretched back more than 15 years. In 1950, the United States began to aid the French in their war against the Vietnamese with $10 million of military assistance. By 1954, the United States was funding 78 percent of the French war, and by 1955, with the French withdrawal, the United States assumed responsibility for training Vietnamese forces. Although U.S ground combat troops were not introduced until 1965, the commitment to intervene, as *The Pentagon Papers* show, was made prior to the French defeat at Dien Bien Phu in 1954. A nation whose historical memory has never been very good, America found itself embroiled in a war whose origins and causes were explained only in such abstract terms as "defending freedom" and "stopping Communist aggression," and whose origins had already receded into the mists of history.[16] It is no wonder, then, that the dominant popular perception of the war developed in ways that construed the conflict as a baffling quagmire.

These, then, are some of the factors explaining the inability of American film to come to terms with Vietnam. Why should we expect film to do what American political culture has been unable to do? Furthermore, as we saw in Chapter 1, Hollywood has frequently shied away from politically controversial subjects, especially where points of disagreement might develop with official foreign policy. The legacy of the McCarthy period had been a kind of overt depoliticizing of American film, and this carried over into the treatment of Vietnam. Thus, the paradox was that while American culture was becoming radicalized by the war in the late 1960s, American films continued for a long time to avoid the subject.

The films about Vietnam produced during the 1980s are distinguished by two distinct periods and styles. The first half of the decade tended to emphasize revisionist vigilante fantasies in which an American warrior, usually superhuman, returned to Vietnam to rescue a comrade and/or symbolically win the war by destroying huge numbers of the enemy. Films in this group include *Uncommon Valor* (1983), *Missing in Action* (1984), *Missing in Action II* (1985), and *Rambo II* (1985). Not all of the Vietnam films produced during the first half of the decade, however, exemplify this style. *The Killing Fields* (1984), for example, detailing the destruction of Cambodia, is clearly not a Cold War fantasy. In 1986, Oliver Stone's *Platoon* marked the shift to a larger and more ideologically diverse group of films. These included in 1987 *Full Metal Jacket, Good Morning, Vietnam, Hamburger Hill, The Hanoi Hilton, Dear America*, and *Gardens of Stone*; in 1988, *Braddock: Missing in Action III* and *Off Limits*; and in 1989, *Casualties of War, 84 Charlie MoPic, Jacknife*, and *In Country*. During the 1980s, the Vietnam film emerged on American screens as a clearly recognizable category with increasingly numerous representatives.

Before exploring these films, it will be helpful to return briefly to an earlier period to establish the manner in which selected features of earlier productions were both extended and rejected by the subsequent works. It is important to point out, however, that productions in the 1970s were not among the first to deal with the conflicts in Southeast Asia or with the American presence there. Julian Smith notes that between the 1940s and the mid-1960s there were more than a dozen American films dealing with the struggle against communism in Southeast Asia. Many of these were low budget, but they included *A Yank in Viet-Nam* (1964), *The Quiet American* (1958), *The Ugly American* (1963), *Operation C.I.A.* (1965), and *Saigon* (1948).[17] During the height of American involvement, however, only John Wayne's *The Green Berets* (1968) attempted a representation of the conflict and a justification for the American presence.

Produced at a time when U.S. troop strength exceeded five hundred thousand, the film attempted to explain why it was important for America to fight in Vietnam. Viewing the film today, however, one is struck by its gross failure of political understanding. The Vietnamese conflict is presented as if it were a struggle between armies operating from fixed territorial positions, as if it were a part of World War II. John Wayne and his company of Green Berets are sent to Vietnam to fortify a U.S. military outpost, from which they launch a strike against a North Vietnamese general in command of the Vietcong, as the film creates the impression that the Vietcong were a centralized army commanded by a single figure. The film justifies American intervention by portraying the Vietcong as unremittingly savage. They terrorize and kill the villagers rather than living and working among them with their support. In addition, this is a war without racial hatred, either between Americans and Asians or between whites and blacks within the U.S. military. The Green Berets adopt a little orphan named Ham Chunk who desires nothing so much as to be an American. No one in Vietnam resents the American presence, and there is no indication of the political stakes motivating the conflict. As in many subsequent productions, the Vietcong remain a shadowy, distant, and ill-defined presence.

Even in 1968, *The Green Berets* was an anachronism, harking back an earlier world, to earlier film styles and forms of military combat. A film about the American presence that did not present search-and-destroy missions, free-fire zones, or strategic hamlets was destined to fail even at the level of propaganda. After so politically and artistically clumsy an effort, and one that was so critically reviled, it is perhaps not surprising that Hollywood avoided films centered on a portrayal and analysis of the war. It would be a decade before major productions again returned to Vietnam. Before turning to these initial major productions—*The Deer Hunter, Coming Home* and *Apocalypse Now*—it will be helpful to consider the insightful and incisive analysis provided by two smaller productions of 1978. *Go Tell the Spartans* (1978) is one of the few productions to deal with the Indochina war before the introduction of American ground combat forces. Set in 1964, when Vietnam was still a police action, the film details the attempts of a resourceful American major, Asa Barker (Burt Lancaster), to equip and defend a deserted village that American officers have declared has strategic value. Though the film is set early in the decade, the attitudes of the characters are far more typical of the late 1960s and early 1970s. Barker, for example, believes that Vietnam is "a sucker's tour going nowhere, just round and round in circles." A corporal under Barker's command uses hard drugs, anticipating the arrival of the drug culture in the war. One sergeant is so burned out that he commits suicide. The cynicism and despair in the command represent in embryo the motivational and disciplinary breakdown that would afflict American forces a few years later. Lieutenant Hamilton, who naively believes the rhetoric about defending liberty and justice in Vietnam, is quickly killed by the Vietnamese guerrillas. Neither Hamilton nor his ideals survive for very long.

The film is especially significant for evoking the fragility of the South Vietnamese government and its desperate position in the mid-1960s. Barker has to bribe a corrupt South Vietnamese regional commander to obtain an artillery defense of the village, and when his forces are finally under attack, he cannot get American air support because it has been held in reserve due to coup threats in Saigon. Eventually, Barker and his command are wiped out, and the sole survivor, Corporal Courcey, walks through a graveyard of French soldiers while being watched by an exhausted, scarred Vietnamese guerrilla. Courcey, badly wounded, tells the guerrilla he is going home. Broken by battle, both men limp off in opposite directions as the credits appear over the graveyard. The historical symbolism here is potent; the American presence is clearly portrayed as inheriting the French burden with equally disastrous results. And with the American decision to leave, the country and its people are left in ruins.

The Boys in Company C (1978) is not as politically coherent, but it does angrily portray some especially sordid features of the American war that later films have studiously avoided. That these facets had been virtually eliminated by the 1980s productions gives us one measure of how the passage of years transforms history into mythology. The first half of the film subscribes to the conventions of the World War II film by following the fortunes of a melting pot of Marine recruits from their induction and training in boot camp to their arrival in South Vietnam. The two sections of the film, however, are in marked contrast. The boot camp sequences stressing discipline and morale-building clash with those in Vietnam, where there is a complete breakdown of discipline, an abuse of authority by the officers, and a lack of direction or purpose to the war itself. The film powerfully evokes the drug culture of the battlefield. Newly arrived in Vietnam, the soldiers find a plentiful supply of heroin, and one plans to ship drugs home inside body bags. Officers abuse their authority. One, for example, knowingly fires artillery at retreating U.S. soldiers and proves to be such an irritant to his men that he invites an attempted fragging. The film is one of the few to deal with this phenomenon. The role of the Green Berets is portrayed as an explicitly repressive one. A friendly South Vietnamese boy is arbitrarily arrested, tortured, and executed by a Special Forces major and a South Vietnamese police colonel who is also a drug runner. The torture and execution, in turn, elicit racial tensions. Tyrone Washington (Stan Shaw), one of the black recruits from Chicago, accuses his captain of treating the boy as a "yellow nigger," arguing that he wouldn't have abandoned the boy to torture and murder if he had been white.

The film climaxes with a soccer game whose visual and narrative functions anticipate the surfing sequences in Francis Ford Coppola's *Apocalypse Now* (1979) and that become a means of symbolizing the war. The soccer match is an early instance of the pervasive reliance by American filmmakers upon metaphor as a means to explicate the historical meaning of the conflict. The Americans are asked to lose so that their South Vietnamese opponents will look good and will be an inspiration to the South Vietnamese Army. Consistent with a popular historical interpretation found in *The Pentagon Papers* and elsewhere, the game presents the war as a contest the United States didn't really try to win and adds the implication that it may not have been worth winning, since the drug-running South Vietnamese colonel supports the Vietnamese team. As one of the recruits says, "If winning this game is good for him [Colonel Trang], how can it be good for us?" The metaphor becomes incoherent, however, as the recruits find that they can't throw the game. They do win it and return to combat, acknowledging that "Winning that stupid game was more important than saving our ass." Although the film ends with a reassertion of traditional genre values (i.e., renewed commitment to the conflict), this is not quite enough to negate the evocation of racism, torture, and bankrupt authority that has gone before. Despite its schizophrenic qualities, *The Boys in Company C* has a political sharpness at isolated moments and a willingness to portray some of the most unsavory aspects of the war, though this may be more a function of the period when the film was made. Racism, fragging, and drug running would have been much closer to the surface of the war's experienced reality in the middle 1970s than they are a decade later. (It should be noted in this regard that the film's director, Sidney Furie, performed an ideological flip-flop when he subsequently directed *Iron Eagle*.)

Neither *Go Tell the Spartans* nor *The Boys in Company C* attracted much attention upon release. Instead, because of the publicity and discussion that surrounded the big-budget productions *The Deer Hunter*, *Coming Home*, and *Apocalypse Now*, it might be said that 1978–1979 marks the beginning of sustained recognition by Hollywood of the war. Each of these films, however, treats the war in a very oblique fashion. Except for its effects upon domestic life, the conflict itself is invisible in *Coming Home*. *Apocalypse Now* uses the war as a framework for metaphysical ruminations, and *The Deer Hunter* examines it by constructing false historical metaphors. The latter film won the Oscar for best picture, and this critical reception underscored acceptance of the subject by the industry and the larger culture. Director Michael Cimino, however, deals less with the war than with the rhythms of working-class culture in a Pennsylvania steel town. The first third of the film centers on the friendship of Mike (Robert DeNiro), Steven (John Savage), and Nick (Christopher Walken) as they gather for a wedding and their ritual hunting trip. The war is an intrusion disrupting their lives and this mythical town. As Auster and Quart point out, the portrayal of the town is heavily romanticized. It is apparently a place "untouched by American dreams of mobility and economic success" and without any apparent unemployment or alienation.[18]

By contrast, the war is presented as total savagery and depravity. Mike, Steven, and Nick are captured by the guerrillas, kept in cages with rats, and brutally tortured in a game of Russian roulette. As many have pointed out, the Russian roulette sequences are sheer fabrication. There is no evidence that the National Liberation Front (known to Americans as the Vietcong) ever practiced this form of torture, but the film implies that Ho Chi Minh endorsed it because prominently displayed on the wall of the torture hut is a portrait of Ho. Through Mike's courage and daring, the three friends manage to kill their captors and escape. Mike, the deer hunter, survives Vietnam relatively intact. Steven sustains wounds and is crippled, and Nick is seduced by the pleasures of Russian roulette and perishes playing the game in Saigon. At the end, the survivors toast Nick and sing "God Bless America." Having returned the surviving characters to the womb of their ethnic American town, the film closes with the song and an affirmation of isolationist sentiments. It is paradoxical that a war of foreign intervention should be expressed via an isolationist film. In *The Deer Hunter*, the world outside the United States is a place of corruption and violence. Saigon, in particular, is presented as a hell of strip joints, crime, violence, and decay. Beyond the film's isolationism, it is difficult to locate a coherent political focus.

Coming Home presents the war through its aftershocks, its effect upon the lives of men and women back home. The story is set following the Tet Offensive in 1968 and focuses on the relationship of Marine Bob Hyde (Bruce Dern), his wife, Sally (Jane Fonda), and Luke (Jon Voight), the crippled veteran whom Sally comes to love. Bob's gung-ho patriotism is soured by his experiences in Vietnam, although we never see them. Instead, he recalls them to Sally: anecdotes about decapitations and American brutality. Bob internalizes the violence of the war and becomes a deranged and threatening character. As the representative of a malignant national psyche engendered by the war, the film requires his removal so that it may construct a symbolic narrative of reconciliation and catharsis. Accordingly, Bob conveniently commits suicide by walking into the ocean, thus clearing the way for Sally and Luke to resume their relationship. The growth of Sally's political consciousness is registered through her ability to achieve an orgasm with Luke, something she has been unable to do with her patriotic husband. Luke moves from being an intensely bitter character to an incarnation of the 1970s' sensitive male. He is capable of crying, of comforting other injured vets, of allowing Sally to paint flowers on his chest, and of suggesting, when Bob confronts Sally with a loaded gun, that there are some things they ought to "talk about."

Weakened by its schematic political symbolism, *Coming Home* treats public expressions of war resistance with ambivalence. Luke's sole act of protest occurs when he chains himself to the gate of a Marine recruiting depot, but the political nature of his rebellion is diffuse because he acts alone, as American heroes always have. Furthermore, his explanation is offered in terms that are more emotional than political: "If we want to commit suicide, we have plenty of reasons to do it right here at home. We don't have to go to Vietnam to find reasons to kill ourselves." When Sally picks him up at the police station afterward, Luke tells her he is not a very nice person, apparently because he has publicly protested the war. At the end of the film, Luke tells a high school class to be wary of patriotic feelings and appeals because the war is essentially an experience of death and brutality. They should remember, when they are being asked to enlist, that they do have a choice. His speech is emotional and quite poignant, but the political dimensions of the war remain outside its focus.

The emergence of the war in the late 1970s as an acceptable subject for narrative films seemed to require that a minimum of historical or political

analysis be applied to the subject. Instead, a psychological focus on personal relationships or a displacement of the war into cultural metaphor
or mythic imagery tended to prevail. By relegating potentially divisive
questions of politics or history to the background, Hollywood films were
clearly in a better position to appeal to a broad spectrum of the movie-
going public. By comparison, the specificity and acuteness of *The Boys
in Company C* seems remarkable indeed. Francis Ford Coppola's *Apocalypse
Now* was the most extreme manifestation of this early trend toward a
metaphorical treatment of the war. (It should be noted here that this is
a strategy the films share with literary treatments of the war. In his study
of Vietnam war novels and films, John Hellmann has examined these
shared allegories ''in which an archetypal warrior-representative of the
culture embarks on a quest that dissolves into an utter chaos of dark
revelation.''[19]) Coppola adapted Joseph Conrad's novel *Heart of Darkness*,
transferring the Vietnam war onto a mythological plane. The film is a
bravura and stunning exercise in the creation of wide-screen imagery,
but all too often the visual spectacle overwhelms a coherent dramatic and
historical perspective. The confusion was built into the film from the outset
because Coppola had no organized or sustained view on the war.[20]

The film's confusions are most apparent in the celebrated sequence
where the air cavalry attacks a South Vietnamese village that harbors some
guerrillas. The attack is viewed from the sky, and the editing sweeps us
into the emotional exultation of launching death from the air. There is
some evidence that Coppola intends to present the character of Colonel
Kilgore, who leads the attack, as a madman in the satiric tradition
established by Stanley Kubrick's *Dr. Strangelove*, but the editing creates
an emotional identification with the airborne attackers, defeating a satiric
perspective that depends upon emotional distance rather than identification in order to work. While the film is somewhat successful at evoking
the hallucinatory qualities of the war that Michael Herr captured in his
book *Dispatches* (Herr also wrote the narration for Coppola's film), the
farther upriver Willard travels in his search for Kurtz, the more removed
from Vietnam Coppola's film grows, until his reference point finally
becomes James Frazer's *The Golden Bough*, a work of anthropological
mythology. As the bull is slaughtered in the climatic imagery during the
death of the king ritual, Coppola's film severs all connection with Vietnam, illustrating how a poorly conceptualized production may quickly
founder at enormous expense. In this respect, several observers have
pointed out that Coppola's production seemed to mimic the U.S. debacle
in Indochina—both enterprises were dragged down by poorly considered
ambitions.[21] Vietnam, however, does not have to be understood in terms
of the quagmire imagery, and Coppola's film shows very clearly how that
metaphor results not in insight but in occluded vision.

The first cycle of major productions was a tentative undertaking, an initial, somewhat hesitant attempt to grapple with the meaning of the war. All these films suggested the war was best understood not in terms of history or politics, but through personal relationships, psychology, or mythology. Subsequent films were less reticent in presenting scenes of combat and carnage but, as we shall see, all operated within sharply constrained boundaries. Although a number of subcategories or styles now constitute the Vietnam film cycle, the productions as a whole exhibit a remarkably coherent and unified perspective on how the war is to be understood and remembered. The films of the 1980s will be discussed from two standpoints, emphasizing the similarity of vision and rhetoric employed and the areas of politics, culture, or history that are notably absent. What is omitted can be as significant as what is included. Social memory, proceeding to reconstitute the war as a remembered historical event for new generations, is as much an act of forgetting as it is of remembrance, operating through a remarkable dialectic of memory and suppression.

The major productions of the 1980s fall roughly into two categories, corresponding to each half of the decade. Initially, production emphasized films featuring powerful vigilante heroes and narratives centering on the rescue of Americans missing in action. These include *Uncommon Valor* (1983) and the Chuck Norris series beginning in 1984 with *Missing in Action*, continuing with *Missing in Action II* (1985), and ending in 1988 with *Braddock: Missing in Action III*. Sylvester Stallone's sequel to *First Blood*, *Rambo: First Blood Part II*, represents the ideological and stylistic climax of this cycle. The release of *Platoon* in 1986 marked a shift in the latter part of the decade toward films that elegized and celebrated the courage of American soldiers in combat. Other films in this category include *84 Charlie MoPic, Hamburger Hill, Gardens of Stone,* and *The Hanoi Hilton.* While these two categories have a different focus, they are unified by shared assumptions about the nature and causes of the war and by common lines of ideological reasoning. As if to make up for lost time, and certainly as part of the political appropriation and ideological suturing of the past that typified the Reagan years, the American cinema rushed to create fictional testaments to the war. Outside the cinema, the early 1980s saw a flurry of Vietnam-related activity. The Vietnam Veterans' Memorial was dedicated in Washington, D.C., in 1982. In 1983, the University of California sponsored a major academic conference on the war, and PBS presented its multipart history of the war, *Vietnam: A Television History.* Louis J. Kern points out that these events seem to mark "the end of society's denial of the experience of the war."[22]

Compared with the efforts of Chuck Norris and Sylvester Stallone, *Uncommon Valor,* which kicks off the first cycle, is the least ideological, despite having John Milius (*Red Dawn*) as co-executive producer. Gene Hackman plays Colonel Jason Rhodes, a father tormented by the conviction that his son is still being held in Laos, and he rounds up some members of his son's former platoon. Financed by an oil tycoon, the group trains to mount a commando mission into Laos to rescue missing Americans, among whom Rhodes hopes will be his son. The film clearly shows how compatible the Vietnam war could be with conventional genre formulas and, therefore, how the delay in bringing accounts of the war to the screen had more to do with its politically controversial nature than with the limitations of generic formulas. The narrative is broken up into episodes drawn from commando films like *The Dirty Dozen* (1967). The first section details Rhodes's attempts to recruit his small elite team; the second shows their training, filled with humorous and prophetic vignettes; and the third deals with the mission itself, during which some of the men are killed. While *Uncommon Valor* is, therefore, quite compatible with the war genre, it does begin to identify and develop certain modes of framing the war that subsequent films in the cycle will employ. Throughout the decade, Vietnam will be presented as a war the United States did not try hard enough to win and one in which bureaucrats betrayed the fighting men by abandoning their efforts in the field and by refusing to persist in securing the release of Americans held in captivity.

Before his team leaves for Laos, Rhodes makes a speech saying that as veterans they have been rejected by the United States because they lost. He describes the war as a business, noting that losing is like going bankrupt and everybody wants to forget something like that. He chastises the ineffectual politicians and bureaucrats and honors the men who laid their lives on the line: "While the politicians sit on their asses, I'm going to ask you to lay yours on the line. This time nobody can dispute the rightness of what we're doing." This last remark alludes to the controversy that surrounded the war and to the antiwar protests. Such allusions are common to the Vietnam films of the 1980s, but they rarely examine the controversy or the antiwar movement, or the issues motivating them, in detail. Instead, a strategy of caricature and denunciation of the protesters tends to prevail in these films, with the added implication that the United States lost partly because of the protests. The antagonism toward the antiwar protesters that runs through many of the Vietnam war films was certainly influenced by similar feelings in many sectors of the general public, but it also indicates the more diffuse and traditional discomfort in the film industry regarding public expression of oppositional politics. In the 1950s, as we have seen, the industry had turned on its own members accused of un-American political activity, blacklisting and publicly disgracing the alleged left-wingers. Given this antecedent discomfort with public political protest, it is not surprising that Hollywood's Vietnam productions are generally so hostile to those Americans who actively opposed the war. The industry's own history had supplied an ideological frame to help generate and contextualize this suspicion and hostility, and it will be important to note the way it inflects the other productions in the cycle.

Rhodes's remark that no one can dispute the rightness of what they are now doing indicates the functional importance of the MIA dilemma for these films. Compared with the politically divisive issues that surrounded the war itself, the plight of missing Americans and the humanitarian issues compelling their return were problems around which everyone could mobilize. They could provide a safe political focus for films portraying the war. At the beginning of *Uncommon Valor*, a television announcer says that the Vietnam war will never be over until the fate of all the MIAs is resolved. While the MIA issue potentially enabled Hollywood to appeal on politically nonprovocative, humanitarian grounds to a heterogeneous audience, the cycle was simultaneously motivated by additional concerns and performed another function that was far more controversial. In many of these films, a vigilante hero defies corrupt politicians and bureaucrats by waging a single-handed, second invasion of Southeast Asia, generating a narrative symbolism in which the United States refights the war and wins it. The vigilante films are usually set after the war, when the ideological victories claimed by the narratives cannot be contested by the history of the war and can function as a symbolic negation of real defeats or unpleasant political contradictions. Permeating all these films is an anxiety about the historic defeat and an inability to comprehend it. The success of Rhodes's mission is a bittersweet one. He and his team rescue a group of American POWs, but he discovers his son has died in captivity. The overall victory of the mission, however, in locating and rescuing the POWs permits a symbolic restoration of national honor, following the American defeat and withdrawal from Southeast Asia. It is the first of many symbolic compensations in the cycle. In his *Missing in Action* series, Chuck Norris launched several violent rescue missions into Southeast Asia to restore loved ones to their families and, by doing so, to reclaim national honor; the Vietnamese, in contrast, are portrayed as brutal and blood-thirsty savages. Norris's films, however, are not the most important examples of this cycle. As with the films of resurgent America examined in a previous chapter, Sylvester Stallone's work functions as the essential register of the social anxieties and political currents of the time.

In the second Rambo film, Stallone's Green Beret returns to Vietnam. But before discussing that film, it will help to examine the character's initial incarnation in *First Blood* (1982), where he wreaked havoc not on some distant Third World country but on a small town in the northwestern United States. The film opens with a dazed Rambo wandering through the forests of the Pacific Northwest. He enters the town of Hope and is treated with contempt and brutality by the local police force. He is told to get a haircut and a bath, then leave town. When he refuses, the police arrest him, hose him down like an animal, and beat him, causing Rambo to flash back to his captivity and torture in Vietnam. He goes berserk. Attacking the police and escaping to the streets outside, running and grunting like an animal, Rambo takes to the hills and the forests, where he immediately acclimates himself as if he were in the jungles of Vietnam. The remainder of the film becomes an elaborate vengeance scenario with the police stalking Rambo through the forests and discovering themselves outclassed when he begins to hunt them. Rambo then returns to the town to spread destruction. Stallone clearly intends Rambo's mistreatment by the police to evoke the climate of social intolerance that he feels surrounded society's treatment of returning Vietnam veterans.

Unlike the subsequent two Rambo films, however, *First Blood* portrays Rambo as a psychopath who has been made dysfunctional by the war. He sets a series of elaborate traps in the forest that mutilate and wound the police; however, these are so spectacularly conceived and the suffering of the officers is so extreme that a problem develops within the film. It becomes difficult for the audience to endorse the brutalizations Rambo engineers because they are far in excess of his own mistreatment by the police—especially when he returns to town to blow up a gas station and a hardware store, shoot out department store windows, and machinegun the sheriff. In political terms, it was a mistake to visit Rambo's unrestrained savagery upon American society. Unlike the deranged vigilante veterans of such 1970s productions as *Rolling Thunder* and *Who'll Stop the Rain*, whose violence was a metaphor for the returning poisons of the war itself, corrupting U.S. society, Rambo is presented as a martyr longing for acceptance and understanding by a society he continues to love. Thus, the film's point of view and its emotional appeals are badly compromised. Because of this, it was necessary in subsequent Rambo films to remove him to distant Third World countries—Afghanistan and Vietnam—where the destruction and killing he wrought might evoke a less ambivalent response.

First Blood also employs a basic narrative conceit of the vigilante films wherein the American predator hero becomes a master of jungle warfare and guerrilla combat. Rambo's former Green Beret commanding officer, Colonel Trautman (Richard Crenna), warns the local sheriff that he has more on his hands than he realizes. Trautman says that Rambo's job in Vietnam was to kill, to win by attrition; that he was an expert in guerrilla war, the lethal use of hands and knives, the improvisation of weapons from all available resources. He warns that if the sheriff goes after Rambo, he should bring a lot of body bags. In *Rambo*, the sequel, we see additional evidence of Rambo's guerrilla fighting prowess. Upon parachuting from the plane into Vietnam, he jettisons his high-tech equipment, preferring to rely upon a knife, a compass, and a bow and arrow. He outwits and massacres a pursuing group of Vietnamese and Soviet soldiers much as he had done with the local police in *First Blood*. In both films, Rambo uses the forests and jungles as cover, hitting and running at will, materializing from nowhere, and striking with deadly, accurate force. Furthermore, in contrast with Rambo's jungle mobility, the Vietnamese remain confined to a jungle fortress.

These portrayals indicate the film's political confusion. A supreme warrior, Rambo is meant as a surrogate for the U.S. fighting spirit in Vietnam, uncomplicated by the era's politics and ambivalence. Trautman describes his protégé as "the best combat vet I've ever seen. A pure fighting machine with only a desire to win a war that someone else lost, and if winning means he has to die, he'll die. No fear. No regrets. What you choose to call hell [war and torture], he calls home." As a pure distillation of American martial honor, Rambo represents the kind of strength and determination that would have won the war, the films imply, had they been used directly and uncompromisingly. Before going into action in *Rambo*, he asks Trautman, "Do we get to win this time?"

By posing such a question, the film is performing an elaborate historical inversion. American forces in Vietnam employed not guerrilla tactics but counterinsurgency methods. The American strategy was twofold. One component was an aggressive attempt to take the war to the enemy, known as search and destroy; the other component was the effort at pacification, at winning the hearts and minds of the South Vietnamese.[23] The strategy of the North Vietnamese Army (NVA) and the National Liberation Front (NLF) of South Vietnam was based upon the concept of "strategic mobility," which involved positioning battalions in remote areas where they could be easily resupplied and then enticing American forces into the area, where they could be attacked at will. Meanwhile, countrywide guerrilla activities continued to tie down, destroy, and otherwise harass the American forces.[24] Strategic mobility permitted the North Vietnamese and the NLF to tie the American forces to reactive defense roles and to permit the NVA/NLF to attack specific positions at their own discretion. Choosing the moment of attack while otherwise evading the Americans enabled the NVA/NLF to control, within wide limits, the size of their losses.

Herein lay the contradiction upon which the U.S. strategy of winning by attrition foundered. The U.S. strategy had been to raise NVA/NLF losses to a level that was not tolerable or sustainable. Yet by carefully choosing when to fight, the North and South Vietnamese guerrillas could control their losses, regardless of the size of the U.S. force. Defense Department studies in 1966 indicated that the NVA/NLF started the shooting in most of the company-sized firefights. The assistant secretary of defense noted, "Since their losses rise (as in the first quarter of 1967) and fall (as they have done since) with their choice of whether or not to fight, they can probably hold their losses to about 2,000 a week regardless of our force levels. If, as I believe, their strategy is to wait us out, they will control their losses to a level low enough to be sustained indefinitely, but high enough to tempt us to increase our forces to the point of U.S. public rejection of the war.''[25] Strategic mobility is a cardinal principle of guerrilla warfare, where strategems involve initiative, flexibility, surprise, and suddenness in attack and retreat. The chief military strategist of North Vietnam, General Vo Nguyen Giap, described the nature of guerrilla war as follows:

Guerrilla war is the war of the broad masses of an economically backward country standing up against a powerfully equipped and well-trained army of aggression. Is the enemy strong? One avoids him. Is he weak? One attacks him. To his modern armament, one opposes a boundless heroism to vanquish either by harassing or by combining military operations with political and economic action; there is no fixed line of demarcation, the front being wherever the enemy is found.[26]

Giap added that casualties must be avoided even at the cost of territory lost.

In contrast with these tactics, the basic principle of counterinsurgency warfare is to sever the connection between the guerrilla and his base of popular support. Mao Tse-tung noted that the guerrilla swims among the populace like a fish in the sea, to which the response of counter-insurgency strategists has been to drain the ocean. The destruction of villages thought to be supporters of the NLF, the relocation of South Vietnamese into hamlets in newly fortified and secured areas, the reeducation programs of the pacification effort, the destruction of crops and livestock, and the defoliation of large areas of the Vietnamese landscape were efforts to sever the connections between the guerrilla and South Vietnamese peasants.

For the Rambo films, then, to define this symbolic American warrior as an expert jungle fighter is to invert the realities of Vietnam. As Louis Kern has observed in an article about the MIA films, ''To 'win' the war we are symbolically re-fighting on the screen, to reverse the verdict of history, we must be transformed into our enemies (who won in the 'real' world), while they are transformed into us.''[27] In accomplishing this, it should be noted that these films are working, in part, from deep generic roots. The MIA films tell new, contemporary versions of the venerable, early American captivity narrative in which innocent whites are kidnapped and tortured by Indians or other representatives of mythic savagery. Furthermore, Rambo's embrace of savagery in his quest for vengeance helps make of him a distant cousin of the savage, questing heroes of American Westerns, and the folklore and imagery of the Western had influenced the presentation of the Green Berets in the popular press of the early 1960s.[28] Discussing the captivity narratives and the wilderness tradition in American culture where violence entailed a process of regeneration, Richard Slotkin has noted how the questing hero became transformed into his savage enemy, required to "fight the enemy on his own terms and in his own manner, becoming in the process a reflection or double of his own dark opponent."[29]

Portraying Rambo as a jungle fighter entails a substitution of familiar mythic frameworks in denial of a troubling historical referent and a willful obfuscation of the strategic and tactical distinctions between revolutionary warfare and the counterinsurgency responses that attempt to contain it. Rambo symbolically transforms the American military from a counterrevolutionary to a revolutionary presence in the jungles of Vietnam, permitting American culture to symbolically reclaim its revolutionary heritage, but only by virtue of a falsification of history. The incompatibility of this heritage and America's counterrevolutionary role in Vietnam is one of the historical contradictions that helped to motivate the use of mythic narratives and characters in these films. Myth helps resolve troubling historical contradictions by reconciling the antagonisms and oppositions that inform them. To the extent, though, that myth may compel belief, it can produce its own substitute reality. Thus, Rambo—a character generated by Reagan-era anxieties about national weakness—encodes an elaborate historic reversal, becoming an emblem of U.S. commitment to Third World revolution and freedom (in Vietnam and Afghanistan). But to uncover and represent this mythic virtue, Rambo has to struggle against the decay of contemporary political institutions.

Like other films in the cycle, *Rambo* assigns much of the blame for the lost war to duplicitous, treacherous politicians and bureaucrats. A bureaucrat named Murdock seeks to derail government hearings on the MIA issue by sending Rambo to an empty POW camp, hoping that when he returns empty-handed, the committee will be able to bury the MIA issue. Rambo instead finds an MIA, and Murdock orders the rescue helicopter to abort its mission, stranding Rambo and the American. This was another mission the United States didn't really want to win, the film implies, as Trautman says to Murdock, "It was a lie, wasn't it, just like the whole damn war?" But in order to recoup the past for contemporary uses, as these films in the cycle aim to do, governmental authority and the individual's bond with the state—which had been damaged by the war—must be reestablished. Despite all the government treachery and duplicity portrayed in the film, therefore, the narrative resolutely insists that patriotism remains every American's duty. At the end of the film Rambo casts aside his rifle and discovers speech. "I want what they [the rescued MIAs] want and what every other guy who came over here and spilled his guts and gave everything he had wants—for our country to love us as much as we love it."

American films will concede that the war might have been a mistake, might have been imprudent or an exercise in poor judgment, but they will continuously affirm the virtues of duty to the state and patriotic love of country. This reaffirmation becomes a principal means of reconstituting the history of the war in cinematic terms for a new generation, despite the fact that the war itself led many to question these very principles. At the end of *First Blood*, Rambo again discovers language and delivers a speech that contains the major allegations which would continue to shape and inform films about Vietnam for the remainder of the decade: "It wasn't my war. You asked me. I didn't ask you. I did what I had to do to win, but somebody wouldn't let us win. I see all of those maggots at the airport protesting me, spitting at me, calling me a baby killer, and all kinds of vile crap. Who are they to protest me unless they had been there?"

We are already familiar with the allegation that the United States did not wish to win the war. In addition, the speech includes a castigation of antiwar protesters as "maggots" and an argument that seeks to invalidate the protests on the grounds that the demonstrators had not fought in Vietnam and therefore had no legitimate position from which to speak. Subsequent films would echo these charges. As for the imagery of the airport protesters, the film minimizes the broad-based and diverse nature of antiwar protest as it developed during the latter half of the 1960s. The movement was composed of priests, teachers, housewives, college students, lawyers, politicians, liberals, and pacifists as well as radicals, advocating positions ranging from unconditional withdrawal to a cease-fire and a negotiated settlement. The antiwar movement was not a single current, nor did it have one goal or even a consensus on how to achieve its aims. This diversity was the source of its enormous vitality as well as its profound political weakness. While it is true that the movement did not represent most of the public, nor even receive the support of the majority, its size and tenacity created very real constraints for Washington policymakers. Nearly half a million Americans, for example, gathered on the Mall in Washington, D.C., in November 1969 to protest the war. Noting the reluctance of the president to call up the reserves because of the domestic political situation in 1967, Pentagon analysts described the increasing influence that domestic unrest was exerting on policy:

When the President and the Secretary of Defense, as well as other Congressional leaders and politically attuned decision makers in the government began to search for the illusive point at which the costs of Vietnam would become inordinate, they always settled upon the mobilization line, the point at which Reserves and large units would have to be called up to support a war which was becoming increasingly distasteful and intolerable to the American public. Domestic resource constraints with all of their political and social repercussions, not strategic or tactical military considerations in Vietnam, were to dictate American war policy from that time on.[30]

Rambo's outburst about the protesters at the airport obfuscates the scope and the scale of the antiwar movement, discounts the motivations of the demonstrators, and reduces their arguments to caricatured terms. In addition, the second *Rambo* film implies that the protesters are, in effect, dupes of the Soviets because their opposition to the government's war policies has hobbled the nation in ways that have ensured the success of Soviet expansionism. This allegation that domestic political opposition is an aid to Soviet agitation is a traditional Cold War argument. In *Rambo*, Stallone portrays the Vietnamese as dupes of the Russians, pulling the war, for a 1980s audience, back into the circuits of Cold War thought that had originally inspired it. Disturbed by the Communist victory in China, American officials regarded Vietnam as the first postwar test for drawing the line against wars of national liberation ostensibly orchestrated by Moscow or Peking. Stallone reconstitutes Vietnam in just these terms, with the added proviso that since the U.S. defeat, the Russians have claimed the country for use as a military base. Captured by the Vietnamese, Rambo discovers they are under the command of a vicious Soviet officer.

Despite the ideological resonance of Stallone's film, its dimensions were so outsized and over-the-top that they apparently exhausted the vigilante warrior/MIA cycle. The political discourse of these films was reductive and lacked the sophistication needed for extension and development. Furthermore, as noted in Chapter 2, the tides of the Cold War were shifting in the latter half of the decade, and the rescue-and-invasion formulas grew somewhat less salient in the period's most popular films, at least as a means for comprehending the Vietnam war. In addition, public attitudes toward the combat troops who served in Vietnam were becoming more supportive and affirmative. The Rambo dramas featuring Stallone's emotionally bruised vet longing for love and acceptance by his countrymen gave way to less ambivalent and ironic presentations of heroic soldiering in the jungles of Vietnam. In the post-Rambo narratives, soldiers in Vietnam no longer pleaded for acceptance as Stallone's warrior did. The films showed them quietly, resolutely, unself-consciously bearing up under the terrifying violence of jungle combat. Pegging Vietnam narratives to the MIA dilemma, as a means of generating politically acceptable protagonists for an uncertain audience, was no longer necessary in the latter half of the decade. Heroes were now found in abundance, and they were located unambiguously among the combat soldiers who, throughout the 1970s, had been portrayed in films as antisocial loners or crazed vigilantes. The vigilante/MIA cycle, accordingly, became depleted; and the vigilante heroes and their rescue missions that were an indelible part of the mythology of resurgent America diminished in the latter half of the decade. The appearance and popularity of *Platoon* in 1986 signaled a decisive shift in the political and narrative focus of

major Vietnam productions. Did this shift, however, entail a corresponding ideological change, or were the allegations and arguments of the
vigilante films simply absorbed by the post-*Platoon* productions? As we
will see, something of the latter occurred.

Platoon inaugurated a series of productions that have been termed
"noble grunt" films, focusing on the courage and fortitude of the
American soldier and resulting from a search by filmmakers for heroes
who would be acceptable to the public[31] and politically responsive to the
emerging national constructions of the war's meaning and significance.
To the extent that these films furnished a primary source of information
on the war for a younger generation, their images became part of the
newly constructed meanings being assumed by the war. *Platoon, Hamburger Hill, 84 Charlie MoPic, The Hanoi Hilton*, and *Gardens of Stone* celebrate
American tenacity, bravery, and commitment to duty, values these films
see as fundamental to the performance of U.S. soldiers in Vietnam. Indeed, Vietnam productions in the second half of the decade attempted
a rehabilitation of the image of the American fighting man, even though
some, like *Jacknife* and *In Country*, focused on the traumas of postwar adjustment by returning veterans. The films collectively idealize and elegize
the Americans fighting in Southeast Asia. *Platoon, 84 Charlie MoPic,* and
Hamburger Hill, in particular, concentrate on the texture of daily life in
the jungle or in combat, and the power of the portrayals has been resonant for many who served there. Each of these films deliberately restricts
its focus to the microcosmic level, to the physical and emotional struggles of the grunt, the foot soldier, whose imperative was often merely
to survive another day. The consequence of this deliberate limitation of
focus is the construction of a restrictive account of the meaning of Vietnam. As such, the selectivity of social memory is especially apparent here.
These films reconstitute the war in terms that are intensely political,
despite their apparent disavowal of political issues.

The most explicit demonstration of these political functions is not,
ironically, contained in the films themselves but is part of a promotional
advertisement for Chrysler Jeep Eagle that precedes *Platoon* on videotape.
A brief analysis of this remarkable advertisement will help us to understand how the microcosmic focus of the films—centered on the soldiers'
struggle for survival and not upon the larger political or historical issues
from which the war sprang—helps to construct the war in ambiguous
terms that are capable of being inflected in quite specific ideological directions. It is important to understand how the ad functions as a vehicle
of persuasion and as a rewriting of the history of the war, but it is also
necessary to see how the political vagueness of a film like *Platoon* invites
the attachment of such an advertisement and, indeed, may even facilitate
it. Preceding the film, the spot is not clearly marked as an advertisement
until its end. Lee Iacocca, clad in a trench coat, wanders through a sunlit

field as if deep in sobering thought. He approaches a Chrysler Jeep and pauses, his mouth grimly shut, lips tightly pursed. The acting, of course, is carefully staged, as is this speech that follows:

This Jeep is a museum piece. A relic of war. Normandy, Anzio, Guadalcanal, Korea, Vietnam. I hope we will never have to build another Jeep for war.

This film Platoon is a memorial, not to war, but to all the men and women who fought in a time and in a place that nobody really understood. Who knew only one thing, they were called and they went.

It was the same from the first musket fired at Concord to the rice paddies of the Mekong Delta. They were called, and they went. That in the truest sense is the spirit of America. The more we understand it, the more we honor those who kept it alive.

I'm Lee Iacocca.

He then walks off-frame, the shot lingers on the Jeep and slowly fades out, to be succeeded by the Chrysler Jeep Eagle corporate logo in red, white, and blue against a dark screen. On videotape, the film proper then begins.

The advertisement provides an interpretive frame in which the home viewer may place the film, and since more people are likely to encounter Platoon as a videotape viewed in the home than as a film seen in a theater, this framing device becomes an important social document. Note the way in which the Iacocca speech removes the specificity of the war and transforms it into one of many the United States has fought. Vietnam becomes undifferentiated from World War II and Korea. It is collapsed onto a timeless and mythological plane where it serves as an example of the American spirit, unchanged since its first manifestation at Concord during the Revolutionary War. Vietnam, furthermore, is defined as something that cannot be understood. Iacocca notes that neither the place nor the era is something anyone really comprehends. This claim is an effective way of inoculating contemporary representations against the divisive politics that surrounded the war during the late 1960s and early 1970s. It is politically safer to claim that no one truly understood the war than to acknowledge the way it threatened to split the country over contending accounts of its meaning. If the war was an irrational event not susceptible to human understanding, then what can be salvaged from those dark and murky times?

Ironically, what is salvaged by contemporary films was among the most hotly contested of all the issues surrounding Vietnam: the claims of duty and patriotic service. One of the peculiarities of the Vietnam war is that not everyone who was called went, and not everyone who went was happy to have done so. Desertion rates, for example, in the Army and the Marine Corps climbed steadily from 1965 to 1973, as did the incidence per thousand of individuals classified 1-A by the Selective Service who requested appeals. On the fields of fire, fragging incidents climbed from 126 in 1969 to 333 two years later.[32] Many veterans, furthermore, were active in protest movements against the war. It is, therefore, a highly selective and an ahistorical version of Vietnam that Iacocca urges us to remember. The simple fact is that Vietnam was not like World War II or Korea or the Revolutionary War, and this advertisement should be understood as a dramatic example of contemporary political communication, an attempt by one of the corporate agencies that supplied the war effort to guide our interpretation of it. Let us now consider the ways in which the ambiguous and restrictive dramatic and narrative focus of *Platoon*, and the films it inspired, invites the attachment of such an advertisement.

Oliver Stone's film caused a sensation because of its richly textured evocation of the jungle's physical presence and the ordeals of marching through it, camping, and fighting there. The opening sequence, for example, makes palpable the oppressive heat, the dense foliage, and the threats posed by red ants, snakes, thirst, fatigue, and an enemy who knows the jungle better than you do. A tension exists, however, between this layer of surface realism and the elaborate network of literary conventions and religious symbolism that Stone employs. In an excellent discussion, Thomas Prasch explores the way the documentary qualities of the film operate to lend conviction to the literary and religious conventions.[33] The narrative of the film is cast as a bildungsroman about the spiritual and moral education of Taylor (Charlie Sheen), who has come to Vietnam because he wants to do his duty like his father in World War II and his grandfather in World War I. Speaking in voice-over narration (a convention employed by many of the films in this cycle), Taylor remarks that he wants to discover something he does not yet see and to learn something he does not yet know. He is torn between two father figures, one a demonic creature named Barnes (Tom Berenger), horribly scarred both physically and emotionally by the war, the other a Christ figure named Elias (Willem Dafoe), who safeguards Taylor from harm and intervenes to prevent the Americans from brutalizing Vietnamese villagers they have captured. As Prasch points out, the documentary texture of the film attaches a great deal of apparent authenticity to these narrative conventions and symbols, deflecting attention from the question of whether a bildungsroman structure and Christian iconography are adequate means for understanding the Vietnam conflict.

Charting Taylor's spiritual education at the hands of Elias and Barnes, studying his transformation from a novice to a seasoned warrior, Stone portrays the war as a hellish confrontation with the forces of the irrational, drawing the best and the worst from Americans. In his opening narration, Taylor says, "Somebody once wrote that hell is the impossibility of reason. That's what this place feels like, hell. I hate it already, and it's only been a week." Later in the film, Taylor adds that what he has seen in Vietnam threatens the loss of his sanity, that everything is a blur, and that he can no longer tell right from wrong. These are also the terms offered by Lee Iacocca for understanding Vietnam, but to view the war as an exercise of the irrational is to defeat and negate the possibility of historical understanding. Taylor goes on to eulogize the grunts in a way that demonstrates both the poignancy and the limitations of the film's microcosmic focus. Taylor says that these soldiers are mostly poor, from small towns, with little schooling and nothing going for them: "They're the poor and the unwanted, yet they're fighting for our society and our freedom. They're the bottom of the barrel. Maybe that's why they call themselves grunts, because a grunt can take it, can take anything. They're the best I've ever seen, grandma, the heart and soul." The narration is heartfelt and moving, but it illustrates the film's lack of interest in the political context of the war. Taylor's claim that they are fighting for American society and American freedom stands unchallenged. Since this was the official explanation for the war offered by a succession of presidents, the lack of inquiry into this claim amounts to an endorsement.

Taylor's self-professed struggle to preserve his sanity is bound to the competing claims that Barnes and Elias hold for him. In the Barnes-Elias dichotomy, Stone opts for a dualistic mode of understanding and explanation centered on a mythically presented struggle of good versus evil; it is one that many other films on the war also employ, most notably *Casualties of War* (1989). The savagery of Barnes and the saintly, humane principles of Elias split the platoon after an assault on a Vietnamese village during which Stone evokes with extraordinary and horrifying detail the way that emotional hysteria can amplify a revenge killing into a large-scale massacre. Barnes executes an old woman and is about to shoot her child when Elias intervenes, beating him and threatening him with a court-martial. Reiterating the familiar explanation that Vietnam was a war the United States did not wish to win, Barnes replies that Elias is "a water-walker like those politicians in Washington trying to fight this war with one hand tied around their balls." Barnes eventually frags Elias and, in turn, is killed by Taylor. In his final meditation as he is airlifted from the field, Taylor says, "I think now, looking back, we did not fight the enemy. We fought ourselves, and the enemy was in us." He adds that Barnes and Elias will be with him for the remainder of his days, fighting for possession of his soul.

Through this symbolism, *Platoon* constructs a metaphysical account of the war not unlike Coppola's portrayal in *Apocalypse Now*: as an inner, psychic conflict of good and evil in the American heart and soul. Although, for Stone, the significance of Vietnam may have been that Barnes's savage principles were triumphant (at one point Barnes declares,

"I am reality"), in Taylor's closing admission—"Those of us who did make it have an obligation to build again, to teach to others what we know, and to try with what's left of our lives to find a goodness and meaning to this life"—something of the spirit of Elias remains as the underlying example that the film affirms. To claim, however, that in Vietnam the United States confronted not the Vietnamese but the darkness in its own soul is to lapse into solipsism and to obviate the historical context of the war even while presenting its existential dimensions in unprecedented detail.

Like *Platoon*, *84 Charlie MoPic* relies upon a richly detailed, surface realism as a mode of historical reconstruction. As in *Platoon* and *Hamburger Hill*, an extraordinary amount of attention is devoted to the small problems and nuisances of daily survival. As in *Platoon*, the focus is equally restricted, equally microcosmic, and one that avoids analysis or extended inquiry. Unlike *Platoon*, however, *84 Charlie MoPic* masquerades as a documentary to give its images and narrative the immediacy of the apparently real. A pseudo-documentary, the entire film is told through a subjective camera as MoPic, a combat cameraman, follows a dangerous, seven-man reconnaissance mission to the Central Highlands. The action is presented as he sees it through the lens of his camera, and the gimmick works well in making us a participant on the mission. Leaves smack directly into the lens, the cameraman occasionally trips and drops the camera, and when the patrol hides from a contingent of Vietnamese, the images become decentered and uninformative because the camera is "hiding" as well.

This pseudo-documentary style operates to lend a legitimacy (to the extent that the style is accepted as a presentation of the "real") to the terms by which the film seeks to understand the Vietnam war. Here, as in the other films following *Platoon*, the war is to be salvaged and understood by focusing upon the honor accruing to soldiers who courageously discharge their duties. The portrait of the team members in *84 Charlie MoPic* stresses their quiet courage and absolute loyalty to each other. Each of the men in the reconnaissance team is interviewed by MoPic, who asks about their home life but not about their opinions on the war. One man, a poor South Carolina father of four, replies, "I don't figure right or wrong about it. People like me just go day to day, spend their time trying to figure how to get food on the table." He adds that his father taught him "You're supposed to do your job the best you can, no matter you like it or not. You do your job, leave right or wrong to others." He adds that he loves the black leader of the team like a brother, that he would kill or die for him and knows that O.D. would do the same for him. The camaraderie and mutual devotion of the men in the team imbue their portrait with the honor accruing to those who, in Iacocca's words, were called and went, those who did their duty with bravery and through unspeakable suffering, despite having questions or reservations about the war. These principles are the basic terms through which this group of films seeks to understand the war. It is, however, a curious, if not cautious, affirmation, one predicated upon a refusal to "figure right or wrong" about the war. This refusal does not seem far from the more nihilistic credo of the men of *Hamburger Hill*, who find solace from friends' deaths in the chant "It don't mean nothin'."

In *Hamburger Hill*, which studies the bloody assault of troops of the 101st Airborne Division on hill 937 in the Ashau Valley in 1969, the bonds of camaraderie help to insulate the soldiers from the violence exploding around them and to fire their animosity toward those who were protesting the war. During a lull in the fighting, one of the Americans gets a letter from his girlfriend telling him that she won't send any more letters because her friends at college have told her it is immoral to write to him. Sergeant Worcester tells of being hit with bags of dog shit thrown by pro-testers when he returned on leave, and he talks bitterly about college kids who call parents and tell them how glad they are that their boys are being killed by the heroic soldiers of North Vietnam. "That's why I'm here," he says, implying that his being here is the answer to the shameless tactics of the antiwar protesters, who are portrayed only through these allusions. The film evokes in extraordinarily powerful detail the horrendous sacrifice and prolonged suffering of the Americans as they attempt to take the hill and, in such a context, the focus on the front lines serves as an implied critique of the antiwar resistance. As constructed by the film, this sacrifice nullifies the antiwar cause by virtue of the immense pain endured by the men in battle compared with the protesters, whose principles were not tested in lethal combat.

Francis Ford Coppola's *Gardens of Stone* contributes to this collective celebration of the courage and honor of the Vietnam combat soldier through a portrait of the home front and the relationship of the elderly Sgt. Clell Hazard (James Caan), serving in the elite Old Guard at Arlington National Cemetery, and the young Jack Willow, who yearns to trade the Old Guard for active service in Vietnam. Willow does get to serve and is killed; the film opens with his funeral, lending the entire narrative a mournful tone.[34] Echoing Taylor in *Platoon*, Jack speaks (during the funeral) in voice-over from a letter he had sent to Clell. Writing from Viet-nam, he says he now has no answers, only questions, whereas when he was first inducted, "I was so young, so sure I had the answers. But I don't think I have the answers any more, just questions." As in *Platoon*, *84 Charlie MoPic*, and *Hamburger Hill*, the war is portrayed as something that corrupts American innocence and ideals, but these corrosive effects, paradoxically, furnish the basis for heroism and the challenge necessary for evaluating the devotion and courage of the combat troops. In this respect, the films are able to couple an acknowledgment of the special destructive qualities of Vietnam with a contrary insistence upon the importance of maintaining traditional soldierly virtues. The films feint in a critical direction only to fall back into the terms of more traditional generic portraits, in which Hollywood films have typically stressed the gallantry of the American soldier. Young Willow is a gung-ho soldier who believes that a good soldier in the right place can make all the difference, whereas the embittered Hazard believes Vietnam is a war unlike other wars, that there is "nothing to win, no way to win it." Willow's youth and idealism are sacrificed in the war, but it has not been in vain because it spurs Hazard's decision at the end of the film to enlist for service in Vietnam, where he can train soldiers properly and, he hopes, teach them what they need to know to save a few of their lives. Clell's attitude embodies the general perspective shared by this group of films. He acknowledges that the war might be an instance of bad judgment on the part of the United States, but that "if we're going to fight this war, we ought to God-damn fight it right."

These films suggest that although the United States may not have done all it could to win the war, however misguided or ill-thought-out the official policy, the service of the ground forces remains an important example of national honor. This perspective is certainly a reaction to, and an attempt to atone for, the controversy and animosity the combat troops aroused among segments of the general population at the time of their return to society, when they were rejected because of the pervasive hostility the war had aroused. But this perspective is also a way of rearranging the political coordinates of the Vietnam era, removing the sting of controversy and ugly social realities, and sanitizing and detoxifying a difficult political period in the interests of making it palatable to a new generation. In this respect, the feints in a politically critical direction that are part of the rhetoric of this cycle of films evoke the ghostly trace of the now-fading political controversies associated with the war, but in a way that ensures they will not be engaged or explored. As an example of the way the films couple a more generic portrait of martial honor with deceptive critical feints, Clell's perspective is given some contrast by the attitudes of his liberal girlfriend (Anjelica Huston), a reporter for *The Washington Post*. She believes that the war is a criminal activity, not merely a mistake, that it is "genocide." However, she is not permitted to explain her position in any detail, and her denunciation of genocide is experienced as simplistic rhetoric because the opinion remains unexplained and because the film cuts immediately to the next scene. These critical feints operate in the films to evoke enough of the political atmosphere of the era to ensure a superficial authenticity by conjuring the effigy of political opposition and controversy, only to bat it aside as a straw figure.

The most important use of this strategy in Coppola's film lies in its handling of the antiwar movement. As we have seen, the antiwar movement has remained invisible and offscreen in most of these productions, but in *Gardens of Stone* it is personified in the character of Don Brubaker, head of Attorneys Against the War. As the imagery of antiwar protesters in the other films might lead us to expect, Brubaker is a caricature, and the sequence in which he appears is remarkably shrill and strident. Encountering Clell at a party, he is insulting and abusive. He calls Clell a chicken shit, a Nazi, a baby-killer, and begins pushing him. The implicit violence of Brubaker's language and actions makes a mockery of his anti-war politics and reduces the movement to the most stereotyped slogans. Clell is goaded into a fight, and when he dispatches the man with a broken jaw, we can't help but feel that Brubaker has gotten exactly what he deserves. Brubaker's cartoonish presence smears the antiwar movement, and by focusing on this single character the film fails to acknowledge the movement's true size.

The events in the film take place in 1968 and 1969, which makes these omissions quite remarkable. In 1969, during the March Against Death, forty-five thousand people gathered near Arlington National Cemetery and then began a march on the White House, each person carrying a placard bearing the name of a dead soldier or a destroyed Vietnamese village. For a film that seeks to evoke the atmosphere in Arlington National Cemetery in 1969, the omission of the demonstration helps to create a willfully selective, if not distorted, historical reconstruction. We have seen, however, that antiwar protest has offered a fundamental challenge to films whose aim is a suturing of historical wounds, a challenge that is either reduced through caricature or ignored altogether. To ignore it, though, is to transmute history into myth. This is the process enacted by *Gardens of Stone*, as by most of the other films in this cycle, but Coppola's film goes even farther by co-opting the antiwar movement itself. In another letter, Jack explains that the real antiwar protesters are the soldiers who are fighting in Vietnam. Speaking about Clell's girlfriend, Jack says, ''Remember, she's a civilian, Sarge. There's no way for her to really and truly know that nobody hates this war more than those who have to fight it.'' By feinting to the Left, by implying that the war was a hateful and hated affair arousing opposition, the opposition can be made to vanish, either by breaking its jaw or by absorbing it within the example of Jack Willow, honorably discharging his duty despite his doubts about the conflict.

Reconstruction of the image of the military in Vietnam, badly damaged throughout the 1970s, has mostly centered on the foot soldier, but in *The Hanoi Hilton* it is extended to the pilots helping prosecute the air war over North Vietnam. The film studies the determined efforts of a group of American airmen to sustain themselves with dignity under a barrage of beatings and torture by their vicious North Vietnamese captors in Hanoi's Hao Lo prison. The main character is Lt. Commander Patrick Williamson (Michael Moriarty), who, in a prelude before the main credits, makes a speech that furnishes the ideological frame in which the narrative is to be experienced and judged. Aboard an aircraft carrier in the Tonkin Gulf in 1964, Williamson is asked by a reporter why he is there and why the United States is involved. He says, "Well, I think we ought to be here. The South Vietnamese want to establish a country with values similar to our own. I think we ought to help them." He is asked what those values are, and he replies, "Freedom, [the] right to think for yourself, to follow your own faith, you know, individual freedom." He then adds, "I'm serving my country. I'm here to serve my government." The film then cuts to the credit sequence with rousing martial music. As in *Platoon*, when Taylor remarked that he was in Vietnam to fight for American society and American freedom, Williamson's claims about helping the South Vietnamese who want democracy are accepted by the film at face value as an adequate explanation of the causes of the war.

By virtue of preceding the credits and the narrative proper, the prologue is invested with a privileged status. Furthermore, Williamson's invocation of the importance of individual freedom establishes a contrast with the North Vietnamese, whose beating and torture of the prisoners reveals their disdain for this freedom. (In a Cold War twist, one of the most vicious of the torturers is a Cuban atheist named Fidel.) The airmen sustain themselves through their belief in each other and a commitment to personal decency. As in the other films we have examined, this focus upon the courage, fortitude, and camaraderie of the Americans helps to suture the divisive past for a contemporary audience and, to a limited extent, to redeem the war for new generations. About to be executed, one of the prisoners reflects in voice-over:

None of the men here . . . are ordinary. They are the bravest of the brave, people who go on even when deserted by friends and countrymen. What they carry inside of them is something very extraordinary. It is a spirit that makes all men unique. It makes them heroic. I do not believe my death will help win the war. It seems that people at home no longer care anyway. I die not so much for love of country as for love of countrymen. God bless you all.

The film contrasts the spirituality and courage of the captive Americans with the crass political opportunism and outright stupidity of antiwar activists. The captives are periodically interviewed by visiting journalists. During one interview, an arrogant television reporter deliberately conceals the torture marks on one captive's arm while pompously announcing that Bertrand Russell has convened a war crimes tribunal. In another sequence, a Jane Fonda caricature—self-important, insipid, condescending, and arrogant—interviews the men and is completely oblivious to the way she is being manipulated by their captors. She does not believe the stories of torture, says that the men seem well-fed, and gushes over the brutal camp commander, even embracing him before leaving and flashing the peace sign. A final smear against the antiwar activists comes from the camp commander. Attempting to demoralize the Americans, he tells them the real war is not being waged on the Mekong Delta but on the Washington Mall and at Berkeley, and that what isn't won on the battle-field, "your journalists will win for us on your very own doorstep." His remarks revive the familiar argument that the antiwar movement gave aid and comfort to the North Vietnamese.

Of all the films considered in this chapter, *The Hanoi Hilton* tries the hardest to discredit the resistance movement. Opposition to the war is acknowledged by these films only in terms of venal protesters and only with the most reductive rhetoric and slogans. Again, however, these por-traits of opposition to the war are historically misleading. Demonstrators marching in the street in the late 1960s were only the most visible and extreme sign of a much wider opposition. Opinion polls registered this larger, more silent group (a group whose opposition to the war was simultaneously coupled with antagonism toward the protesters). A Gallup poll taken in the winter of 1970 indicated that 46 percent of those polled favored an immediate U.S. pullout or a pullout within a year, while 38 percent stuck by President Nixon's policy of a gradual, phased withdrawal of U.S. troops. Only 7 percent favored military escalation. As Gallup remarked, the poll seemed to indicate that Americans were split into roughly equal groups differing only on the terms favored for American withdrawal.[35] Hollywood films have had extraordinary difficulty coming to terms with this pervasive, if deceptively silent, opposition, and they have tended to concentrate instead on the more easily ridiculed figure of the public protestor.

In a departure from these conventions of contemporary Vietnam pro-ductions, the antiwar movement is a patently strong presence in Oliver Stone's *Born on the Fourth of July*. Raised by his parents to revere God and country and to hate communism, sensitized by President Kennedy's warning that there will be no free America unless people are willing to sacrifice their lives, Ron Kovic (Tom Cruise) enlists in the Marines, eager for Vietnam, but returns paralyzed from a bullet wound. Embittered by the war and his paralysis, Kovic joins Vietnam Veterans Against the War, and at the 1972 Republican National Convention makes a speech against the war and the Nixon administration. Afterward, outside, he and other vets clash with the police. This scene, and an earlier sequence detailing a campus protest that elicits a violent police response, depict the social divisions that were tearing the country apart and that most major pro-ductions of the 1980s chose to ignore or to impugn through caricature. Like those other productions, however, *Born on the Fourth of July* understands the war not primarily in historical or political terms, but metaphorically, as a national and emotional trauma of the first magnitude that shattered the dreams and ideals of a generation of American youth. Kovic is embittered about Vietnam because he connects his personal loss with the wastage of the best of a generation. He insists he loves his country but not the government that sponsored the war, and in his speech on the convention floor he obliquely acknowledges the war as a struggle for national independence that antedated the introduction of U.S. troops.

These are rare and provocative perspectives for a film to offer in the 1980s, but they are given oblique and allusive expression. The reception of *Born on the Fourth of July*, evoking hostility in many quarters, indicated that these remain dangerous admissions because the wounds of the war are not yet healed and the political and ideological divisions it opened are still not closed. Despite its rather more critical discourse, however, *Born on the Fourth of July* is not fundamentally different from the other productions. It, too, understands the war as a primarily American experience, a tragedy in which the real enemy was the divisions inside American society and the American psyche, much as Taylor reflected at the end of *Platoon*. The shattering of Kovic's body parallels the shattering of society during the war, and in the film's concluding sequence, as Kovic is about to address the 1976 Democratic National Convention in New York, his final remarks invoke the necessity of personal and social healing: "Just lately I've felt like I'm home, like maybe we're home."

This presentation of Vietnam as a physical and moral tragedy corrosive to the American character, while simultaneously challenging Americans to maintain honorable and moral behavior, receives its most schematic representation in Brian De Palma's *Casualties of War*. In the film, an American patrol captures a Vietnamese girl and takes her through the bush, raping, beating, and stabbing her over a period of days, ultimately shooting her to death. The patrol's Sergeant Meserve (Sean Penn) has been thoroughly brutalized by the war; against him stands only the ineffectual Erickson (Michael J. Fox) as the voice of reason and decency. Horrified by the girl's torture and killing, Erickson says it seems that in Vietnam things are backward, that because they might die at any time, people act as if it no longer matters how badly they behave. But, he concludes, that is precisely why they have to restrain their darkest impulses, because it matters more than they know. *Casualties of War* offers a starkly dualistic account of the war as the patrol is split between Erickson and Meserve, between the forces of decency and savagery, good and evil. Eventually Erickson brings charges against the sergeant and the other members of the patrol, but this does not alleviate the guilt he feels for not preventing the girl's death. Luckily for him, however, in the film's concluding moments, in what must stand as the most amazing contextualization of the war in any of the films of this period, Vietnam turns out to have been a dream. After the war, back in the United States and civilian life, Erickson miraculously encounters the Vietnamese girl's double on a streetcar. She is now well-groomed and carries a load of books, obviously a college student. As she leaves the car, he calls to her in Vietnamese, and she turns and tells him that he has had a bad dream that is now over. They part, and Erickson glances up at the sky, visibly relieved. Vietnam turns out to have been just a bad dream, one that has left no visible scars on the victims, who return to comfort the victimizers in their time of need.

To the extent that films like *Platoon, Casualties of War,* and *Born on the Fourth of July* employ metaphors of bodily and spiritual corruption and dualities of decency and savagery contending for the American heart as modes for understanding the war, the visual and narrative strategies have changed very little since Francis Ford Coppola's metaphysical exercise *Apocalypse Now.* Indeed, the appearance of Stanley Kubrick's *Full Metal Jacket* in 1987 dramatically illustrated the degree to which Vietnam continued to linger in the cinematic imagination not as a historical event but as a symbolic and metaphysical one. Vietnam is entirely absent from the first half of Kubrick's two-part film. The initial section details the extraordinary brutalities inflicted upon Marine recruits in boot camp, as Kubrick reverses a convention of the war film whereby a drill instructor's harsh treatment effectively molds a weak recruit into a disciplined and distinguished soldier. The brutality is intensified in Kubrick's film (due in no small part to a spectacularly scatological performance by Lee Ermey) and has the opposite effect on Private Pyle, making him into a psycho killer. Internalizing the brutality that Kubrick sees as central to the military institutions of a modern state and accepting the love of rifle and killing as first principles, Pyle shoots his drill instructor and turns the gun on himself. The second section of the film follows the adventures of Private Joker (Matthew Modine) in Vietnam during the Tet Offensive as he and other Americans scour the ruins of Hue for NVA.

Neither section, however, connects with Vietnam as a war rooted in a specific time and place. Instead, they provide another vehicle for Kubrick's continued meditations upon the dehumanization of the individual by social institutions. There is no essential difference or distance, for example, between the Marine recruits at boot camp chanting "What makes the grass grow? Blood, blood, blood! What do we do for a living, ladies? Kill, kill, kill!" and a helicopter machine gunner in Vietnam sniping at fleeing peasants while saying with a laugh, "Anyone who runs is a VC. Anyone who stands still is a well-disciplined VC." Joker asks how he can shoot women and children, and the gunman replies, "Easy. You don't lead them as much." Then he adds with an excited laugh, "Ain't war hell?" As these sequences indicate, the film's narrative collapses onto a single dimension regardless of the time or place in which it is set, as Kubrick again evokes the *merkwürdigliebe,* the love of death, he explored in *Dr. Strangelove* (1964). The Marine Drill Instructor vowed to turn his recruits into "a weapon, a minister of death praying for war," and the subsequent episodes in the film bear this out as the U.S. role is defined as the infliction of slaughter and death. The film's point of view remains ambiguous and puzzling because the North Vietnamese are defined in similar terms. We see the bodies of their massacre victims in Hue (as Kubrick re-creates as fact an episode that remains murky and poorly substantiated), and in the film's climax several Americans are brutally shot to pieces by a Vietnamese sniper. All distinctions between the sides collapse as the film concentrates purely on killing and the existential imperative to survive in what several characters refer to as "a world of shit." For Kubrick, Vietnam was an exercise unleashing the primal savagery of human beings, with that savagery refined by and given an institutional basis in the Marine Corps. Given these perspectives, it is surprising that *Full Metal Jacket* did not elicit more controversy than it did.

As it did for Coppola in *Apocalypse Now*, Vietnam provided Kubrick with a basis for philosophically inclined reflections on the dark side of human life and behavior. As visually compelling as their films were, however, the Vietnam they constructed was a symbolic and mythological one, predicated on the omission of its historical specificity. But this is a function common to most of the films in the cycle. Throughout this chapter we have been noting the ideological filtering of history enacted by the contemporary Vietnam productions. A primary means of accomplishing this filtering is the omission of politically unacceptable or unpleasant features of the war. We have already noted the treatment of the domestic political context in the United States—the portrayal of opposition to the war as a dishonorable activity—but this is by no means the only instance of selective reconstruction. Viewing these films, one really has no idea why the war was fought, against whom it was waged, and on whose behalf. The forces of the NLF in South Vietnam and of the NVA, if they appear, invariably do so as distant, shadowy figures materializing like ghosts from the night or the jungle. During the war, the NLF was the subject of extensive analysis and data collection, and its organization was quite well understood. But it remains indistinct or invisible in the films, despite the fact that its remarkable success at infiltrating secured areas and recruiting peasant support constituted one of the major strategic obstacles for U.S. forces.

We have previously noted how film treatments of Vietnam have tended to ignore the roots of the struggle in the anticolonial wars fought against the French and the Japanese. They have, moreover, omitted depiction of the regime in South Vietnam, a government (actually a series of regimes) riddled by corruption and without widespread popular support. *Off Limits* (1988), an otherwise routine police thriller, is one of the few productions that attempts to evoke the corruption of Saigon, although it is unable to politically contextualize that corruption. Defense Department analysts admitted that the Vietcong had captured the Vietnamese nationalist movement, while the government of South Vietnam was regarded by many Vietnamese as the refuge for those who had allied themselves with the French in a battle against their nation's independence and whose mantle the United States had now assumed.[36] To ignore the political dimensions of the war in this way has entailed an overreliance upon misleading symbols and metaphors. Indeed, watching these films, one can erroneously believe that the NLF did not constitute a political presence in the countryside and that there was virtually no South Vietnamese ally at all. The strategic relationship between the U.S. forces and the army of South Vietnam is ignored by these films, even though it is central to an understanding of the war's controversial nature. Until the late 1960s, for example, U.S. forces were bearing the brunt of the fighting while the army of South Vietnam was assigned responsibility for the pacification program, an alignment that the policy of Vietnamization, following Tet, attempted to redress.

Furthermore, the endemic weakness and corruption of the Saigon government has been overlooked, as has the way that the ever-present threat of its collapse helped to motivate the steady increase of U.S. forces. Eventually, the deployment of those forces reached a ceiling because of domestic opposition to the war, but also because the U.S. presence was wrecking the South Vietnamese economy. A rapidly escalating inflation threatened to produce civil strife that could bring down the government the United States was pledged to protect.[37] The weakness of the Saigon government in 1965 led the United States to institute its program of air strikes against North Vietnam, called Rolling Thunder, its most sustained attempt to take the war to the North Vietnamese. An initial motive for commencing Rolling Thunder was to boost the morale in South Vietnam by demonstrating American resolve, but the air strikes continued even after American intelligence analysts realized that the bombing was not disrupting the guerrillas' supply lines or damaging Hanoi's morale. Except for *The Hanoi Hilton* and obliquely in *Bat 21* (1988), and more recently in *The Flight of the Intruder* (1991), the air war against Vietnam has not figured in the films, perhaps because of the key role the air strikes played in mobilizing opposition to the war. The ferocity of the air war, in which sorties against North Vietnam reached about 4,000 per week in 1968, with a high number of noncombatant casualties, and the secret expansion of the air war against Cambodia and Laos, became political flashpoints and created a fire storm at home. In a draft memorandum to the president in 1967, an assistant to Defense Secretary Robert McNamara noted that "The picture of the world's greatest superpower killing or seriously injuring 1000 non-combatants a week, while trying to pound a tiny backward nation into submission on an issue whose merits are hotly disputed, is not a pretty one. It could conceivably produce a costly distortion in the American national consciousness and in the world image of the United States."[38]

These considerations indicate only some of the ways that film treatments of the Vietnam war have tended to strip it of its social, historical, and political details and significance. In their place, the war is presented as a kind of bleak, existential landscape of violence and death, devoid of larger meanings. This representation lends itself especially well to an overtly symbolic and philosophical design as found in films like *The Deer Hunter, Apocalypse Now, Casualties of War, Platoon,* and *Full Metal Jacket.* A complementary focus, emerging from the presentation of Southeast Asia as an existential arena where a conflict without apparent meaning was being waged, is the celebration of brotherhood, camaraderie, and honor among the ground troops that is found in *84 Charlie MoPic, Hamburger Hill, Platoon, Gardens of Stone,* and others. This transformation of the Vietnam soldier into an ideal warrior hero works to repress and deny other components of the veterans' experience, specifically the remarkable opposition to the war by many veterans (expressed in myriad ways, from deserting to demonstrating). It also represses and denies the role played in the development of that opposition by the extreme brutality of the war (e.g., the free-fire zones, where anything living was to be killed, the defoliation and poisoning of the ecosystem and the people in it, the destruction of ancestral villages and the forced relocation of the villagers to strategic hamlets). Finally, it denies the political perceptions that shaped much of that opposition: the view of the war as a criminal enterprise or as a war against the anticolonial aspirations of a Third World country.[39] By substituting images of ideal warrior heroes for all this, history can be rewritten and difficult political issues avoided.

Both modes of cinematic construction—the metaphysical and the microcosmic—should be seen as creative solutions emerging from the avoidance of politics. Walter Wanger's recipe for the most effective means of presenting war to the American public—avoiding the politics and concentrating on the personal drama—still seems salient as a means for understanding Hollywood's representation of the Vietnam war. Unfortunately, for younger generations the portrait of Vietnam that emerges has lost its unique political and historical specificity, that which made it a war unlike any other the United States has fought. Instead, it has come to be seen as a journey into the heart of darkness, into an irrational region of savagery and destruction that defies coherent explanation. Coppola may have been more prescient than he knew when he transposed Conrad's metaphor to Vietnam, for in one way or another, American films have been extending and transposing, but still working within, the basic terms of that metaphor. In the introduction to his study of the antiwar movement, Charles DeBenedetti notes that although the war was fought in Southeast Asia and involved the Vietnamese, for proponents and critics alike discussion has tended to center upon American needs, perspectives, and motives: "Fundamentally, the war was always about America."[40] On film, too, it has always been about America. The Vietnamese disappear.

As the war undergoes conversion on celluloid from history to epic national myth, purged of the political divisions and moral controversies it aroused, it comes to be seen as a tragedy that elicited brutality and the best within the American heart. This is the function of mythology: to paper over the cracks and fissures of historical experience and oppositional political values. It is also the ideological function of film narratives, and in the Vietnam films that have now been produced, we find image and narrative working to suture the ruptures in our national consciousness, to cleanse and restore but also to omit and alter the contents of the recent unendurable past. Perhaps the most striking measure of the success of this ritual exorcism of the past was the popular acquiescence in the Bush administration's decision to wage war in the Persian Gulf. The challenges posed by the Vietnam experience to the conduct of American foreign policy apparently have been successfully managed, partly by constructing a symbology that sees Vietnam as a distant and incomprehensible event. Certainly the films about resurgent American military power and martial honor that we have been examining here and elsewhere did not create the cultural willingness to mobilize in support of a new war in a distant land involving a poorly understood culture. But neither were these films indifferent to the social currents and political atmosphere that helped to bring about this latest crusade. Films supply us with images and narratives that permit a political and social coding of the meaning of the past and the present. Looking back at the films of the 1980s—at the portrayals of aerial bombings of renegade Middle Eastern countries or at the solipsism of American military ventures in foreign lands (the disappearance, for example, of the Vietnamese and their culture from films of the Vietnam war)—it is difficult not to see the shape of our most recent war prefigured in these not-so-distant images and to feel the yearning they express for that profound and sobering national political leap from symbol to reality.

NOTES

1. See the essays in Noam Chomsky, *Towards a New Cold War* (New York: Pantheon, 1982).

2. Richard H. Schultz, Jr., and Alan Ned Sabrosky, "Policy and Strategy for the 1980s: Preparing for Low Intensity Conflicts," in *Lessons from an Unconventional War: Reassessing U.S. Strategies for Future Conflicts*, ed. Richard A. Hunt and Richard H. Schultz, Jr. (New York: Pergamon Press, 1982), p. 204.

3. Barry Dornfeld, "*Dear America*: Transparency, Authority and Interpretation in a Vietnam War Documentary," in *From Hanoi to Hollywood: The Vietnam War in American Film*, ed. Linda Dittmar and Gene Michaud (New Brunswick, NJ: Rutgers University Press, 1990), p. 296.

4. See David A. Cook, *A History of Narrative Film*, 2nd ed. (New York: W. W. Norton, 1990), pp. 882–884.

5. Albert Auster and Leonard Quart, *How the War Was Remembered: Hollywood and Vietnam* (New York: Praeger, 1988), p. 34. Julian Smith makes a similar point in *Looking Away: Hollywood and Vietnam* (New York: Scribner's, 1975), p. 23.

6. These and other public statements about the justification of the war are in *The Pentagon Papers*, vol. 2 (Boston: Beacon Press, n.d.), pp. 802, 807.

7. Frances FitzGerald, *Fire in the Lake* (Boston: Little, Brown, 1972), p. 41.

8. Quoted in Mark Green and Gail MacColl, eds., *Reagan's Reign of Error* (New York: Pantheon, 1987), p. 32.

9. *The Pentagon Papers*, vol. 2, p. 22.

10. Ibid., vol. 1, pp. 42–52.

11. Ibid., p. 180.

12. Ibid., p. 242.

13. Ibid., p. 295.

14. Ibid., p. 252.

15. Ibid., p. 324.

16. A detailed portrait of the roots of American involvement in Southeast Asia and of the early relationship of Ho Chi Minh and the OSS can be found in Archimedes L. A. Patti, *Why Vietnam? Prelude to America's Albatross* (Berkeley: University of California Press, 1980).

17. Smith discusses these productions in *Looking Away*, pp. 104–126. A comprehensive listing of fiction and documentary films about Vietnam produced between 1948 and 1989 is in Dittmar and Michaud, *From Hanoi to Hollywood*, pp. 350–373.

18. Auster and Quart, *How the War Was Remembered*, p. 62.

19. John Hellmann, *American Myth and the Legacy of Vietnam* (New York: Columbia University Press, 1986), p. 102.

20. See Jeffrey Chown, *Hollywood Auteur* (New York: Praeger, 1988), pp. 59–84.

21. See, for example, Eleanor Coppola's *Notes* (New York: Simon and Schuster, 1979).

22. Louis J. Kern, "MIAs, Myth, and Macho Magic: Post-Apocalyptic Cinematic Visions of Vietnam," in *Search and Clear: Critical Responses to Selected Literature and Films of the Vietnam War*, ed. William J. Searle (Bowling Green, OH: Bowling Green State University Popular Press, 1988), p. 48.

23. The contradictions between these two strategies are explored in Richard A. Hunt, "Strategies at War: Pacification and Attrition in Vietnam," in Hunt and Schultz, *Lessons from an Unconventional War*, pp. 23–47.

24. The concept of strategic mobility is defined and discussed in *The Pentagon Papers*, vol. 4, p. 305.

25. Ibid., p. 465.

26. Russell Stetler, ed., *The Military Art of People's War: Selected Writings of General Vo Nguyen Giap* (New York: Monthly Review Press, 1971), p. 105.

27. Kern, "MIAs, Myth, and Macho Magic," p. 48.

28. For discussion of this context, see Hellmann, *American Myth and the Legacy of Vietnam*.

29. Richard Slotkin, *Regeneration Through Violence: The Mythology of the American Frontier, 1600–1860* (Middletown, CT: Wesleyan University Press, 1973), p. 563.

30. *The Pentagon Papers*, vol. 4, pp. 527–528.

31. Pat Aufderheide makes this point in her discussion of the "noble grunt" film "Good Soldiers," in *Seeing Through Movies*, ed. Mark Crispin Miller (New York: Pantheon, 1990), pp. 81–111.

32. Data on fragging, desertion rates, and draft appeals are in Guenter Levy, *America in Vietnam* (New York: Oxford University Press, 1978), pp. 156–157; and in Robert Smith, "Disaffection, Delegitimation and Consequences: Aggregate Trends for World War II, Korea, and Vietnam," in *Public Opinion and the Military Establishment*, ed. Charles C. Moskos, Jr. (Beverly Hills, CA: Sage, 1971), pp. 221–251.

33. Thomas Prasch, "Platoon and the Mythology of Realism", in Searle, *Search and Clear*, pp. 195–215.

34. The film's funereal tone may also be due to Coppola's personal tragedy. During filming, his son died in an accident.

35. Quoted in Charles DeBenedetti, *An American Ordeal: The Anti-War Movement of the Vietnam Era*, Charles Chatfield, assisting author (Syracuse, NY: Syracuse University Press, 1990), p. 271.

36. *The Pentagon Papers*, vol. 2, p. 414.

37. See ibid., vol. 4, pp. 338–344, 364.

38. Ibid., p. 484.

39. These aspects of the cinematic portrayal of the Vietnam combat soldier are fully discussed in Harry W. Haines, "The Vietnam Veteran," in Dittmar and Michaud, *From Hanoi to Hollywood*, pp. 81–97.

40. DeBenedetti, *An American Ordeal*, p.4.

Chapter Five

Future Imperfect

In the preceding chapters, we have seen that the representational space afforded to politics in contemporary American cinema is rarely uncontested by the competing claims of narrative, spectacle, formula, and convention. The Cold War films were ideologically driven exercises in mythmaking that eventually collapsed due to a shifting international scene and the formulaic nature of their own ideology—but not before some of the most popular stars of the period were put through their paces in a series of action-adventure narratives. More interesting were the films dealing with Latin America. They attempted in a more self-conscious manner to negotiate the star-centered narratives and melodramatic conventions of Hollywood filmmaking in order to discover some political ground on which to contest the administration's policies in the Caribbean basin. The Vietnam films, by contrast, clearly showed the linkages between history and popular memory and the manner in which, by reconstructing social memory, history may be transformed by operating upon the representations that embody it for the public. The films studied in Chapters 2–4 display in varying ways and at various levels structural tensions between the political material that animates the narratives, derived as it is from the cultural world outside the films, and the requirements for acceptable representation, understood in terms of the historical stylistics of the American cinema. As the foregoing analysis has tried to show, the two are rarely homologous.

The films examined in the previous chapters engage politics in a direct and immediate way. The issues of resurgent American military power, revolution in Latin America, and the legacy of the Vietnam war were major foci of political debate and discussion throughout the 1980s. The cinematic narratives spun from these controversies emphasize the political material that informs them and place it in the foreground. Not all of the period's most striking political films, however, operated in this fashion. What of a more indirect approach to political representation? Visions of the future, understood as projections of the political present, in science fiction films of the 1980s offered a harsh portrait of ongoing socioeconomic decay. The erosion of U.S. economic power in the 1980s, and the problems of the social infrastructure associated with an ailing economy, may be symptoms of declining imperial power, and the ideological celebrations enacted by the Cold War films and, to some extent, the Vietnam war films operate as symbolic denials of this development. In this respect, the science fiction films of the 1980s, through the mediation of fantasy and the displacement of a future setting, indirectly address the declining social and economic health of American society. Their futuristic visions of social disintegration, of vast inequities of wealth and poverty, and of repressive state policies designed to maintain those divisions correlate with a domestic political landscape afflicted by the crack cocaine epidemic and the looming threats of homelessness, unemployment, and dispossession. Moreover, manipulation of the media, in these films, is one symptom of the decay of political control and democracy these films warn against. Throughout their narratives, ersatz, media-manufactured images disguise and prettify the realities of political power and economic decay. By reflecting upon this dialectic of social decline and political denial, these films are able, in the guise of fantasy, to chart some of the crises of contemporary society and, in doing so, to contextualize them within that more comprehensive set of dilemmas of politics and representation known as postmodernism. A brief consideration of postmodernism as a style and a cultural moment will be helpful here because many of the confusions and anxieties of the Reagan period can be understood as emblematic of the postmodern moment and because the group of films that we will study in this chapter employs visual and political designs that attempt to envision, and often contest, the shape of a postmodern future and the crisis of political belief and control that it entails. Furthermore, both postermodernism and the political and cultural concerns of the Reagan period can be understood as symptoms of, and responses to, an ongoing process of social fragmentation, a process imagined and visualized in stark terms in many of the decade's science fiction films. (Not all of the period's science fiction films, of course, operated in this way. Steven Spielberg's *E.T. The Extra-Terrestrial* [1982] and Ron Howard's *Cocoon* [1985] exhibit the nostalgia for a reconciliation with the past that was a defining feature of the era's political culture.)

Construed in various ways by different writers, postmodernism is an elusive concept, its meaning frequently quite fluid, but it can be understood as a phenomenon issuing, in part, from the transformation

of society from an industrial phase to a postindustrial organization, from
the coordination of labor and machinery for the production of goods to
an information-based society with a large service sector where control
over knowledge and the technologies of information generation is basic
to social control and the political management of new forms of social relationships. Writing about the contours of the postindustrial society, Daniel
Bell noted:

The sense was present—and still is—that in Western society we are in the midst
of a vast historical change in which old social relations (which were property-
bound), existing power structures (centered on narrow elites), and bourgeois
culture (based on notions of restraint and delayed gratification) are being rapidly
eroded. The sources of the upheaval are scientific and technological. But they
are also cultural. . . . The use of the hyphenated prefix post- indicates, thus, that
sense of living in interstitial time.[1]

As Andreas Huyssen points out, "postmodernism" involves questions
of both politics and culture.[2] In the cultural arena, beginning in the
1970s, the term began to be applied to a wide range of media and cultural
productions, first including architecture and later, theater, painting, film,
music, and dance. The term has come to designate a break or rupture
with the cultural politics of the modern period. This break has ramifica-
tions for cultural production at both stylistic and political levels. The art-
works of high modernism, which in their day posed a challenge to the
moral and perceptual conventions of established society, no longer do
so. The transgressions at the level of code carried out by Pablo Picasso,
James Joyce, Igor Stravinsky, or Vassily Kandinsky no longer promise
to open up a redemptive space beyond art or society or to contain a
therapeutic aesthetic effect when measured against the ills of contemporary culture. Paradoxically, the ugliness of many of the works of
aesthetic modernism, so perceived in their day, no longer seems so
disturbing. As Fredric Jameson has remarked, "Not only are Picasso and
Joyce no longer ugly; they now strike us, on the whole, as rather
'realistic.'"[3]

The failure of modern art to sustain a social critique, the breakdown of
the modernist era at the level of aesthetic code, intersects with a corresponding collapse of the systems of political and social belief that had
sustained modern, industrial culture until very recently.[4] These grand
beliefs—social progress through industrial productivity, the emancipation
of the worker, the rationality of the human personality, the inevitability
of class struggle, the dialectic between capital and labor—and other coordinates of the modern world no longer seem to provide an adequate mapping of our own postindustrial period. "In close sequence, we have lived
through the 'end of ideology', the 'end of religion', the 'end of Marxism',

the 'end of scientificity' and the 'end of evolutionism'."[5] Huyssen remarks that postmodernism operates inside a field of tension "which can no longer be grasped in categories such as progress vs. reaction, Left vs. Right, present vs. past, modernism vs. realism, abstraction vs. representation, avantgarde vs. Kitsch. The fact that such dichotomies, which after all are central to the classical accounts of modernism, have broken down is part of the shift I have been trying to describe."[6]

Daniel Bell has argued that the breakdown of such simple dichotomies is itself a symptom of the onset of postindustrial society.[7] This breakup of political frameworks and ideologies based on limited variable models has helped to produce a set of as-yet-irresolvable political and aesthetic dilemmas. As the grand beliefs that had hitherto sustained social and political reforms collapse or become less relevant for contemporary society, a crisis for political and economic reform, and for its aesthetic representation, is entailed. As we will see in the remainder of this chapter, considerable cultural anxieties seem to surround this transition, marked in part by an apparent lack of faith that the new order can be administered in a socially just manner or be controlled at all. The future slouches darkly closer in the films we'll be examining here; and, as we will see, its social structure, extrapolated from the present, is experienced as the threat of dehumanization and antidemocratic organization.

What seems to have been lost in the political strata of contemporary postmodern society is a belief in the redemptive character or the teleological direction of contemporary life. Hopes for the future as a better place and time are declining: "That such visions are no longer possible to sustain may be at the heart of the postmodern condition."[8] In this respect the collapse of the grand political paradigms and disillusionment with the potential for political reform and the seemingly intractable problems of contemporary society can incline postmodernist cultural production toward pessimistic projections of future social development: "The postmodern political condition is tremendously ill at ease with Utopianism of even a non-Messianic type, which makes it vulnerable to easy compromises with the present as well as susceptible to 'doomsday myths' and collective fears stemming from the loss of future."[9] And vulnerable as well to a fixation (seen throughout the Reagan period) upon the nostalgic past. In its desire to restore historical continuity by reclaiming the American past of small town and small government, and its attempt to reclaim political and ideological certitude in American society, the Reagan period was a reaction against this crisis of belief in history and politics. But by seeking salvation in the past, it was itself a manifestation of the problems it sought to avoid.

This sensitivity to political and representational crisis and an inclination to conceive the future in bleak terms of loss and defeat characterized a major cycle of political films in the 1980s. Standing in stark contrast with the relentlessly upbeat fantasies of Spielberg and Lucas was a group of comically charged, pessimistic, sometimes despairing dystopian thrillers. Spanning the entire decade, they include, but are not limited to, *Alien* (1979) and its sequel *Aliens* (1986), *Escape from New York* (1981), *Outland* (1981), *Blade Runner* (1982), *The Running Man* (1987), *Robocop* (1987) and its sequel *Robocop 2* (1990), and *Total Recall* (1990). Fred Glass has termed these films "new bad future" films,

The NBF scenario typically embraces urban expansion on a monstrous scale, where real estate capital has realized its fondest dreams of cancerous growth. Amnesia-stricken characters and advanced gadgetry tangle against the backdrop of a ruined natural environment, while drug gangs compete with private security forces to provide the most plentiful opportunities for employment. The heroes, by themselves or with rebellious groups, go up against the corruption and power of the ruling corporations, which exercise a media-based velvet glove/iron fist social control. This repressive structure of society provides the films' rationale for lots of action and bloodletting.[10]

In *Escape from New York*, for example, American society has been overwhelmed by crime and social decay, and a quasi-fascist police state now rules. Manhattan has been turned into a giant prison colony, its borders secured by deadly force.

While Ronald Reagan was proclaiming the glories of unfettered capitalism, and the need for increased defense spending and a reduction in social services, this cycle of dystopian thrillers began to reflect upon the likely outcome of such policies many generations from now. These films extrapolate from the contemporary ills of capitalism to a future where the social disintegration they register has greatly intensified. Pollution of the environment, urban decay and overcrowding, drugs, violent crime, outlaw gangs, media manipulation and domination of political discourse, corporate concentration and irresponsibility in the pursuit of profit, and an integrated web of corporate and political power—these pathologies of the contemporary world, projected into the future, become a means for linking the grim dystopias of cinematic fantasy with recognizable contours of our contemporary reality. The politics of the dystopian science fiction films, then, issue from real anxieties and salient features of the political landscape of the 1980s. As Glass has pointed out, many of these films "envision the world that will emerge without . . . an apocalyptic break with history."[11] This view differentiates these films from their close cousins, the postnuclear, postapocalyptic fantasies (e.g., the *Mad Max* series and its numerous offshoots). James Combs has noted the underlying crisis such films address: "An absence of optimistic images of the future suggest [*sic*] a real decline in the faith that the structure of power is equal to the task of ruling over vast time and space. The appearance of apocalyptic and death imagery in the arts offers confirmation of the pervasiveness of a 'deluge mentality' that expects the worst and finds power unable and unwilling to cope with the historical abyss that lies just ahead."[12] The postmodern crisis of belief in political reform and control is all too apparent in the visions of social decay and decrepitude these films offer.

Two of these critical dystopias—*Blade Runner* and *Total Recall*—are based on the fiction of Philip K. Dick. Another film, *Outland*, employs a scenario remarkably close to the plots of Dick's novels—a corrupt corporation operates a mining colony on one of Jupiter's moons and exploits its workers by feeding them mind-destroying drugs. The contours of the future worlds in the dystopia films, and the films' own social critiques, are quite congruent with Dick's grim future projections. It will be useful to examine the terms of Dick's social forecasting because his work can be viewed as a set of parallel reflections, companion texts to the dystopia films that, on at least two occasions, exerted a direct influence and inspiration, and because a consideration of the terms of his literary visions will help to clarify the social orientation of the dystopia films. Like these films, Dick's fiction was preoccupied with what one writer has termed "the present caught in the future."[13] In his novels and short stories of the 1950s and 1960s, Dick conjured up postindustrial landscapes of the future where fascistic corporate states waged economic and military aggression on a global and an interplanetary scale. Collectively, these novels and stories describe a future where the earth has been stripped of economic resources and society is settling into an advanced state of decay, while colonists flee Earth for other planets where they can establish mining operations, labor camps, and tourist colonies. The media have induced a state of public apathy and act as mouthpieces for the state, disseminating narcotizing talk shows and religious programming. Drugs are plentiful and are used as a means of escape from unpleasant realities.

Dick was particularly concerned with the colonization of the mind, as well as of external reality, by an omnipresent consumer society as advanced capitalism veered, in his view, toward a totalitarian system. The production of commodities, developing apace with the exhaustion of the world's natural resources, produces, in Dick's grim tales, worlds overtaken by simulacra, duplicates, pseudo realities, mechanical objects, and androids that are indistinguishable from humans. Serial production and cyborg mimicry have undermined the epistemological foundations of the human world. In *Do Androids Dream of Electric Sheep?*, the novel on which *Blade Runner* was based, the bounty hunter Rick Deckard finds himself becoming ever more machinelike, cold, and unfeeling in his relentless pursuit of the androids who desire life with an all-too-human hunger. In the novel, Deckard's motivation for hunting the androids is to earn enough money to buy a real animal. Animals have become extinct and have been replaced by electric surrogates that are virtually in-distinguishable. Deckard owns an electric sheep that he despises, and he yearns for a real ostrich or horse. The terror and despair, as well as the frequent comedy, of Dick's novels lie in the loss of distinction bet-ween the organic and the inorganic, the real and the simulacra.

Dick's pessimistic worlds where social relations and humanly produced objects turn against their makers and tower over them as alien things illustrate the Lukacsian conception of reification. The Hungarian philosopher and Marxist literary critic Georg Lukacs lamented the loss of the human in a social and technological world given over increasingly to mass production. "The transformation of the commodity relation into a thing of 'ghostly objectivity' cannot therefore content itself with the reduction of all objects for the gratification of human needs to com-modities. It stamps its imprint upon the whole consciousness of man; his qualities and abilities are no longer an organic part of his personality, they are things which he can 'own' or 'dispose of' like the various ob-jects of the external world."[14] Similarly, the Marxist critic Walter Benjamin, in his famous essay on the work of art in the age of mechanical reproduction, lamented the loss of "aura," of authentic feeling and social interconnection, in the era of mass production. That Dick is concerned with these problems, with reification, with the psychological consequences issuing from the internalization of the mechanical by the human mind, is apparent in remarks he made as part of a speech titled "Man, Android, and Machine," that he intended to deliver at a convention in London in 1976: "The greatest change growing across our world these days is probably the momentum of the living towards reflection, and at the same time a reciprocal entry into animation by the mechanical."[15] In a world of androids and electric sheep, where simulacra embodied lost or decayed attributes of human feeling, the mechanical could paradoxically come to seem more human than the human. "We humans, the warm-faced and tender, with thoughtful eyes—we are perhaps the true machines. And those objective constructs, the natural objects around us and especially the electronic hardware we build, the transmitters and microwave relay stations, the satellites, they may be cloaks for authentic living reality in-asmuch as they may participate more fully and in a way obscured to us in the ultimate Mind."[16]

For Dick, the dehumanization of contemporary life and labor, the reduc-tion of people to instruments and tools in the production process, has engendered on a massive scale the social production of inauthentic human activity.

And I would include, in this, the kind of pseudo-human behavior exhibited by what were once living men—creatures who have, in ways I wish to discuss next, become instruments, means, rather than ends, and hence to me analogues of machines in the bad sense, in the sense that although biological life continues, metabolism goes on, the soul—for lack of a better term—is no longer there or at least no longer active. And such does exist in our world—it always did, but the production of such inauthentic human activity has become a science of government and like agencies now.[17]

Fredric Jameson has suggested that the erosion of key social, political, and epistemological boundaries and distinctions, the breakdown of the signifying chain of language and communication, and the replication of pseudo events and images indistinguishable from their referents are hallmarks of the postmodern process.[18] The films in the dystopian cycle share these anxieties and examine similar processes of boundary rupture and effacement in a future where vital distinctions between human and machine, human and alien, freedom and exploitation on personal, political, and economic levels have become confused and effaced. The loss of these distinctions is symptomatic of the contemporary political crisis these films address and, in turn, represent.

Films in the critical dystopia cycle, then, conjoin some of the analytic tools of classical Marxism (e.g., reification) with a Left-leaning critique of advertising and the media in the political economy of advanced capitalism. This is clearly found in *Blade Runner*, an early and key film in the cycle and one that helped to establish the role that decor may play in evoking a grim future world. The story, lifted from Dick's novel *Do Androids Dream of Electric Sheep?*, focusing on the search by bounty hunter (or blade runner) Deckard for a group of Nexus-6 replicants who have escaped from a slave labor camp on an off-world colony, unfolds inside a grimy, perpetually rainy, dark, gray, cluttered megalopolis. A profusion of architectural styles competes in the city. Blocks of high-rise, high-tech opulence coexist with decayed, crumbling tenements. On the streets, a chaotic visual and cultural esperanto typifies the city's social and economic life. This future city is a kind of integrated global market as American corporate advertising—Pan Am—competes with ads for Japanese-produced electronic hardware and even food (sushi bars), a mix of national styles and markets that clearly embodies the loss of American economic hegemony. A huge electronic billboard hanging on the skyline alternates advertisements for Coca-Cola with a seductive Japanese woman and Japanese lettering. Denizens of the city speak a language called Cityspeak, which is, Deckard tells us, "a mish-mash of Japanese, Spanish, German, what have you." Advertisements issuing from hovercraft in the sky remind city dwellers of the pleasures to be found on off-world colonies: "A new life awaits you in the off-world colony, the chance to begin again in a golden land of opportunity and adventure."

The film's dense, richly textured cityscapes were designed by Syd Mead, who has elaborated on the visual design of the film's architecture and, in particular, its mix of opulence and decay:

Imagine vast structures resting on pylons with pyramidal bases, expressly designed to accommodate logical entry and egress from buildings that may have populations of thousands. Entire blocks of older, three-to-four story buildings are gutted, leaving their street facades intact. Electrical transformers and extensive arrays of tubing are routed, for convenience, up the facades of the "new" city high above the now sha-dowed streets. Add garish lighting, vast imaging screens and thick curb-line pillars supporting mechanical equipment above, and you have a rather depressing "alley" environment which is a negative caricature of the normal city street. The result: a maze of mechanical detail overlaid onto barely recognizable architecture producing an en-crusted combination of style which we humorously labeled "retro-deco." . . . Every-thing had to have a patina of grime and soot over a makeshift high-tech feeling.[19]

An opulent, high-tech empire sits atop the crowded multicultural ghetto below.

These rainy, dark streets through which a detective hero moves are, as many commentators have noted, indebted to the American film noir. Beyond that, however, as Giuliana Bruno has pointed out, "The link between postmodernism and late capitalism is highlighted in the film's representa-tion of post-industrial decay. The future does not realize an idealized, aseptic technological order, but is seen simply as the development of the present state of the city and of the social order of late capitalism."[20] Bruno goes on to point out that the film presents us not with a real geography but with an imaginary one. The film's city is "a synthesis of mental architectures, of topoi. Quoting from different real cities, postcards, advertising, movies, the text makes a point about the city of postindustrialism. It is a polyvalent, interchangeable structure, the product of geographical displacements and condensations."[21] In this sense, the rupture of cultural and geographical codes embodied in the design of the city's architecture evokes a postmodern landscape. *Blade Runner* embodies in visual terms the dissolution of social and cultural boundaries (and extends this dissolution via a narrative deal-ing with replicants to a subjective and psychological realm). In his essay on the symbolic functions of architecture, "Building Dwelling Thinking," Martin Heidegger remarked that boundaries define not the edges of things, where they stop, but the places from which they begin their essence, their definition.[22] Taking his cue from Heidegger, Kenneth Frampton has noted the antithesis between the bounded public space as an embodiment of the social community and its institutional basis and the placelessness of the modern environment. Only the bounded public domain, he notes, will per-mit architectural form and the communities it delineates to stand against "the endless processal flux of the Megalopolis."[23]

The rupture and explosion of architectural boundaries and styles in *Blade Runner*, by contrast, visualize the collapse of social community and history in a world of endlessly metastasizing pseudo realities and simulacra. Furthermore, this collapse of national culture and community is linked with a declining U.S. share in the world economy. The omnipresent Japanese food, language, electronic goods, and corporate advertising in this future city clearly speak to American anxieties about the Asian economic giant that made steady inroads into American markets and business operations throughout the 1980s. (Director Ridley Scott would be much more explicit in this antipathy toward Japan in his 1989 film *Black Rain*.) The economic chaos and rampant multiculturalism that prevail on the crowded streets of the film's cityscape are dynamic embodiments and prefigurations of the anxieties accompanying the contraction of U.S. economic power in the world market. Visual design here clearly speaks to contemporary dilemmas.

But the dense, high-tech look of the film—the megalopolis and its huge buildings with twinkling lights, evoked through forced perspective and elaborate movements by hovercars on diagonals in apparent depth—coupled with Vangelis's soaring music score emphasizes decor to the extent that it becomes a primary subject of the film and a major carrier of its discourse. There is a problem here. Concerned to criticize the mechanization of human life, Dick as author never becomes overwhelmed by the futuristic technologies he evokes. In the film, however, the size, scale, and immense visual intricacy of the urban and technological decor overwhelm the viewer, confusing and making equivocal the film's discourse. The elaborate special effects embody a technological fascination that runs counter to the major conceptual premise of the novel, which is that entropy and "kipple" are overtaking the human world. In Dick's novel, as in the film, the characters wander listlessly amid a landscape marred by overproduction; but in the novel technology is running down, as are human lives, and this is given a kind of ontological basis in the law of "kipple," the tendency of all organic and inorganic objects to dissolve into a shapeless and decayed mass. One of the characters in the novel describes it this way: "Kipple is useless objects, like junk mail or match folders after you use the last match or gum wrappers or yesterday's homeopape. When nobody's around, kipple reproduces itself. For instance, if you go to bed leaving any kipple around your apartment, when you wake up the next morning there's twice as much of it. It always gets more and more." The first law of kipple is that kipple drives out nonkipple. "No one can win against kipple. . . . It's a universal principle operating throughout the universe; the entire universe is moving toward a final state of total, absolute kippleization."

The only correlative of kipple in the film is the accelerated decrepitude of the replicants, which are programmed to have a life span of only four

years. This is a fail-safe device engineered by their corporate makers to prevent the replicants from becoming fully human. While the replicants live,
they gradually evolve human emotions. The film's narrative counterpoints
Deckard's hunt for the replicants and his attempts to quash his growing
empathy for them with the attempt of their leader, Roy Batty, to search for
his corporate makers to demand more life, an extension of their program.
Harrison Ford plays Deckard in a very cold, almost affectless way in order
to suggest the android qualities of the human. By contrast, Roy Batty, fully
human in every way, undertakes a quest that is a Promethean attempt to
recover and reinstate the fires of creation in his own being.

Despite the ambiguities of the film's visual design, its narrative does
borrow the political contours of Dick's fiction and, in doing so, begins
to reinforce some basic conventions of the dystopia cycle. For example,
consistent with the presentation of the corporate state in other films, the
Tyrell Corporation's tentacles of power have an interplanetary reach. The
corporation has designed the Nexus-6 replicants to supply slave labor to
the off-world colonies and the state's security apparatus. The police and
bounty hunters, in turn, are employed to provide security for the corporation's economic operations and to prevent the replicants from returning to Earth—and, should they return, to eliminate them. "Commerce
is our goal here at Tyrell," the president of the corporation says. "More
human than human is our motto."

The amorality and ruthless quest for power of the film's corporate state
extend both outward through physical space and inward through psychic
space. "I am the business," the beautiful replicant Rachael (Sean Young)
admits sorrowfully when she realizes that she is not human, as she has
believed, but merely an android. Tyrell has implanted a false memory
system inside Rachael, which had been derived from the real memories
of his niece. "If we give them a past, we create a cushion or pillow for
their emotions and consequently we can control them better," Tyrell says,
explaining the need to use an ersatz past for the replicants in order to
subject them to the corporation's control. Paradoxes of time and memory
are thereby evoked as distinctions between past and present, real event
and remembrance, collapse. The android self with its stock of implanted
memories embodies the internalization of commerce, and to the extent
that it can function successfully as a human simulacrum it also embodies
the estrangement of the real self in a world of copies. In this dystopic,
postmodern landscape, the photographic image also becomes a
simulacrum, no longer able to certify truth. Rachael carries a photograph
that she believes shows her as a little girl sitting on her mother's knee.
The photograph ostensibly documents her past, but it is a fake, correlated
with a memory implant. Photography, as a medium capturing a
manipulated past, can no longer function as a document of the present,
the ostensibly true.

Like other films we have been examining throughout these chapters, *Blade Runner* very clearly shows the limits restricting a commercial film-maker working for the major studios. Despite its flamboyant film noir style, the movie is considerably more hopeful than Dick's novel. The film's androids, developing human emotions, eventually attain the capacity to experience real empathy. Rachael is able to fall in love with Deckard, and Deckard's life is spared by Roy Batty, who, in his final seconds of ex-istence, has come to cherish all life, anyone's life. Dick's androids, by contrast, could not experience empathy, and this was the major factor enabling their detection. When Deckard makes love with Rachael in the novel, it is a cold and empty experience, and he realizes it was a ploy on her part to dissuade him from hunting her fellow replicants. The end of the novel saw the characters forever trapped by the emotional devasta-tion and epistemological confusions wrought by the endless reproduction of ersatz life forms. In the final pages, Deckard, yearning for a live animal, discovers a toad in the desert and triumphantly returns home with it, achieving a kind of redemption and transcendent peace with his discovery. At home, however, he finds that it, too, is merely an electrical simulacrum. His wife calls an animal accessories store to order one pound of artificial flies and to make arrangements for periodic tongue adjustments because it will have to be put through its feed cycle regularly. In the film, by contrast, an affirmative ending was added by the studio, which feared that the film would otherwise be too depressing and confusing for a com-mercial audience. As the film ends, it transpires that Rachael does not have a termination date after all, that she can live as long as a normal human being. She and Deckard leave the city, flying to a lovely country setting (in a series of shots that were apparently lifted from outtakes for Stanley Kubrick's *The Shining*). Although this final scene provides a way out of the black box of the narrative, it doesn't entirely diminish the portrait of powerful corporations extending the principles of commodity production (e.g., planned obsolescence) to newly invented life forms and the inflection of the decor of the cityscape with a political critique.[24] It does, however, represent a commercial concession that violates the political logic of the novel. It should be noted, however, that the direc-tor's cut of *Blade Runner* was restored and was presented in limited public screenings in 1991.

Furthermore, the emphasis upon spectacle in *Blade Runner* and in the other critical dystopias points up the instability of political content within the formal structures of commercially marketed films. The foregrounding of spectacle (e.g., the emphasis upon special effects) threatens to under-mine the possibility of political critique. The spectacular image functions as a concentrated form of capital making visible the vast economic resources behind the production of that image. In a $50 million film, ac-cording to Hollywood wisdom, every dollar should be visible on screen.

Fascination with, and consumption of, the spectacular image integrates the spectator, via the evocation of his or her pleasure, into the networks of production that have made such an image possible. This, in turn, can impose a profound limit upon the political discourse of the films. Their critique of the corporate domination of contemporary life and culture, for example, cannot advance in a coherent fashion through reliance upon the spectacular image, since the spectacular special effect image itself reproduces and embodies the capital-intensive, consumption-oriented social relationships these films ostensibly criticize. Spectacle, in this case, enforces political equivocation. As Guy Debord has noted, spectacle can be "the guardian of sleep."[25]

Throughout previous chapters, we have observed how the visual and narrative structures of American films define the political realm in a provisional and limited way. The political discourse of American films is rarely free of ambiguity, ambivalence, and contradiction. The use of spectacle by the dystopia cycle furnishes another illustration of the ways that formal design may contradict, or be opposed to, critical social or political content. These remarks are not meant to negate the critical function of these films, but merely to qualify it, for despite the limitations of coding political discourse as spectacle in the blockbuster film, the dystopia cycle does offer a nightmare exploration of the social and psychological legacies of postindustrial society. In the information age, computers and electronic communication have replaced the heavy industry of the modernist period, political control is exercised via information monopolies and mass media networks, and information has become a commodity and control over its circulation a means of accumulating capital—these phenomena are regarded by the films as developments that pose challenges to established personal identities and social stability. Moreover, these narrative features are clear analogues of contemporary crises developing in the United States throughout the 1980s: the closing of many industrial plants and the growth of endemic unemployment in those regions of the country that depended on them, the rise of the information professions for which an earlier generation of skilled labor had not been trained and was unemployable, the growth of service-sector jobs carrying few benefits and paying wages insufficient to live on, and the use of the media to engineer political imagery and campaign messages that ignore or obfuscate the foregoing.

Anxiety over the inability to define the integrity of the boundaries of the human self in an era of rampant mass production is central to most of the films in the cycle and is a key means of coding, in futuristic terms, contemporary processes of social and political disintegration. The films posit a breakdown of self, of subjectivity, of the body itself; and these visions of disintegrating individuals, of android selves, or of psyches overwhelmed by the flux of daily life can be seen in part as grim fictional transformations of a larger and more pervasive contemporary phenomenon: the threats to personal survival in the economy of the 1980s, of which the explosive growth of the homeless underclass in American society was the most dramatic and visible sign. Inflation, the gutting of social services, and the loss of low-cost housing combined in the 1980s to deny hundreds of thousands of Americans the basic human right to shelter and economic survival. Throughout the decade, these tattered, dazed ghosts of former lives and selves grew in numbers in the major cities, bereft of jobs, food, clothing, and networks of social support. As this population grew, and despite the myth that they were all the result of new policies regarding release of the mentally ill into the community, a collective anxiety passed through those still working, still with families, in the realization that they, too, could be cast adrift or cannibalized by the economy. No wonder threats to the self and to personal and psychological survival are experienced so intensely throughout the dystopia cycle.

Furthermore, consistent with the critique of reification and the economic injustices in contemporary American society, corporations integrated with the state and the media are the frequent culprits and villains in these films. In *Blade Runner*, the rebellion led by Roy Batty is a quest not just for self-knowledge but for political freedom as well. The rebellion against the father (in the form of Tyrell) is also a rebellion against the corporate state. As simulacra, the androids are members of a series without an originating term. The human appearance of the Nexus-6 androids, especially their assumption of emotions, challenges the status of the authentically human. Rachael's ability to fall in love, in contrast with Deckard's cold, methodical bounty hunting, makes her seem more human than he. As J. P. Telotte has pointed out, the doubling of the human body and the creation of artificial humans are narrative devices present throughout the history of science fiction films.[26] What distinguishes the use of this motif in the current cycle is its integration with an extrapolated vision of the social decay of contemporary society. The logic of production eventually extends to the human body itself, "more human than human." Tyrell boasts to Roy that they made him as well as they knew how, to which he angrily replies, "But not to last."

An earlier film by Ridley Scott, *Alien* (1979), is informed by many of the same anxieties, which, as in *Blade Runner*, seem to be partly based in and motivated by popular fears about the occupational displacement, the need for retooling, and the job loss accompanying the shift from an industrial-based economy to one based on information and computer networks,[27] as well as the anxieties about the ability to survive in an economy that does not secure basic human needs for all of its citizens. *Alien* deals with the battle aboard a commercial towing vehicle, the Nostromo, between its human crew and an alien intruder organism. As in *Blade Runner*, corporate capitalism has expanded to an interplanetary scale. The Nostromo is returning to earth with 20 million tons of minerals for refinery processing. The company to which the ship belongs has pro-grammed the computer, known as Mother, to alter the ship's course so that it can bring back one of the alien organisms for use in the company's weapons research division. Unknown to the crew, the company has placed an android on board. Science Officer Ash, the android, has been designed by the company to ensure the safe return of the alien organism, even at the cost of the crew members' lives. As this is indeed what happens—the creature wipes out all of the crew members but one—the company's economic imperatives are seen as especially ruthless. (It is in this regard that the ship's name, Nostromo, is contextualized. It comes from Joseph Conrad's novel of the same name, about a nineteenth-century silver mine and the macro forces of capitalism, imperialism, and revolution.)

The ship itself is something of an anomaly. In its guidance, medical, and command centers, it contains an array of advanced electronic gadgetry that beeps, blips, and gleams. Its systems seem completely automated. The crew sleeps in a state of suspended animation during their long years traveling through space, and they are awakened by a previously pro-grammed command from the ship's computer. In the bowels of the ship, Parker (Yaphet Kotto) and Brett (Harry Dean Stanton) maintain the Nostromo's engines. In contrast with the gleaming, orderly, sterile quarters above, Parker and Brett's world is cramped, dark, and wet, punctuated by the hiss of steam and the pounding of engines. It is the world of heavy industry, and Parker and Brett, as proletarians, worry about being underpaid and exploited by their superiors. The visual design of the ship, then, suspends in symbolic dialectical tension two moments of history, two different social and economic systems, the industrial and the postindustrial. The Nostromo contains a vestige of the old within the forms of the new. Despite being programmed and run by the computer, the ship requires its crew of laborers to stoke the engines. Downstairs, the ship rumbles, hisses, and clangs while upstairs are the click of keyboards and the beeping of urgent electronic messages.

In addition to this visual metaphor, the film portrays the ship as if it were animate. In one of the opening shots, a computer projects an elaborate array of data on the visor of a helmet, but the helmet is empty. No one's face is visible inside, yet the data projection continues indepen-dent of human presence or witness. As the camera subsequently tracks through the empty ship, a rubber toy is glimpsed hanging in front of one of the computer screens, and a piece of paper flutters briefly, as if stirred by an unseen presence. The ship is silent, apparently without human presence (all of the crew are in hypersleep) but very much animate. The ship's design deliberately confuses mechanical and organic features. The insides appear to be part of a living organism, with pipes and tubing sug-gesting a skeletal and circulatory system. This fusion of the mechanical and the organic is a key element of the film's visual design, and it extends beyond the design of the Nostromo to include the rock formations on the deserted planet where the alien is found and the huge alien spaceship discovered on that planet. Through a vague gestalt all of these shapes and objects suggest organic life forms, tissued, ribbed, veined, with vertebrae and spines. Exploring the deserted planet, the crew enters an alien spaceship through huge vaginal openings and discovers the skeleton of a dead alien fused with its observation platform. Remarking upon these boundary confusions, one of the crew comments, "It's fossilized. It looks like it's growing out of the chair." The boundaries of the body and of organic life itself are no longer certain. Capitalizing on these confusions, the alien invades the bodies of its human hosts and uses them to nurture its own embryonic life form until, in a bloody birth, it bursts through the stomachs of its hosts, destroying them in the process. Loose on board the ship, the alien fuses with its design, hiding in its corridors, camouflaged among its piping and tubing. It destroys most of the crew by advancing upon them silently and invisibly, striking from the depths of the ship.

The crew is as much a victim of the ship (the ship as a visual incarnation of a historical transition from industry to information, from class struggle to more diffuse structures of exploitation encompassing proletarian and professional alike) and its company's directives as it is of the alien. The film examines the breakdown and extinction of human identity and social relations during a period of historical transition. The crew members have few emotional bonds linking them together. Instead, strictly professional identities and relationships prevail. Each member of the crew efficiently attends to his or her duty, and their social system is so thoroughly coded by the machinery of their work and its attendant responsibilities as to bypass and make irrelevant the ties of friendship, the tensions or desires of sexuality, and the social marking of gender. The crew is composed of males and females, and it is accepted that each gender is capable of leadership and professional responsibilities. In this respect, the film is almost postfeminist in its view of the relations between men and women.[28] However, the affectless and mechanical nature of their relationships make the crew members little more than extensions of their electronic machinery and computer screens. Through its narrative and its metaphorical visual design, the film posits human identity as an anachronism in a superrationalized society where regimentation and mechanization have bypassed the class consciousness of Parker and Brett, which belongs to an earlier, eclipsed moment of history. Aboard the Nostromo, professionals as well as proletarians are considered expendable by the company. Faced with the alien threat and with betrayal by Mother and the company, the human group has few internal resources to use in its defense. Lacking internal cohesiveness and bonds of camaraderie, its members become easy targets for the alien.

The film's visual design and narrative address the increasingly peripheral nature of human beings and human labor in a mechanized world where organisms become commodities (in this case the alien as a future weapons system) and where the mechanical simulacrum (Ash) becomes indistinguishable from the human and, alone among the crew members, employs the language of humanism. Ash defends his decision to allow the alien on board on the grounds that he is thereby saving the life of one of the wounded crew members. The human members of the crew seem like affectless androids, while the android (treacherously, it transpires) lays claim to humanist compassion. The vital distinctions that shape human society have broken apart. The resulting anxieties are given political inflection by equating the loss of the human with reification and market production. The company, Mother, and Ash form the coordinates of an oppressive social world that excludes from its operations and its values the human group aboard the Nostromo. Dallas (Tom Skerritt), the captain, says of their relationship with the company, "Standard procedure is to do what the hell they tell you to do." As in *Blade Runner* and *Robocop*, the alienation of human life and relationships in a future world where the products of social labor return to dominate their makers, as do Ash and Mother, evokes the famous passage by Marx: "It is nothing but the definite social relation between men themselves which assumes here, for them, the fantastic form of a relation between things."[29] From this standpoint, the title of the film designates not only the alien organism that decimates the crew but also the human crew itself, displaced by the logic of Mother and the company, enclosed by the mechanized world of the Nostromo, adrift in the void of space.[30]

As we have seen, the films in the dystopia cycle emphasize the reification of social life, the translation of the products of human labor into animate things that come to seem more human than human and that represent the dispersal of signs, the breakdown of codes, the dissolution of boundaries which typify a postmodern condition. It is in this disruption of code, sign, and boundary that the political discourse of these films resides, but it is linked to an enveloping pessimism that signifies the contemporary crisis of belief in the possibility of political control and reform. The center cannot hold, yet as it tears apart, reformatory or revolutionary possibilities fail to appear. Instead, exploitation and coercion are dispersed across the social spectrum. These issues receive their most intelligent and deliberate working out in the pair of films made by Dutch director Paul Verhoeven, *Robocop* and *Total Recall*.

Before exploring those, however, it should be emphasized that the dystopia cycle is not as uniform or homogeneous a group of films as it may appear to be. These films do not present a uniformly Left-leaning analysis or critique of contemporary culture and society. Like the cycles of films we have examined in previous chapters, this one, too, is marked by internal contradictions and ambivalences. While its critique and mistrust of the corporate state place it at some distance from the established ideologies of the Reagan period, this critical detachment can be an antidialectical one that, at times, threatens to lapse back into the structures of thought and society it seeks to criticize. At their most conservative, the dystopia films may even be inflected with Cold War perspectives. The sequel to *Alien*, for example, directed by James Cameron, fresh from the success of *The Terminator*, uses the formulas and anxieties of the dystopia cycle to construct a futuristic Cold War parable about imperial intervention in the Third World. Preserved in suspended animation for 57 years following her escape from the Nostromo and its alien visitor, Ripley (Sigourney Weaver) has been drifting through space in her shuttle when the company rescues her and persuades her to return to LV-426, the planet from which the alien was retrieved. The company has been maintaining a colony of Terra-formers on LV-426. These 70 families have been working to install an atmosphere processor manufactured by the company that will generate a breathable atmosphere on the planet. The company, however, has lost contact with the Terra-formers and, alarmed by Ripley's warnings of the destructive potential of the alien, decides to send her with a company of colonial Marine Corps to investigate.

Whereas the first film concentrated on the moral and physical displacement of the human characters by a ruthless corporation and a stark, information-based environment, the sequel is presented more straightforwardly as a Cold War combat film. The bulk of the action focuses on the clashes between the Marines and the colony of aliens. Cameron's staging of the combat footage enables him to rework the dystopia formulas in a less radical, more conservative direction that resonates with the anxieties of resurgent America. The Marines are a counterinsurgency presence with airborne and land-rover strike capabilities. They boast state-of-the-art weaponry, but their encounter with the aliens is marked by the anxieties about weakness and defeat so familiar in the Reagan period. The film contains several allusions to Vietnam. Before embarking on their mission, one of the Marines asks his commanding officer, "Is this going to be a stand-up fight, sir, or another bug hunt?" In other words, will they be allowed to fight (a popular explanation of the Vietnam defeat, as we have seen, was that the military was not allowed to try hard enough), or will they spend their time and energy searching for an unseen and elusive enemy? *Aliens* employs a familiar convention of the Vietnam films: The Marines are commanded by a green, flustered lieutenant who makes crucial strategic errors. When the aliens attack, the Marines are not permitted to fire their weapons because they are too close to the colony's nuclear processor. Not being allowed to fight, in an obvious metaphoric parallel to Vietnam, many of the soldiers are killed and the remainder quickly withdraw. Shamed by the outcome of events, one of the survivors tells Carter Burke, the company's representative, "Maybe you ain't been keeping up on current events, but we just got our asses kicked, pal." The current events symbolically alluded to include not only Vietnam, of course, but the whole smorgasbord of perceived strategic defeats for the United States, from Afghanistan and Iran to Nicaragua.

The struggle for LV-426 faithfully reflects Reagan-era perceptions about the nature of Third World revolution. Threatening the colonists, the aliens are an outside force. They are not indigenous to the planet, thus mirroring in science fiction terms the Reagan administration's assertions about Third World revolutions directed from abroad by Moscow. As in Grenada, where the United States intervened ostensibly to aid threatened American students, the Terra-formers on LV-426 are a beleaguered collection of families, and it is the threat to the family that generates Ripley's outrage and compels her to accompany the Marines. (Family values are reasserted as well through a subplot dealing with the maternal bonding that develops between Ripley and a surviving child.) The film's ultimate imperial fantasy lies in its easy acceptance of the use of nuclear weapons for defeating Third World rebellions. Most of the Marines are wiped out by the aliens, and Ripley and the survivors decide that the only way to be sure of victory is to leave the planet and nuke it from space, which is exactly what they do. "It's the only way to be sure," Ripley emphasizes. In Vietnam, policymakers could only dream of this option, but as a futurist in tune with the political currents of his time and as a filmmaker who wishes to translate dominant cultural anxieties into box-office success, Cameron permits his characters the luxury of this recourse. The only character who tries to dissuade Ripley and the others from nuking the planet is Carter Burke, the corrupt company representative. Burke points out that they can't arbitrarily decide to wipe out another species, that no one has this right. However, in a significant political maneuver, this ecologically based reasoning is invalidated by Burke's hidden agenda. Like Ash in the previous film, Burke is planning to smuggle an alien embryo back to Earth, where he believes he can sell it for millions of dollars to the company's weapon research division. While the film, therefore, condemns the aggressive capitalism of Burke and, to some extent, of the company that stands behind him, it accepts the imperial military policies that are the prop of an interplanetary economic empire. Aliens has the ideological schizophrenia common to many of the period's biggest box-office successes.

In Aliens, Cameron notably revised the technology-is-bad thesis of his earlier film, The Terminator (1984). Unlike Ash in the first film, the android Bishop in Aliens turns out to be trustworthy and heroic, saving the lives of Ripley and the remaining Marines. Moreover, Bishop has his own charming and quirky personality. Referred to as a "synthetic" by Burke, Bishop replies, "I prefer the term 'artificial person,' myself." Moreover, in Ripley's climactic showdown with the alien queen, she operates a mechanical loader that serves as both defensive armor and weapon. Her human body fused with the loader, she knocks the alien queen out of the spaceship.

The Terminator, by contrast, provides a much grimmer, far more pessimistic vision of the future. While this film postulates an apocalyptic break with present history and therefore is not a true member of the dystopia cycle (as here defined), it nevertheless will be useful to examine it briefly because it was so phenomenally popular, helped launch Cameron's career, and does intersect with the cycle. The world in A.D. 2029 is a postapocalyptic world run by machines that triggered a nuclear war to exterminate their human makers. In the film's somewhat nonsensical premise, a huge defense network computer, "hooked into everything," decides to exterminate society. After the war, the surviving humans are rounded up into extermination camps or used as slaves who load bodies into the disposal units that run 24 hours a day. Guerrilla war breaks out between the hunter-killer machines and the few surviving humans. The narrative is constructed as a time-loop paradox in which a soldier of the future, Kyle (Michael Biehn), is sent back to Los Angeles, circa 1984, to protect the woman who will become the mother of the man who leads the guerrillas in their battle against the machines. The machines, for their part, have created a terminator, a cyborg (part man, part machine), and have sent it back through time to hunt and kill Sarah Conner (Linda Hamilton).

The film develops as an extended chase with Kyle trying to protect Sarah and to elude or kill the terminator (Arnold Schwarzenegger). The narrative is a time-loop paradox because the man who sends Kyle back into the past is John Conner, Sarah's son. Furthermore, while hiding from the terminator, Sarah and Kyle make love, with Kyle thereby becoming John Conner's father.[31] Like the replicants in *Blade Runner* and the androids in the *Alien* films, the terminator is virtually indistinguishable from its human opponents. Inside it has a hyperalloy combat chassis controlled by a microprocessor, while outside it is covered with living human tissue—flesh, hair, blood—that has been specially grown for the cyborgs. As Kyle says, "These are new. They look human. Sweat, bad breath, everything. Very hard to spot." Like the dystopia films, *The Terminator* focuses on the loss of human feeling and identity in a totalitarian world. The bleak world of the future is a nightmare of pain, violence, and death, where the surviving humans have to disconnect themselves from their emotions in order to elude the machines. Looking at Kyle's scars, Sarah murmurs, "So much pain." Kyle replies, "Pain can be controlled. You just disconnect it." Sarah responds, "So you feel nothing?"

The film is ferociously edited for maximum emotional impact, but it lacks the political and philosophical nuances of *Blade Runner, Alien,*

Robocop, and *Total Recall.* Indeed, to the extent that the machines act for themselves and are not portrayed as being part of a specified political or economic system that has its roots in the present period, the film's discourse becomes depoliticized. In place of political analysis, the film offers a survivalist ethic. The survivalist movement of the early 1980s was composed of disenchanted individuals convinced that the country was sliding to hell on a greased rail and who, to escape a nuclear war they considered inevitable or a civil conflagration brought about by racial or economic strife, provisioned themselves to survive in the mountains of the western United States. At the end of the film, with the terminator defeated and Kyle dead, Sarah drives off to the mountains, equipped as a guerrilla fighter of the future. She knows a holocaust is coming, and the sky darkens as she drives away. The film's anxieties about nuclear conflict resonate with the tensions of the period and with Reagan's apocalyptic musings, but, as in *Aliens,* Cameron proves himself to be an adept manipulator of the zeitgeist while lacking the ability or the inclination to probe critically at the social roots of the popular fears he manipulates.

The ambivalence about radical politics that runs through some of these films, even as they project the onset of totalitarian forms of social control, is perhaps seen most clearly in *The Running Man.* Conceived as another of Arnold Schwarzenegger's increasingly popular productions during the decade, the film presents a future society, circa 2017, where the economy has collapsed, food and natural resources are in short supply, and a police state uses the media to enforce its rule. Schwarzenegger plays a helicopter pilot named Richards who becomes a state criminal when he refuses to fire on 1,500 unarmed civilians during a food riot. Perversely, the state publicly accuses him of doing so and broadcasts its accusations via the media. As in *Blade Runner,* huge electronic billboards ring the sky in Los Angeles. Programming on the billboards is operated by ICS, an information and entertainment network whose slogan is "Seeing Is Believing." This slogan is an effective signifier of the mechanisms of social and political control. The slogan draws its power and appeal from a modernist faith in the truthfulness and reliability of photographic media and visual reproductions.

In a postmodernist context, however, where the connections between images and their referents have broken, seeing and believing have been sundered from one another, and to assert the contrary is to engage in sophistry and deceit, precisely what the Entertainment Division of the Justice Department in the film desires. A society of the spectacle has emerged, where the criminal justice system has become theater, disseminated to the masses by the ICS television network. The most popular game show is "The Running Man," a show where alleged criminals are hunted and killed on-air—where, as the host, Damon Killian, says, "unstoppable network stalkers give criminals, traitors, and enemies of the state exactly what they deserve." Richard Dawson, who had been a real television game show host, plays Killian. His presence, therefore, effaces the boundaries between "real" game shows and their fictional, futuristic counterparts. The syntax of the show—its rapid editing, excessively loud, manically paced music, and its frenzied, screaming fans—draws from the elements of contemporary television, thereby establishing a clear continuum between contemporary spectacle and its more repressive futuristic counterpart.

The film's political critique, however, soon becomes immobilized by the very spectacle it initially sought to contextualize. Killian pressures the Justice Department to release Richards to his custody so Richards can become a contestant on the show. The film then settles into a prolonged chase format as Richards is stalked by the network's hunters, whom he dispatches in turn. Eventually he hooks up with the political underground and leads them to the studio, where he dispatches Killian, whose death is cheered by the fans with the same mindless glee the deaths of previous running men had elicited. The formulas of action melodrama and the dictates of the happy ending displace a coherent social critique. Earlier in the film, Richards tells one of the rebels, "I'm not into politics, I'm into survival." These words are certainly the register of a dark cultural moment, as the social safety net was cut from under hundreds of thousands of poor Americans during the 1980s, landing them on the streets and in poverty, reducing life to the terms of sheer personal survival. But Richards's words also express the political limitations of pop-Orwellian films like *The Running Man* and conservative dystopias like *Aliens*, which accept as inevitable the corruption and ruthlessness of the corporate states they describe. Moreover, Schwarzenegger's hulking, golemlike presence as a major figure on the pop-cultural landscape offers an iconographic enactment of the virtues of the individual will to power and survival over those of organized political reform.

The political ambivalence and limited self-awareness of the dystopia cycle remain characteristics of its two most outstanding exemplars, Verhoeven's *Robocop* and *Total Recall*. In Verhoeven's work, however, these limitations do not seem to be as much a product of the filmmaker as of the generic requirements for blockbuster production. Indeed, without those formulaic necessities, one feels that Verhoeven would have gone much farther, both in his political critique and in his spectacularly violent tableaus. *Robocop*, for example, the better of the two films, was far more violent in the director's than in the studio's cut. More important, it stands as a grotesquely funny and grim indictment of the economic policies of the Reagan period. The film's sharp satire is the result of a foreign director viewing American culture with the acuteness that only the outsider can possess. *Robocop* was Verhoeven's first American film after a number of Dutch productions, including *Turkish Delight* (1973), *Soldier of Orange* (1978), *The Fourth Man* (1979), and *Spetters* (1981). Verhoeven was determined to emulate and surpass the pyrotechnics and gory theatrics of the contemporary American action films he studied, such as *Rambo*, while charging the formulas with his own philosophical and political interests and perceptions. The result, especially in *Robocop*, is that genuine rarity, a thinking person's action film whose politics are considerably left of center. The film evokes the urban decay of the 1980s and the economic chaos and terror faced by those cut from access to social services, and with fine comic anger it links the transformation of social services into profit-making business operations with the resulting social alienation and disintegration. The social Darwinism that underlay Reagan-era economic reforms—the callous commitment to the survival of the fittest implicit in cutting economic supports from the poorest and most vulnerable sectors of the population—is identified in the film with the activities of characters who are gangsters and criminals presiding over empires of theft and murder. Verhoeven's achievement in this film is to inflect its narrative with this political dimension without ever seeming heavy-handed or to be forcing an ideological point, and without damaging its elegant black humor. The political meanings, quite simply, grow organically from the narrative and its contemporary social referents.

In *Robocop*'s future society, amplifying the domestic reforms of the Reagan period, the private sector is completely deregulated and has taken over so many of the state's social service activities as to become indistinguishable from the state. The Detroit police force is funded and run by Omni Consumer Products (OCP) under a contract with the city. OCP's president, Richard Jones (Ronny Cox), boasts that OCP has traditionally gambled in markets considered nonprofit. Prisons, hospitals, space exploration, and the military are all run as businesses by OCP, whose growth is tied to a government that is amenable to privatizing social services so that they can become profit-making operations. Reagan-era deregulation and privatization conjure up this futuristic nightmare. OCP plans to build a new Delta City where Old Detroit now stands. Control of the police force is part of the OCP strategy because it will enable OCP to break the police union and play upon public fears of escalating crime in order to introduce its newest product, ED-209, an enforcement robot programmed for urban pacification. ED-209 is a supercop that can operate 24 hours a day, needs no food nor rest, and has superior firepower. OCP anticipates that its success in Old Detroit will make ED-209 the hot military product for the next decade. The language of urban pacification and the merging of the police and a military presence in the inner cities enable the film to present the United States as a kind of future Third World country, riven by huge gulfs between rich and poor and where the corporate sector allies itself with the military to maintain its control over the economy. As Richard Jones says, "We practically are the military."

Not since Charles Chaplin's *Monsieur Verdoux* (1947), in which he played a bank-clerk-turned-mass-murderer, has an American film been this blackly humorous in its equation of free enterprise with theft and murder. OCP's chairman of the board, in a speech constructed with direct references to Reagan's economic and tax policies, makes it clear that state benevolence has permitted OCP's corporate expansion in ways that hold hostage the public's welfare. "Old Detroit has a cancer. The cancer is crime, and it must be cut out before we employ the two million workers who will breathe life into this city again. All those shifts in the tax structure have created an economy ideal for corporate growth. Community services, in this case law enforcement, have suffered. I think it's time we gave something back." What OCP wishes to give back is ED-209, which will enable it to reap additional profits from the very problems it has helped to create with the aid of the government-sponsored overhaul of the tax system. Unfortunately, ED-209 kills an OCP employee during its test demonstration. Blasted by the robot's machine gun, the employee's bullet-riddled body symbolically falls atop the miniature model of Delta City. Gazing at the blood-soaked corpse and the model city's wreckage, Jones remarks with fine comic understatement, "I'm sure it's only a glitch." Jones is in league with Clarence Boddicker, the crime boss of Old Detroit. Jones intends to use Boddicker and his gang to create markets for drugs, prostitution, and gambling among the two million workers who will build Delta City. "Virgin territory for the man who knows how to open up new markets," Jones tells Boddicker. In the logic of the film's future world, a market is a market, irrespective of the human or social damage inflicted.

Jones's plans, however, are frustrated when ED-209 misfires and kills the employee. A rival executive presents the Robocop program as a backup plan. In contrast with the entirely mechanical ED-209, Robocop is a cyborg, part human and part machine. A human candidate quickly becomes available when a Detroit police officer named Murphy (Peter Weller) is nearly killed in a shoot-out with Boddicker's gang. One of Murphy's arms has been shot off, and the remainder of his body has been ruined by gun blasts. Surgeons working for OCP are able to fuse Murphy's remaining parts with the Robocop chassis. They sever his remaining arm to achieve total body prosthesis, and they blank his memory circuits. Murphy signed a release when he joined the privatized police force enabling OCP to do "pretty much what we want with him," as one of the executives says. Murphy's body has become a product owned and operated by OCP but, enigmatically, some residual human identity remains. Murphy is troubled by disturbing memory flashes. He continues to see the moment of his execution by Boddicker's gang, and he has brief recollections of his home, his wife, and his child. His semihuman status is revealed to his former partner when she sees him twirling his gun before holstering it. This is something he picked up from "TJ Lazer," a television show. This human trace is ironically derived from a media image, further corrupting the boundaries of the self.

A completed cyborg, Murphy is publicly unveiled by OCP and turned loose on the streets, where he promptly begins arresting or executing criminals. He gains the attention of the television news and appears on "Media Break," a three-minute news digest that punctuates network shows. Murphy's segment occurs as he visits the children at Lee Iacocca Elementary School (as the film pokes fun at corporate celebrities as culture heroes), where he sententiously tells them to stay out of trouble. Murphy's segment is not the only story that appears on "Media Break." The film's narrative is periodically interrupted for these three-minute newscasts, which are among the funniest and the most pointedly satiric moments in the film. These "infotainment" segments make fun of the fast-disappearing distinction between television news and entertainment programming and offer cautionary comic warnings about problems including governmental doublespeak (one story deals with a presidential press conference aboard "the Star Wars Orbiting Peace Platform") and the bogus compassion of for-profit medical clinics. The Family Heart Center, for example, advertises its complete Jarvik line of hearts, its Series Seven Sports Heart by Jensen, and the availability of extended warranties and financing for its products, made available to the consumer because, according to the Heart Center, "We care." These and other spots evoke a future where market forces have permeated all sectors of society and services and have determined the logic of human relationships. Later in the film, a deranged city councilman takes the mayor hostage and holds him at gunpoint, issuing a demand for a new car, "something with reclining leather seats that goes really fast and gets really shitty gas mileage." The social Darwinism that underlay Reagan-era economic policy is targeted by the film's portrait of a future Detroit torn by corporate avarice, the depredations of criminal gangs, and economic collapse. As part of a series of people-in-the-street interviews shown on "Media Break," one man bitterly tells the camera, "It's a free society, except there ain't nothing free. There's no guarantees, you know. You're on your own. It's the law of the jungle." In another sequence, one of the members of Boddicker's gang gleefully remarks, "No better way to steal money than free enterprise," referring to the gang's use of bank robbery proceeds to finance its cocaine manufacturing plant. "It takes money to make money." Theft becomes a form of capital investment.

As a counter to the advanced state of social disintegration that deregulation and unfettered corporate appetites have wrought in the film's world, the narrative focuses on Murphy's quest to learn who he is, to regain his memory, to identify with his own human subjectivity as against his machine self and programmed corporate identity. Shedding his metallic helmet and exposing his scarred but still-human face, Murphy destroys Boddicker and his gang, then goes after Jones. Jones, however, has programmed Robocop with a secret directive prohibiting him from arresting any senior officer of OCP. An attempt to do so will result in product shutdown. "You're our product, and we can't very well have our products turning against us, now can we?," Jones says to Murphy, reminding him of his commodity origins. In a last-minute turn of events, Murphy is able to kill Jones when he resists arrest because OCP's chairman, held hostage by a panicking Jones, promptly fires him. After killing Jones, Robocop returns to work for OCP, but when asked his name, replies, "Murphy." He will not renounce the ties to his human past. OCP remains what it was, Murphy remains a servant in its employ, and the social disintegration the film has described will continue unchecked.

This does not mean, however, that the film's critique collapses or is abandoned. It is too funny a film for that, its humor issuing from political outrage and anger. Its ability to make an audience laugh means granting its viewers the Brechtian distance necessary to see the ties between their (our) world and the film's future world. The audience's laughter is testimony to both the film's anger and the viewer's own political perceptions. In this respect, by insisting on the pleasure of its audience and by inflecting that pleasure with a radical politics, *Robocop* becomes a quite Brechtian film. By itself, however, that is no longer enough. In Brecht's day, his politically charged aesthetic could connect with real political movements outside the theater that could build on and extend the perspectives embodied in his plays. There is, by contrast, no corresponding left-wing political tradition in the United States, and the politics of Verhoeven's film remain suspended in the air with no political frameworks nor organizations to connect to or be grounded by in the lives of the film's spectators. The absence of an alternative politics limits the political use of this very political film. In more general terms, this lack must be seen as the major constraint inhibiting the development of an authentically critical American political cinema. We will return to this point.

Despite these limitations, Verhoeven was willing to inflect commercial formulas in his distinctive manner in another production, *Total Recall*. (The importance of Verhoeven's contribution to *Robocop* can be assessed in terms of its dismal sequel. *Robocop 2* is a poorly conceived film in which the criticism of the social policies of the Reagan period fades into the background in favor of an emphasis upon bloodletting and special effects.) Less of a direct satire of the contours of Reagan's America than *Robocop*, *Total Recall* is set in a more distant future where, as in *Blade Runner* and *Alien*, capital has expanded on an interplanetary scale. As capital enlarges its grip in the future, however, it regresses to earlier political forms. The exceptionally intricate and complex narrative of the film involves conflicts typical of nineteenth-century imperialism and deals with the macro forces of dictatorship and revolution that have been featured in other dystopia films. The complicated narrative of *Total Recall* will bear some detailed description because its design incorporates and expresses the film's political critique. Unidentified economic and political powers on Earth have colonized Mars, where they operate mining colonies to extract turbinium ore that is used to finance programs of military conquest. Defending these mining operations, the administrator of Mars and the film's chief villain, Cohaagen (Ronny Cox), says at a press conference, "Mars was colonized by the Northern Bloc at enormous expense. Our entire war effort depends on their turbinium, and it's ridiculous to think that we're going to give it away just because a bunch of lazy mutants think they own the planet." Cohaagen's political control of Mars is based upon the ownership of air. By controlling the price and availability of oxygen, Cohaagen can enforce his will over the miners. In the film's climax, he attempts to destroy the rebellion by depriving the miners of oxygen.

As in *Robocop*, the private ownership of public resources becomes an index of political corruption and repression, and is meant to resonate with the move toward privatization of social goods and services in the 1980s. The mutants, those who labor in the mines, have organized a resistance movement, under the leader Kuato, that is battling Cohaagen's colonial troops. The attempted revolution receives lots of media coverage on Earth, where a newscaster labels Kuato and his "so-called freedom brigade" as terrorists. As in *The Running Man* and *Robocop*, the media have usurped the power to define reality, only now it is done in a brazen fashion with little attempt to disguise the apparent contradictions between journalistic commentary and the content of the image. Over shots of the Mars militia machine-gunning the rebels at close range, the newscaster claims that order was restored with minimal force. In the world of *Total Recall*, the disjunction between images and their referents has achieved an almost schizophrenic intensity. As additional evidence of this slippage between fiction and reality, the newscaster's description of Kuato's group as a "freedom brigade" is an instance of ideological agglomeration, of equivocation. The film incorporates here a key political term of the era but confuses relevant political distinctions. The term "freedom brigade" resonates with the "freedom fighters" of Nicaragua, the name bestowed upon the Contra army by the Reagan administration. Unlike Kuato's group, however, the Contra army was not an indigenous revolutionary force but was instead organized and kept afloat by the CIA and its network of private donors, without whom it would have collapsed. As we have seen throughout the chapters, ideological equivocation is a defining feature of political representation in the American cinema. An additional and more significant example of this can be found in the film's visual design. Throughout, the imagery is packed with corporate logos and labels advertising well-known products of today, not of the future world of the narrative. Of films released in 1991, *Total Recall* had one of the highest frequencies of product placements. Thus, the film's anti-corporate social critique is somewhat compromised by the extent to which the film itself functions as an extended commercial for contemporary products.

The narrative deals with Cohaagen's attempt to plant a mole among the mutants who will lead Cohaagen and his army to Kuato, who will then be assassinated. The mole is Douglas Quaid (Arnold Schwarzenegger), a construction worker on Earth who has been having a disturbing series of dreams about a prior life on Mars. Stirred by these dreams, Quaid decides to vacation there, but when his wife refuses to accompany him, he decides instead to have a memory implant. He goes to Rekall, Inc., a firm that specializes in providing vacation memories which the firm claims are superior to the real experience. In one of its advertisements, the firm boasts, "You can buy the memory of your ideal vacation cheaper, safer, and better than the real thing. So don't let life pass you by. Call Rekall for the memory of a lifetime." A complete Mars package includes two full weeks of memory plus the ego trip, in which the consumer gets to take not only a vacation from familiar surroundings but also from himself or herself. Rekall will provide an alternative identity as a millionaire playboy or a secret agent or some other glamorous style of life.

With its basis in the Philip K. Dick short story "We Can Remember It for You Wholesale," the film grapples with what has been a recurring theme of the dystopia cycle, the introjection of commodity relationships inside the psyche, with the personality acquiring the characteristics of a product or, in the metaphors employed by the films, a cyborg, a simulacrum, a replicant. Quaid determines that he would like to be a secret agent, whereupon the Rekall salesman creates a new self for Quaid and a scenario that is the narrative of this film. The salesman tells Quaid, "A top operative, back under deep cover on your most important mission. People are trying to kill you left and right. You meet this beautiful, exotic woman. I don't want to spoil this for you, Doug, but by the time the trip is over, you get the girl, kill the bad guys, and save the entire planet."
All of this comes true, but what Quaid doesn't know is that he is not really Quaid but Hauser, a confederate of Cohaagen who has volunteered to have his memory blanked and to be provided with a new identity, as Doug Quaid, a construction worker on Earth. Cohaagen's goal is to manipulate Quaid into returning to Mars, where he will sympathize with the rebels and lead Cohaagen to Kuato. It was necessary to erase Hauser's memory because Kuato is psychic, and during previous attempts on his life he has always been able to intuit the presence of Cohaagen's spies. Quaid does unwittingly lead Cohaagen's forces to Kuato, who is assassinated.

Learning of Cohaagen's scheme and of his own manipulation, Quaid refuses to recognize his real self as Hauser and chooses instead his surrogate but more humane identity as Quaid. As the Rekall salesman prophesied, he defeats Cohaagen and saves the planet by starting a secret Martian nuclear reactor that melts the ice at the planet's core, releasing oxygen and creating an atmosphere. Cohaagen's political control broken, the miners' rebellion succeeds, and at the end everyone comes out to enjoy the new blue skies of Mars.

On an initial viewing, because the viewer does not at first know Cohaagen's master plan, the narrative seems delightfully dense and playfully self-referential. Because subsequent events conform so closely to the scenario of the ego trip Quaid purchases at Rekall, and, because during his memory implant at Rekall, Quaid suffers a schizoid embolism triggering a psychotic reaction, one is not initially sure how much is taking place inside Quaid's head and how much in reality. Reality, however, the film implies, has become an increasingly solipsistic state of mind, and as we shall see, it is here that the film's political critique is located: in the evocation of a solipsistic fantasy world by the corporate state for its citizens in order to erode the distinctions between fact and fantasy, consumer freedom and antidemocratic political control. As replicants, electric sheep, talking taxicabs, and state-dispensed hallucinogenic drugs undermine the authenticity of physical experience and social relationships, distinctions between an engineered and mechanized external world and a colonized internal one collapse. Dick's work charted the contours of this collapse and the transformation of both realms, mental and social, into kipple or waste. In *Total Recall* Verhoeven has a lot of fun playing upon this invasion of the psyche. Taking the logic of consumption to its ultimate extension, the salesman at Rekall tells Quaid that real trips are bothersome. They involve lost luggage, bad weather, rude cab drivers, but with Rekall everything is perfect and is custom designed to fit Quaid's wishes.

However, the ability to engineer memories is predicated upon the loss of an authentic past, of time and history, and ultimately of personality and the body itself. When his marriage is exposed as being a memory implant, his wife tells him, "Sorry, Quaid, your whole life is just a dream." On Mars, having learned of Cohaagen's master plan, Quaid sees a video message from Hauser, who tells him, "It's my body, and I want it back." The fascination with the deceptions and manipulations wrought by images and surrogate, artificial realities that has been a recurrent feature of the dystopia films has one of its roots here, in the anxieties and cynicism that result from an awareness of how easily mediated political realities of the 1980s can become manipulated political realities. Time and again in these films, control of the image and its market becomes a way of extinguishing truth, and in this respect, these narratives about the engineering of reality to secure political or economic power can be regarded as signs of a mistrust of the contemporary mechanisms and institutions of political culture. These visions of futuristic societies of the spectacle were spawned during the era of an exceptionally media-savvy presidential administration. As Quaid is threatened with becoming lost in the fiction created for him by Rekall, *Total Recall* dramatizes the blending of fantasy and reality and the seductive appeal of deliberately engineered fictions that make the film a cautionary fable about social and political mystification.

Produced at the end of the 1980s, *Total Recall* thus has a reflective quality, a sense of looking back and summing up a political period whose logic is expressed in the film's metaphors of getting lost in a land of fantasy that has been constructed to maintain and secure the claims of empire (in the film, these are Cohaagen's schemes to keep control of the Martian mines and the interplanetary military machine they support). Thus, *Total Recall* can be seen as one of the subtlest but most critical imaginative transformations of the political referents of the Reagan period. As with most of the Hollywood films discussed in these chapters, however, the film's political view is limited by its use of the narrative conventions of the commercial cinema, and we should now consider this limitation more closely.

Playing with ambiguities of the image and personality, the narrative seems denser and more multilayered than it really is, unlike a film such as *Hiroshima Mon Amour* (1959), produced in Europe, outside the production practices of the Hollywood cinema, in which narrative relationships of time and space are unstable, in flux, because they are interpenetrated by the subjectivity and desires of the characters. Alain Resnais's *Hiroshima Mon Amour* retains its mystery, despite repeated viewings. The narrative ambiguities of *Total Recall*, by contrast, are sustained only so long as the viewer does not know Cohaagen's master plan and, therefore, do not survive a second viewing. Clearly indicating the formula and narrative limits of contemporary commercial films, *Total Recall* cannot remain an open-ended text. As we have seen, Hollywood narratives are unfolded and resolved in a clear, coherent, often linear fashion. At the end, closure—the resolution of all plot lines and the answering of all outstanding narrative questions—is achieved. For much of its length, *Total Recall* tantalizes its audience with the possibility of a genuinely enigmatic narrative, organized around unanswerable ambiguities. Is Quaid sane or crazy? Is he Quaid or Hauser?

But the puzzles are not allowed to remain unsolved. One sequence in particular threatens to open the narrative onto irresolvable ambiguities, but closure is quickly achieved and the strategy employed—resort to action and mayhem as a certification of Quaid's sanity—shows very clearly the creative boundaries beyond which this kind of film may not go. On Mars, Quaid receives a visit from a physician who claims to be from Rekall.

The physician tries to persuade Quaid that he is suffering a schizoid embolism and that all of the strange events which have befallen him are really taking place inside his head, that he is not on Mars but still strapped in the chair at Rekall. What is more plausible, the physician reasons—that Quaid is the victim of a vast interplanetary conspiracy to convince him he is really a lowly construction worker on Earth and not an invincible secret agent, or that he is simply experiencing a drug reaction at Rekall? If Quaid is really in the grip of a free-form delusion based on implanted memory tapes, a hallucination that he invents as he goes along, then the stability of the narrative is threatened with rupture, becoming an eternally open-ended text with no reliable referents because everything is occurring inside a mad mind. Closure is achieved, however, and ambiguity foreclosed by having Quaid see a bead of stress-induced sweat trickle down the physician's forehead. Quaid thereupon decides that the man is real, not a hallucination, and that he has been sent to prevent Quaid from meeting Kuato. Quaid shoots the physician and then has to battle his way past the very real guards who have been stationed outside his room. In the bloody sequence that follows, the political limitations of the action-oriented dystopia films are apparent. As Fred Glass has noted,

Resolving the scene this way brings us back into the narrative we'd almost lost. But it does so in a manner that reiterates a defining contradiction for NBF [new bad future] films: the curious amalgam of progressive politics and action adventure narrative rooted in intense violence, which may or may not be of the redemptive sort. What will the audience remember most when it leaves the theatre: the politics, psychology, and philosophy—or the blood?[32]

The spectacular violence of *Total Recall* and its bravura display of special effects (for which it won a special Academy Award) vie with the film's political and social critique for the attention of the audience and for the resolution of the narrative ambiguities that function as political metaphors. This is a familiar tension in the dystopia films, where spectacle and violence have been employed to add luster to the grim future prognostications. Although the gun battles and bloodletting constitute the most conventional aspect of the film and certify it as a Schwarzenegger action vehicle, the popular success of *Total Recall* was also a function of its playful and self-consciously puzzling, labyrinthine narrative structure. Getting lost in the narrative of this film offered its audience the pleasures of a fun house with distorted images and mirror reflections undermining one's secure and stable bearings. The uncertainties of self and sanity that inform the narrative, the schizoid qualities of Quaid's own mind and the world he inhabits, are consistent with recurring features of the dystopia films, where the media mystify reality, photographic images document fictional events and ersatz selves, and simulacra and cyborgs mimic and undermine the human body and psyche. As we have previously noted, these visions, coupled with dramas of imperialist corporate appetites transforming globe and galaxy, suggest a loss of hope for the future and a loss of belief in the potential for political justice and democratic control. The dystopia cycle resonates with the latent, underlying anxieties of national decline that the Reagan administration itself alternately intensified, manipulated, and denied. The schizoid worlds of the dystopia films, where madness and simulated realities are omnipresent, amplify the political uncertainties of the 1980s, embodying in displaced cinematic form the easy slippage between reality and fiction, history and ideological desire, represented by the era's political culture. The confusions of fiction and reality—indeed, the very use of fantasy itself—in the dystopia cycle can stand as a comprehensive political metaphor for the spirit of the 1980s, that complex dialectic in the period's elaborate political symbology of evident decline and stubborn ideological denial.

This cycle of films—envisioning a widening gulf between rich and poor, the operation of what were formerly state-run social services by for-profit corporations, and the extension of market values across the entire social spectrum—reflects the 1980s environment of curtailed social services, privatization of the public sector, and regressive tax policies favoring the wealthy. The 1980s have come to be known, in popular parlance, as "the decade of greed," and the multinational and interplanetary corporate empires depicted in these films, coexisting with massive urban decay, are striking visualizations of this spirit. Economic opportunism in these films, and their portraits of a state abnegating social responsibility in order to succor its corporate sector, yield imagery of social disintegration and conflict. More often than not, these films portray the United States as a kind of Third World country ruled by a business elite, with the bulk of its citizens impoverished, imprisoned, or under state surveillance. The dystopia films have been able to extrapolate the pathologies of contemporary society and project them into an even grimmer future where crime, ruthless corporate and political control, and the engineering of reality by the media form an interlocking partnership that eliminates utopian aspirations. In doing so, the films have portrayed the loss of the natural environment, the exhaustion of natural resources, and the extension of political and economic control across both physical and psychological space. The engineering of political and social reality voids the psyche and transforms the personality and the body into a manufactured product subject to the laws of exchange like any other commodity.

As Glass notes, however, this dystopian analysis of a capitalism allowed to develop without any regard for democratic controls or public welfare has been developed amid the blood and carnage of hyperkinetic action films. There is every possibility that the carnage does short-circuit the political analysis and perception of these films. Moreover, the films' unrelentingly grim future projections may serve to reinforce the perceived political passivity of their viewers. No functioning democratic state appears in the films examined in this chapter. Instead, social disintegration and chaos have overwhelmed the possibility of effective political leadership. With social decay experienced as inevitable, and with no available political alternatives, the future looms in these films as a frightening authoritarian nightmare. The lack of social or political alternatives, in these films, to the networks of corruption and decay powering state and society is an imaginative failure that may also be the register of a political failure—that is, the absence of a real-world cultural base that might inspire representations of political alternatives. Rather than visions of political empowerment, these films offer the gratifications of spectacle and the pleasures of formulaic repetition.

Where is the cinematic space beyond action and melodrama from which a filmmaker with an alternative political vision might speak? Where are the unique formulas, conventions, or traditions available to such a filmmaker? That space, as we have seen throughout these chapters, is a minimal one. Either the filmmaker can fall in step with the dominant discourse of the era, as did George Lucas, John Milius, and Steven Spielberg, or the filmmaker can hope to tie an alternative portrait to a counterveiling political current that has achieved some legitimacy and resonance, as Costa-Gavras was able to do with *Missing* and as Oliver Stone attempted to do during the controversy about intervention in Central America with *Salvador*. One reason for the enormous popularity of the Spielberg and Lucas films and of works like *Top Gun* and *Rambo* is that their cultural discourse went largely unchallenged. The collapse of liberalism during the 1980s and the absence of a Left-wing political tradition permitted the Right to enjoy a certain ideological privilege throughout the decade. If we have to look long and hard for those films which sought a dialogue with and a critique of the cultural and political landscape of the 1980s, rather than simply giving voice to its main idées fixes, we should remember both the limited place that film holds in public political life and the presumption that is implicit in asking filmmakers to develop perspectives in their films that are not otherwise available in the culture. The great traditions of political film, those identified with Jean-Luc Godard, Luis Buñuel, Glauber Rocha, and others, emerged from European and Third World countries where contending classes, ideologies, and political traditions are part of the texture of everyday life. By contrast, the tradition of consensus politics in America and the minor differences between the two political parties narrow and foreclose the universe of political discourse that is available to filmmakers and that is accordingly recognized as legitimate by audiences. For a filmmaker to discard a narrative structure centered on the individual protagonist and to employ analytic terms like "class" and "capital" is to risk seeming out of touch with American traditions of discourse and politics. This is not to unnecessarily deny the possibility of films made in a spirit of criticism and resistance but is merely to suggest that film is not the place from which to start. Without an expansion of the coordinates of public discourse and political analysis, films will continue to be informed by the imperatives of spectacle and hyperkinesis, striking an uneasy partnership between formula and politics, and conjuring but not contesting the imagined darkness of the future.

NOTES

1. Daniel Bell, *The Coming of Post-Industrial Society* (New York: Basic Books, 1973), p. 37.
2. Andreas Huyssen, "Mapping the Postmodern," *New German Critique* 33 (Fall 1984), p. 36.
3. Fredric Jameson, "Postmodernism, or the Cultural Logic of Late Capitalism," *New Left Review* 146 (July/August 1984), p. 56.
4. See Jean Lyotard, *The Postmodern Condition* (Minneapolis: University of Minnesota Press, 1984).
5. Agnes Heller and Ferenc Feher, *The Postmodern Political Condition* (New York: Columbia University Press, 1988), p. 4.
6. Huyssen, "Mapping the Postmodern," p. 48.
7. Bell, *The Coming of Post-Industrial Society*, p. 28.
8. Huyssen, "Mapping the Postmodern," p. 40.
9. Heller and Feher, *The Postmodern Political Condition*, p. 4.
10. Fred Glass, "Totally Recalling Arnold: Sex and Violence in the New Bad Future," *Film Quarterly* 44, no. 1 (Fall 1990), p. 2.
11. Ibid.
12. James Combs, *American Political Movies* (New York: Garland, 1990), p. 113.
13. Patricia S. Warrick, *Mind in Motion: The Fiction of Philip K. Dick* (Carbondale: Southern Illinois University Press, 1987), p. 2.
14. Georg Lukacs, *History and Class Consciousness*, trans. Rodney Livingstone (Cambridge, MA: MIT Press, 1968; repr. 1976), p. 100.
15. Quoted in Patricia S. Warrick, "The Labyrinthian Process of the Artificial: Philip K. Dick's Androids and Mechanical Constructs," in *Philip K. Dick*, ed. Martin Harry Greenberg and Joseph D. Olander (New York: Taplinger, 1983), p. 204.
16. Quoted in Warrick, *Mind in Motion*, p. 132.
17. Ibid., pp. 117–118.
18. Jameson, "Postmodernism," p. 66.
19. Mead's accounts of his design of the film's architecture as well as his working sketches may be found on the Criterion laser disc version of this film.
20. Giuliana Bruno, "Ramble City: Postmodernism and *Blade Runner*," *October* 41 (Summer 1987), p. 63.
21. Ibid., p. 66.
22. Martin Heidegger, "Building Dwelling Thinking," in *Martin Heidegger: Basic Writings*, ed. David Farrell Krell (New York: Harper & Row, 1977), p. 332.

23. Kenneth Frampton, "Towards a Critical Regionalism: Six Points for an Architecture of Resistance," in *The Anti-Aesthetic: Essays on Postmodern Culture*, ed. Hal Foster (Port Townsend, WA: Bay Press, 1983), p. 25.

24. However, it should be pointed out that the urban design of *Blade Runner* is not wholly original. It owes much to the set design of Fritz Lang's *Metropolis* (1926), particularly the spatialization of social and political power into upper and lower regions, although much of this is also to be found in Dick's work.

25. Guy Debord, *Society of the Spectacle*, trans. (Detroit: Black & Red, 1983), para. 21. Originally published 1967.

26. J. P. Telotte, "Human Artifice and the Science Fiction Film," *Film Quarterly* 36, no. 3 (Spring 1983), pp. 44–51. In a more recent article, Telotte has explored the symbology of the android self in these films: "The Tremulous Body Politic: Robots, Change and the Science Fiction Film," *Journal of Popular Film and Television* 19, no. 1 (Spring 1991), pp. 14–23.

27. Glass makes this point in "Totally Recalling Arnold," p. 3.

28. This point is made by James H. Kavanaugh in, " 'Son of a Bitch': Feminism, Humanism, and Science in *Alien*," *October* 13 (Summer 1980), p. 95.

29. Karl Marx, *Capital*, vol. 1, trans. Ben Fowkes (New York: Vintage Books, 1977), p. 165.

30. A similar point is made by Thomas B. Byers, "Commodity Futures," in *Alien Zone*, ed. Annette Kuhn (New York: Verso, 1990), p. 40.

31. Psychological and epistemological implications of the time-loop paradox in science fiction literature are explored in Constance Penley, "Time Travel, Primal Scene, and the Critical Dystopia," in *The Cultural Politics of "Postmodernism*," ed. John Tagg (Binghamton: State University of New York at Binghamton Press, 1989), pp. 33–49. The article also discusses the debt Cameron's film owes to Chris Marker's *La Jetée*.

32. Glass, "Totally Recalling Arnold," p. 7.

Afterword: The Place of Politics in Hollywood Films

If we seek to evaluate the efficacy of the indirect, implicit mode of political representation exemplified by the dystopic science fiction films, it must be acknowledged that these films (excluding *Robocop*) bear a more tangential relationship to the politics of the period in which they were made than do those film cycles examined in the other chapters. Those other films placed political issues in the foreground and shaped their narratives around ongoing controversies and debates. As we have seen, those narratives owed as much to convention and formula as to politics, but there can be no doubt that they were topically engaged productions.

What of the dystopic science fiction films? Their political content and relationship to topical events is second order, preventing even the seamless fusion of generic narrative and generic political frameworks exemplified by the new Cold War films examined in Chapter 2. To retrieve the political discourse of the dystopic science fiction films, their narratives need to be decoded in a fashion that is not necessary with the other film cycles we have examined. The dystopic films are of interest to the extent that they collectively offer a kind of counterdiscourse to the uninhibited free-market economics of the Reagan period and its conduct of politics through the sound bite and the management of media information and images. They are also notable for their images of empires running down or generating rebellion due to their own corruption and repressive policies. Indeed, one of the basic characteristics informing the content of the film cycles examined in this book has been the vision of empire at its zenith or in decline coupled with an inability throughout most of these films to articulate alternatives to imperial perspectives.

What President Reagan offered the culture was a final period of ostensible imperial glory, when the military, moral, and industrial power of the United States was evoked in unequivocal and shining terms. The extraordinary phenomenon of the Reagan years was not so much this evocation as its fanciful nature. Visions of empire throughout the 1980s were accompanied by a mushrooming national debt, the ongoing collapse of heavy industry, and the erosion of the social infrastructure, evidenced by the loss of low-cost, affordable housing and health insurance, the gutting of social services, and the lack of resources allocated for the benefit of the next generation. Major urban centers were abandoned. Bereft of federal funds, many teetered on the edge of bankruptcy. One result of these social crises was the growth of a huge underclass. The spread of crack cocaine throughout impoverished urban areas was a sign not just of obvious social decay but of the failure of politics as well. In an earlier decade, urban poverty and unemployment might ignite riots that, however counterproductive in the short run, at least testified to the existence of political anger and collective perceptions of dispossession and economic exclusion. By contrast, the crack house offers an alternative, underground economy for those living in the now abandoned inner cities, but represents the death of politics. The solipsistic despair nurtured by crack addiction erodes the collective consciousness that once sparked riots as the perverse and negative expression of community. Along with the crack epidemic, the dramatic creation and explosive growth of a homeless population offer the clearest evidence that the goals of social justice and economic advancement for all Americans, which were compelling ideals only a generation ago, have been discarded. The logic of society through the 1980s, and into the present, often seems based on exclusion rather than inclusion, denial rather than provision of basic services and benefits.

The significance and fascination of the Reagan period lay in the tacit agreement between the administration and the public not to acknowledge the significance of these developments, even while the policies of those years helped to accelerate the process. In this context, the dystopic science fiction films offer dark reflections on these social currents, picturing an intensification of social conflict and economic injustice in societies where a welter of media images obfuscates the underlying crises. By contrast, the new Cold War films, and in considerably more ambiguous terms the Vietnam war films, endorse the commencement of a new American century in which the United States might resume its role as an arbiter of international conflicts. In this respect, they offer substitute ideological celebrations in place of a recognition of the growing disparity between national achievement and national aspiration. Of those examined in this book, only the films dealing with the revolutions in Latin America sought to define and discern the shape of an alternative political future in terms of policies regarding change in the Third World. Throughout the film

cycles examined in this book, therefore, greater potential exists for reinforcement of, and fidelity to, dominant political perspectives than for a
search for alternatives to accompany a changing world, and a reluctance
to abandon established imperial paradigms will almost certainly be
characteristic of American political culture for years to come. The national
euphoria surrounding the Gulf war victory indicates how deeply rooted
this commitment is, and to this extent, visions of brave homelands and
evil empires will remain a fixture of Hollywood films. Of the rhetorical
strategies adopted by the films examined in this book in their evaluation
of the claims of empire, only the Latin America films clearly announce
an explicitly critical position. The grim social prognostications of the
dystopic science fiction films, ironically, can be viewed as reinforcing
existing trends toward political passivity and feelings of social helplessness
in the face of economic crisis. This potential for a co-optation of their
political content is perhaps the clearest constraint on their political efficacy
and articulateness, and presents itself as a general problem for political
communication where an indirect, implicit mode of representation is
adopted.

The use of fantasy to inflect and embody political perspectives tends
to soften and make ambiguous the linkages between the corrupt future
worlds pictured in these films and the shape of present society. By virtue of its camouflaging of contemporary political ills, the fantasy format
in the dystopia films opens a space for ambivalence, evasion, or denial
of the contemporary referents that underlie the format. While viewers
are free to respond in these terms to the visions and critiques advanced
by the other film cycles, those films, at least, present their political topics
forthrightly, even if the point of view directed upon those topics is not
always coherent. The dystopic science fiction films, by contrast, demonstrate by omission the importance of a clear and coherent point of view
when dealing with political material. Its absence permits a film's political
communication to exemplify, all too easily, the fallacy of equivocation.
As we have seen, however, valuing a committed, coherent political (or,
for that matter, moral or social) point of view has not often been emphasized in the American film tradition. Filmmakers like director John Milius
on the Right, and screenwriter-director Abraham Polonsky on the Left,
are among the exceptions. In their work, and in their interviews, one
usually encounters an internally consistent political worldview. By virtue of the need to appeal to a diverse audience, however, American films
typically seek to soften direct expressions of noncentrist political ideologies
(which makes the extreme jingoism of the new Cold War films rather
special).

A more recent illustration of this occurred during production of Irwin
Winkler's *Guilty by Suspicion* (1991), about a Hollywood filmmaker (Robert
DeNiro) blacklisted as a Communist during the 1950s. Winkler originally

commissioned Polonsky to write the script, and in Polonsky's version real political, as well as social, issues were at stake: The character really was a Communist. Winkler, however, decided it would be more interesting, and more profitable at the box office, if the character was a political innocent, a non-Communist, falsely accused of being a Communist. The Polonsky script was abandoned because Winkler did not believe he could get a contemporary audience to care about a Communist—as if that, rather than freedom of political expression, was what the film ought to be about. Such are the trade-offs and calculations that dilute political expression in the American cinema. As the dystopia cycle indicates, these calculations can result in an equivocating presentation of political issues. Does the audience see the dystopia films as uncomplicated action films, disconnected fantasies about a distant future, or for their potential to function as disguised commentaries on trends in contemporary society? While the last perspective cannot be discounted, it certainly remains true that the dystopic fantasy format is not the most politically efficacious for a filmmaker interested in addressing contemporary urban or economic problems. The format will, however, provide a better chance of getting such a film made and its finding an audience, and therein lies a big part of the problem in making political films in an industry oriented toward making diverting entertainments. The narrative conventions and formulas that it makes sense to use from an economic standpoint are not always well suited for conveying the desired political or social content.

Different potentials for effective political communication characterize the cycles examined in this book. As expressions of official political culture, the potential for a reinforcement of that culture is strongest with the new Cold War films, especially since they were widely viewed and were quite popular. By virtue of their critical distance from the foreign policy and political discourse of the period, the Latin America films would likely meet with resistance from viewers not already inclined toward the terms of their political analysis. The dystopic films, as noted, have probably the most diffuse political impact, since their social analysis recedes behind the camouflage of a future world and the visual spectacle of special effects. Implicit in these evaluations is a recognition that media effects often tend toward a reinforcement of previously held opinions and attitudes. Those who believe in the evil and duplicity of the Soviets would probably find nothing ideologically objectionable in the presentation of the villains in *Rocky IV* and *Rambo III*, while those who are skeptical about the claims of unmitigated Soviet evil might find that the films' cartoonish portrayals strengthen their own, alternative perspectives. By contrast, for audience members who do not hold strong prior opinions on a given political topic that is represented on film, the potential for influence by the media certainly exists. A young viewer, for example, may play at being

Rambo in neighborhood games or derive impressions about the Soviets from Stallone's films. A viewer uninformed about events in Central America and not committed to a view that sees U.S. foreign policy as an exercise of benevolence may be amenable to the persuasive appeals of a film like Oliver Stone's *Salvador*. This is not the place to enter into the extensive literature on media effects.[1] But it is important to note that film may reinforce as well as help instill political perceptions. Does recognition of the ability of mass media content to reinforce existing attitudes have the consequence of inhibiting or constraining the use and place of politics in the cinema? Quite the contrary—what it does is to reemphasize the importance of having a diverse, intensive political culture in place to nurture and inform political filmmaking. Without this, with a narrow spectrum of admissible political opinion, with an electorate that feels distant from the centers and operation of political power, and with campaigning conducted via a cynical manipulation of media messages, the potential for political expression in the cinema becomes highly constrained. As a political medium, film will reproduce only the traditions and conventions of political discourse available in the surrounding culture. If they emphasize consensus and downplay ideology, so will films. If they emphasize debate, ideological difference, and a wide spectrum of political opinion, so will films. That the former condition tends to prevail in contemporary politics helps to account for the dominance of genre and formula, in place of explicit ideology, in many of the films we have studied.

Thus, questions about the place of political filmmaking in the United States, while mediated by and intimately connected with aesthetic issues and conventions, ultimately open onto questions about the American political culture and tradition. Hollywood productions are driven by economic needs to be timely and topical. These qualities can help to generate audience interest and curiosity, which, given the right conditions, can translate into box-office success. But Hollywood films are also bound by decades of industry practice not to depart in fundamental ways from the terms and frameworks of political custom, tradition, and analysis common in American society. Thus, issues of class and ideology tend to be deemphasized or ignored, and political conflicts tend to be portrayed through the clash of colorful characters and personalities. We have seen many consequences of this orientation, from the bonding of generic narratives with generic political perspectives, where conflict is thrashed out between a charismatic hero and a dehumanized villain, to the simple but telling inability of film narratives to identify key players, parties, and issues in real-world political conflicts dramatized on screen. As Terry Christensen has observed, "any discussion of political ideas beyond acceptable democratic values may offend some segment of the audience. Americans are uneasy with ideology, especially any ideology other than their own; most movies respect this by remaining resolutely centrist and issue-oriented."[2]

As we saw in Chapter 1, Hollywood's cautiousness with respect to political content and controversy is a long-standing practice that informed the industry's responses to the crises surrounding the adoption of the Production Code and its general retreat from overtly partisan filmmaking following the anticommunist scares in the 1950s. These impulses to retreat, however, have always existed in tension with a clear liberal, populist, pragmatic American political outlook in the national cinema and with the industry's own recognition that the cultural resonance necessary for economic success at the box office frequently requires some measure of topicality. The films examined throughout this book show clearly how closely the topical and the popular, politics and entertainment, are conjoined as twin currents in the American cinema. Even the rise of the blockbuster, examined in Chapter 1, has not managed to extinguish political content from contemporary film, although it has been accused of doing so. John Milius, whose *Red Dawn* was a key film of the early Reagan years, and who recently made a Vietnam war film (*The Flight of the Intruder*) has accused the current generation of blockbuster filmmakers of ruining American film. They proved, he said, that there was more money in the film market than anyone realized, but in doing so "they made movies into amusement-park rides."[3]

However, while the blockbuster formula has had deleterious effects, both economically and artistically, on contemporary American film, blockbusters have not yet brought the end of topical filmmaking. As the 1990s commenced, for example, an emerging group of black filmmakers, in works like *Boyz N the Hood* and *Straight Out of Brooklyn*, revived the conventions of cinematic realism, as against those of fantasy, in deeply felt portrayals of black America presented in an angry, didactic style that reaffirmed the connections between cinema and social reality. Furthermore, as the new decade began, Hollywood seemed to be moving through one of its fiscally conservative cycles. Several anticipated blockbusters in the summer of 1990 (*Another 48 Hours, Days of Thunder*) failed to deliver huge audiences, and the average production cost of a film had risen to the neighborhood of $25 million. As production and marketing costs climbed, revenues from the box office, video, and pay TV flattened out. In this somewhat more cost-conscious climate, executives at a number of studios (most visibly, Disney) began to rethink the wisdom of inflating production costs on routine films through the addition of high-priced directors and stars. This publicly acknowledged cost consciousness, however, did not displace blockbuster productions. Despite the studios' wish to see the budgets of average films decline, the blockbuster production seems a permanent fixture of contemporary Hollywood. Carolco, for example, forged ahead with *Terminator II* for summer 1991, its budget approaching the unprecedented amount of $100 million.

Despite a continuing if newly cautious emphasis upon blockbusters, in terms of the volume of overall production and the stylistic energy of the films themselves, politics remains very much alive in the American cinema. And as political matters should be, these films are there to be argued over and struggled with. Controversy and argumentation, after all, are the best part of the American film tradition, ensuring its vibrancy and vitality as a popular art. As a measure of this vibrancy and vitality, American films do not speak with a unified ideological voice. Instead, as we have seen, the industry is willing, to an extent, to inflect its productions with diverse, and sometimes conflicting, political perspectives and content. The need to seek the viewers' dollars helps to ensure this relative diversity. At the same time, though, this prevents many films from retaining a coherent and consistent ideological perspective, and this is the reason for caution when surveying the place of politics in American film. Throughout these chapters we have seen examples of political agglomeration, the concatenation of different and sometimes divergent ideological perspectives inside a single film. This structural diversity (or opportunism), rooted in the economics of the industry, is one of the major constraints operating upon the political use of the American cinema. Political representation in American film is also constrained and limited by the intellectual frameworks prevailing in American politics and society, and by the need to embed political material inside traditional entertainment formulas. The problems of the 1980s—urban decay, unemployment, homelessness, crime, drug use, and socially irresponsible financial speculation and investment—were not addressed by American film in a systematic way (i.e., via the sustained inquiry that a cycle of films makes possible and that, in general, lies beyond the agenda-setting capabilities of any single production), except through the fantasy format of the dystopic science fiction films. As noted, this disguise helped to ensure box-office appeal as well as to lend the issues themselves a certain political vagueness and invisibility. That American film chose to deal with some of the decade's most urgent and defining problems through fantasy is both significant and telling.

This book was written from the conviction, and in the hope, that film might play an important cultural role in identifying and addressing the important social, political, and economic problems and issues confronting the nation as the twentieth century nears its close; that film, with its emotional intensity and ability to create unforgettable images, might be a key player in the cultural debates surrounding past crises and those which lie ahead. But, unfortunately, the movies in America can't seem to do that and remain movies—that is, retain their base of popular support. This, then, is the unresolved dialectic informing American political filmmaking: topicality without sustained commitment, passion without analysis. This is not the best combination of attributes to enable film to participate as a mass popular medium in our national political and cultural life, especially during a time of sustained economic and political crisis associated with the erosion of the social infrastructure and the U.S. position in world markets.

In the years to come, more than ever, American films need to reclaim a political vision and point of view, but for this to happen, the crisis of political leadership in American society will also have to be addressed, reorienting national political debates in ways that make them amenable to addressing urgent domestic social problems. Contemporary political culture, however, seems unable to confront or to address the present drift of American society. To this extent, the lacunae and evasions of political culture will constitute the gaps and omissions of cinematic images and narratives. Hollywood, though, needs politics (and politicians increasingly need the professional image-maker). Reactionary or progressive, forward-looking or nostalgia-driven, politics furnishes the topicality essential for popular success. In the years to come, American films will continue to reflect and refract the social crises and defiant ideological celebrations that will surround the changing status of the United States as a global power, even while the film industry publicly proclaims, as it always has, that its business is entertainment, not politics. But its practice tells us otherwise, and there is always the chance that a rare filmmaker will succeed in creating images which clarify the structures of power and give voice to those in need. Otherwise, as the actor Paul Winfield observed,[4] without a sustaining social vision in the film industry and a commitment to the power of ideas, it's all just about making money.

NOTES

1. The interested reader can consult *Selective Exposure to Communication*, ed. Dolf Zillmann and Jennings Bryant (Hillsdale, New Jersey: Lawrence Erlbaum, 1985), *The Process and Effects of Mass Communication*, ed. Wilbur Schramm and Donald F. Roberts (Chicago: University of Illinois Press, 1971), or *Perspectives on Media Effects*, ed. Jennings Bryant and Dolf Zillmann (Hillsdale, NJ: Lawrence Erlbaum, 1989).

2. Terry Christensen, *Reel Politics* (New York: Basil Blackwell, 1987), p. 213.

3. "20 Questions: John Milius," *Playboy* 38 (June 1991), p. 160.

4. "One on One: Stanley Kramer and Paul Winfield," *American Film* 16 (May 1991), p. 47.

Bibliography

Abercrombie, Nicholas, Stephen Hill, and Bryan S. Turner. *The Dominant Ideology Thesis*. London: George Allen & Unwin, 1980.

Acheson, Dean. *Present at the Creation*. New York: Norton, 1969.

Armstrong, Robert, and Janet Shenk. "El Salvador—A Revolution Brews." *NACLA Report on the Americas* 14, no. 4 (July–August 1980): 2–36.

——— . "El Salvador—Why Revolution?" *NACLA Report on the Americas* 14, no. 2 (March–April 1980): 3–35.

Aufderheide, Pat. "Good Soldiers." In *Seeing Through Movies*, ed. Mark Crispin Miller. New York: Pantheon, 1990.

Auster, Albert, and Leonard Quart. *How the War Was Remembered: Hollywood and Vietnam*. New York: Praeger, 1988.

Bell, Daniel. *The Coming of Post-Industrial Society*. New York: Basic Books, 1973.

Bernstein, Basil. "A Sociolinguistic Approach to Socialization, with Some Reference to Educability." In *Directions in Sociolinguistics*, ed. John J. Gumperz and Dell Hymes. New York: Holt, Rinehart and Winston, 1972.

Biskind, Peter. "Blockbuster: The Last Crusade." In *Seeing Through Movies*, ed. Mark Crispin Miller. New York: Pantheon, 1990.

Blumenthal, Sidney. *Our Long National Daydream*. New York: Harper & Row, 1988.

Brownlow, Kevin. *Behind the Mask of Innocence*. New York: Knopf, 1990.

Bruno, Giuliana. "Ramble City: Postmodernism and *Blade Runner*." *October* 41 (Summer 1987): 61–74.

Byers, Thomas B. "Commodity Futures." In *Alien Zone*, ed. Annette Kuhn. New York: Verso, 1990.

Carr, C. "War on Art: The Sexual Politics of Censorship." *Village Voice*, June 5, 1990, pp. 25–30.

Carroll, Noel. *Mystifying Movies: Fads and Fallacies in Contemporary Film Theory*. New York: Columbia University Press, 1988.

Chanan, Michael. *The Cuban Image*. London: BFI, 1985.

Charters, W. W. *Motion Pictures and Youth: A Summary*. New York: Macmillan, 1935.

Chomsky, Noam. *Towards a New Cold War*. New York: Pantheon, 1982.

Chomsky, Noam, and Edward S. Herman. *The Political Economy of Human Rights*, vol. 1. Boston: South End Press, 1979.

Chown, Jeffrey. *Hollywood Auteur*. New York: Praeger, 1988.

Christensen, Terry. *Reel Politics*. New York: Basil Blackwell, 1987.

Combs, James. *American Political Movies*. New York: Garland, 1990.

Comolli, Jean-Luc, and Jean Narboni. "Cinema/Ideology/Criticism." In *Movies and Methods*. vol. 1, ed. Bill Nichols. Berkeley: University of California Press, 1976.

Cook, David A. *A History of Narrative Film*, 2nd ed. New York: W. W. Norton, 1990.

Coppola, Eleanor. *Notes*. New York: Simon and Schuster, 1979.

Crawford, Alan. *Thunder on the Right*. New York: Pantheon, 1980.

Curran, James, Michael Gurevitch, and Janet Woollacott. "The Study of the Media: Theoretical Approaches." In *Culture, Society and the Media*, ed. Michael Gurevitch, Tony Bennett, James Curran, and Janet Woollacott. New York: Methuen, 1982.

Dallek, Robert. *Ronald Reagan: The Politics of Symbolism*. Cambridge, MA: Harvard University Press, 1984.

Davis, Mike. "The New Right's Road to Power." *New Left Review* 128 (July–August 1981): 28–49.

DeBenedetti, Charles, with Charles Chatfield. *An American Ordeal: The Anti-War Movement of the Vietnam Era*. Syracuse, NY: Syracuse University Press, 1990.

Debord, Guy. *Society of the Spectacle*. Detroit: Black & Red, 1983. Originally published 1967.

DeFleur, Melvin L., and Sandra Ball-Rokeach. *Theories of Mass Communication*, 4th ed. New York: Longman, 1982.

Doherty, Thomas. "Hollywood Agit-Prop: The Anti-Communist Cycle, 1948–1954." *Journal of Film and Video* 40, no. 4 (Fall 1988): 15–27.

Dornfeld, Barry. "*Dear America*: Transparency, Authority and Interpretation in a Vietnam War Documentary." In *From Hanoi to Hollywood: The Vietnam War in American Film*, ed. Linda Dittmar and Gene Michaud. New Brunswick, NJ: Rutgers University Press, 1990.

Facey, Paul W. *The Legion of Decency*. New York: Arno Press, 1974.

FitzGerald, Frances. *Fire in the Lake*. Boston: Little, Brown, 1972.

Foster, Hal, ed. *The Anti-Aesthetic: Essays on Postmodern Culture*. Port Townsend, WA: Bay Press, 1983.

Frampton, Kenneth. "Towards a Critical Regionalism: Six Points for an Architecture of Resistance." In *The Anti-Aesthetic: Essays on Postmodern Culture*, ed. Hal Foster. Port Townsend, WA: Bay Press, 1983.

Gabriel, Teshome H. "Third Cinema as Guardian of Popular Memory: Towards a Third Aesthetics." In *Questions of Third Cinema*, ed. Jim Pines and Paul Willemen. London: BFI, 1989.

Gitlin, Todd. "Media Sociology: The Dominant Paradigm." *Theory and Society* 6, no. 2 (September 1978): 205–253.

Glass, Fred. "Totally Recalling Arnold: Sex and Violence in the New Bad Future." *Film Quarterly* 44, no. 1 (Fall 1990): 2–13.

Gomery, Douglas. "Corporate Ownership and Control in the Contemporary U.S. Film Industry." *Screen* 25, no. 4–5 (1984): 60–69.

Green, Mark, and Gail MacColl, eds. *Reagan's Reign of Error*. New York: Pantheon, 1987.

Grossberg, Lawrence. "Strategies of Marxist Cultural Interpretation." *Critical Studies in Mass Communication* 1 (December 1984): 392–421.

Gustafson, Robert. "'What's Happening to Our Pix Biz?' From Warner Bros. to Warner Communications, Inc." In *The American Film Industry*, ed. Tino Balio, rev. ed. Madison: University of Wisconsin Press, 1985.

Haines, Harry W. "The Vietnam Veteran." In *From Hanoi to Hollywood: The Vietnam War in American Film*, ed. Linda Dittmar and Gene Michaud. New Brunswick, NJ: Rutgers University Press, 1990.

Hall, Stuart. "Encoding/Decoding." In *Culture, Media, Language*, ed. Stuart Hall et al. London: Hutchinson, 1980.

Harvey, Sylvia. *May 68 and Film Culture*. London: BFI, 1980.

Heidegger, Martin. "Building Dwelling Thinking." In *Martin Heidegger: Basic Writings*, ed. David Farrell Krell. New York: Harper & Row, 1977.

Heller, Agnes, and Ferenc Feher. *The Postmodern Political Condition*. New York: Columbia University Press, 1988.

Hellman, John. *American Myth and the Legacy of Vietnam*. New York: Columbia University Press, 1986.

Holmlund, Christine Anne. "New Cold War Sequels and Remakes." *Jump Cut* no. 35 (1990): 85–96.

Hunt, Richard A. "Strategies at War: Pacification and Attrition in Vietnam." In *Lessons from an Unconventional War: Reassessing U.S. Strategies for Future Conflicts*, ed. Richard A. Hunt and Richard H. Schultz, Jr. New York: Pergamon Press, 1982.

Huyssen, Andreas. "Mapping the Postmodern." *New German Critique* 33 (Fall 1984): 5–52.

Inglis, Ruth A. "Self-Regulation in Operation." In *The American Film Industry*, ed. Tino Balio, rev. ed. Madison: University of Wisconsin Press, 1985.

Jameson, Fredric. "Postmodernism, or the Cultural Logic of Late Capitalism." *New Left Review* 146 (July/August 1984): 53–93.

Jarvie, I. C. *Movies as Social Criticism: Aspects of Their Social Psychology*. Metuchen, NJ: Scarecrow, 1978.

Jay, Martin. *The Dialectical Imagination*. Boston: Little, Brown, 1973.

Jowett, Garth. *Film: The Democratic Art*. Boston: Little, Brown, 1976.

Kahn, Gordon. *Hollywood on Trial*. New York: Boni and Gaer, 1948.

Kann, Peter B., and Phillip Jennings. "Trashing History: Did Hanoi Make This Movie?" *The Wall Street Journal*, August 28, 1990, p. A8.

Katz, Elihu, and Paul F. Lazarsfeld. *Personal Influence*. New York: Free Press, 1955; repr. 1964.

Kavanaugh, James H. "'Son of a Bitch': Feminism, Humanism, and Science in *Alien*." *October* 13 (Summer 1980): 91–100.

Kern, Louis J. "MIAs, Myth, and Macho Magic: Post-Apocalyptic Cinematic Visions of Vietnam." In *Search and Clear: Critical Responses to Selected Literature and Films of the Vietnam War*, ed. William J. Searle. Bowling Green, OH: Bowling Green State University Popular Press, 1988.

Kirkpatrick, Jeane. "Dictatorships and Double Standards." *Commentary* 68, no. 5 (November 1979): 34–45.

Klapper, Joseph T. *The Effects of Mass Communication.* New York: Free Press, 1960.

Kolker, Robert Phillip. *The Altering Eye.* New York: Oxford University Press, 1983.

———. *A Cinema of Loneliness,* 2nd ed. New York: Oxford University Press, 1988.

Kuspit, Donald. "The Contradictory Character of Post Modernism." In *Postmodernism—Philosophy and the Arts,* ed. Hugh J. Silverman. New York: Routledge, 1990.

Lasswell, Harold W. "Propaganda." In *Encyclopedia of the Social Sciences,* vol. 12. New York: Macmillan, 1934.

Lazarsfeld, Paul F., Bernard Berelson, and Hazel Gaudet. *The People's Choice.* New York: Columbia University Press, 1944; repr. 1968.

Lazarsfeld, Paul F., and Robert K. Merton. "Mass Communication, Popular Taste and Organized Social Action." In *The Process and Effects of Mass Communication,* ed. Wilbur Schramm and Donald F. Roberts. Chicago: University of Illinois Press, 1971.

Leff, Leonard J., and Jerold L. Simmons. *The Dame in the Kimono: Hollywood, Censorship, and the Production Code from the 1920s to the 1960s.* New York: Grove Weidenfeld, 1990.

Levy, Guenter. *America in Vietnam.* New York: Oxford University Press, 1978.

List, Chris. "*El Norte*: Ideology and Immigration." *Jump Cut* no. 34 (1989): 27–31.

Lovell, Terry. *Pictures of Reality.* London: BFI, 1980.

Lukacs, Georg. *History and Class Consciousness,* trans. Rodney Livingstone. Cambridge, MA: MIT Press, 1968; repr. 1976.

Lyotard, Jean. *The Postmodern Condition.* Minneapolis: University of Minnesota Press, 1984.

Maltby, Richard. "Made for Each Other: The Melodrama of Hollywood and the House Committee on Un-American Activities, 1947." In *Cinema, Politics, and Society in America,* ed. Philip Davies and Brian Neve. New York: St. Martin's Press, 1981.

———. "The Political Economy of Hollywood: The Studio System." In *Cinema, Politics, and Society in America,* ed. Philip Davies and Brian Neve. New York: St. Martin's Press, 1981.

———. *Harmless Entertainment: Hollywood and the Ideology of Consensus.* Metuchen, NJ: Scarecrow, 1983.

Marchetti, Gina. "Class, Ideology and Commercial Television: An Analysis of *The A-Team.*" *Journal of Film and Video* 39, no. 2 (Spring 1987): 19–28.

Marx, Karl. *Capital,* vol. 1, trans. Ben Fowkes. New York: Vintage Books, 1977.

Mattelart, Armand. *Multi-National Corporations and the Control of Culture,* trans. Michael Chanan. Atlantic Highlands, NJ: Humanities Press, 1979.

———. *Mass Media, Ideologies and the Revolutionary Movement,* trans. Malcolm Coad. Atlantic Highlands, NJ: Humanities Press, 1980.

McEvoy, James III. *Radicals or Conservatives?: The Contemporary American Right.* Chicago: Rand McNally, 1971.

McQuail, Denis, *Mass Communication Theory,* second edition (Beverly Hills: Sage, 1988).

Merton, Robert K. *Social Theory and Social Structure.* New York: Free Press, 1968.

Miles, Sara, and Bob Ostertag. "D'Aubuisson's New ARENA." *NACLA Report on the Americas* 23, no. 2 (July 1989): 14–39.

——. "FMLN: New Thinking." *NACLA Report on the Americas* 23, no. 3 (September 1989): 15–38.

Miller, Mark Crispin. "Advertising: End of Story." In *Seeing Through Movies*, ed. Mark Crispin Miller. New York: Pantheon, 1990.

Mills, C. Wright. *The Sociological Imagination*. New York: Oxford University Press, 1959; repr. 1982.

"Nicaragua: Haunted by the Past." *NACLA Report on the Americas* 24, no. 1 (June 1990): 10–39.

O'Connor, John E., and Martin A. Jackson. *American History/American Film*. New York: Frederick Ungar, 1988.

Patti, Archimedes L. A. *Why Vietnam? Prelude to America's Albatross*. Berkeley: University of California Press, 1980.

Pearce, Jenny. *Under the Eagle*. Boston: South End Press, 1982.

Penley, Constance. "Time Travel, Primal Scene, and the Critical Dystopia." In *The Cultural Politics of "Postmodernism*," ed. John Tagg. Binghamton: State University of New York at Binghamton Press, 1989.

The Pentagon Papers, vols. 1–4. Boston: Beacon Press, n.d.

Polan, Dana. *Power and Paranoia*. New York: Columbia University Press, 1986.

Powdermaker, Hortense. *Hollywood: The Dream Factory*. Boston: Little, Brown, 1950.

Prasch, Thomas. "*Platoon* and the Mythology of Realism." In *Search and Clear: Critical Responses to Selected Literature and Films of the Vietnam War*, ed. William J. Searle. Bowling Green, OH: Bowling Green State University Popular Press, 1988.

Ray, Robert B. *A Certain Tendency of the Hollywood Cinema, 1930–1980*. Princeton: Princeton University Press, 1985.

Reagan, Ronald. *Speaking My Mind*. New York: Simon and Schuster, 1989.

Reagan, Ronald, and Richard C. Hubler. *Where's the Rest of Me?* New York: Dell, 1981. Originally published 1965.

Rocha, Glauber. "Glauber Rocha: Cinema Novo and the Dialectics of Popular Culture." In *Cinema and Social Change in Latin America: Conversations with Filmmakers*, ed. Julianne Burton. Austin: University of Texas Press, 1986.

Roffman, Peter, and Jim Purdy. *The Hollywood Social Problem Film*. Bloomington: Indiana University Press, 1981.

Rogin, Michael. *Ronald Reagan: The Movie*. Berkeley: University of California Press, 1988.

Rosen, Phillip, ed. *Narrative, Apparatus, Ideology*. New York: Columbia University Press, 1986.

Ryan, Michael, and Douglas Kellner. *Camera Politica*. Bloomington: Indiana University Press, 1988.

Schickel, Richard. "The Crisis in Movie Narrative." *Gannett Center Journal* 3, no. 3 (Summer 1989): 1–15.

Schultz, Richard H., Jr., and Alan Ned Sabrosky. "Policy and Strategy for the 1980s: Preparing for Low Intensity Conflicts." In *Lessons from an Unconventional War: Reassessing U.S. Strategies for Future Conflicts*, ed. Richard A. Hunt and Richard H. Schultz, Jr. New York: Pergamon Press, 1982.

Sklar, Robert. *Movie-Made America*. New York: Random House, 1975.

Slotkin, Richard. *Regeneration Through Violence: The Mythology of the American Frontier, 1600–1860*. Middletown, CT: Wesleyan University Press, 1973.

Smith, Julian. *Looking Away: Hollywood and Vietnam*. New York: Scribner's, 1975.

Smith, Robert. "Disaffection, Delegitimation and Consequences: Aggregate Trends for World War II, Korea, and Vietnam." In *Public Opinion and the Military Establishment*, ed. Charles C. Moskos, Jr. Beverly Hills, CA: Sage, 1971.

Sontag, Susan. "Fascinating Fascism." In *Movies and Methods*, vol. 1, ed. Bill Nichols. Berkeley: University of California Press, 1976.

Stauth, Cameron. "Requiem for a Heavyweight." *American Film* 15 (January 1990): 22–27, 57.

Steinfels, Peter. *The Neo-Conservatives*. New York: Simon and Schuster, 1979.

Stetler, Russel, ed. *The Military Art of People's War: Selected Writings of General Vo Nguyen Giap*. New York: Monthly Review Press, 1971.

Talbot, David, and Barbara Zheutlin. *Creative Differences: Profiles of Hollywood Dissidents*. Boston: South End Press, 1978.

Telotte, J. P. "Human Artifice and the Science Fiction Film." *Film Quarterly* 36, no. 3 (Spring 1983): 44–51.

Thompson, Anne. "Field of Dreams: 15th Annual 'Grosses Gloss.'" *Film Comment* 26, no. 2 (March–April 1990): 59–66.

Torres-Rivas, Edelberto. "Guatemala—Crisis and Political Violence." *NACLA Report on the Americas* 14, no. 1 (January–February 1980): 16–27.

Tucker, Robert W. "The Purpose of American Power." *Foreign Affairs* 59, no. 2 (Winter 1980/1981): 241–274.

Volosinov, V. N. *Marxism and the Philosophy of Language*, trans. Ladislav Matejka and I. R. Titunik. Cambridge, MA: Harvard University Press, 1973.

Wanger, Walter. "OWI and Motion Pictures." *Public Opinion Quarterly* 7, no. 1 (Spring 1943): 100–110.

Warrick, Patricia S. "The Labyrinthian Process of the Artificial: Philip K. Dick's Androids and Mechanical Constructs." In *Philip K. Dick*, ed. Martin Harry Greenberg and Joseph D. Olander. New York: Taplinger, 1983.

——— . *Mind in Motion: The Fiction of Philip K. Dick*. Carbondale: Southern Illinois University Press, 1987.

Wills, Garry. *Reagan's America: Innocents at Home*. New York: Doubleday, 1987.

Wolfe, Alan. "Sociology, Liberalism and the Radical Right." *New Left Review* 128 (July/August 1981): 3–27.

Wood, Robin. *Hollywood from Vietnam to Reagan*. New York: Columbia University Press, 1986.

Index

ABOUT THE AUTHOR

STEPHEN PRINCE is Assistant Professor of Communication Studies at Virginia Polytechnic Institute and State University. He has written articles for publications such as *Cinema Journal, Wide Angle, Journal of Film and Video,* and *Journal of Popular Culture,* and is the author of *The Warrior's Camera: The Cinema of Akira Kurosawa.*